180 DAYS
of PRAYER

WITH THE SAINTS

180 DAYS
of PRAYER

WITH THE SAINTS

WYATT NORTH

CONTENTS

ST. TERESA OF AVILA

ST THERESE OF LISIEUX

ST. BERNARD OF CLAIRVAUIX

ST. JOHN OF THE CROSS

ST. FRANCIS OF ASSISI

ST. CATHERINE OF SIENA

DAY 1

In today's meditation, Teresa presents a powerful metaphor for the human soul, particularly with respect to the body and how the whole human being relates to God who seeks to "fill" each person with His presence. As you consider today's meditation, think about how deeply God desires to know you, and what greater intimacy with God might mean for you as you go about your daily life.

Meditations from St. Teresa

I thought of the soul as resembling a castle, formed of a single diamond or a very transparent crystal, and containing many rooms, just as in Heaven there are many mansions.

If we reflect…we shall see that the soul of the just man is but a paradise, in which, God tells us, He takes His delight.

What, do you imagine, must that dwelling be in which a King so mighty, so wise, and so pure, containing in Himself all good, can delight to rest? Nothing can be compared to the great beauty and capabilities of a soul; however keen our intellects may be, they are as unable to comprehend them as to comprehend God, for, as He has told us, He created us in His own image and likeness.

As this is so, we need not tire ourselves by trying to realize all the beauty of this castle, although, being His creature, there is all the difference between the soul and God that there is between the creature and the Creator; the fact that it is made in God's image teaches us how great are its dignity and loveliness. It is no small misfortune and disgrace that, through our own fault, we neither understand our nature nor our origin. Would it not be gross ignorance…if, when a man was questioned about his name,

1

or country, or parents, he could not answer? Stupid as this would be, it is unspeakably more foolish to care to learn nothing of our nature except that we possess bodies, and only to realize vaguely that we have souls, because people say so and it is a doctrine of faith.

Rarely do we reflect upon what gifts our souls may possess, Who dwells within them, or how extremely precious they are. Therefore we do little to preserve their beauty; all our care is concentrated on our bodies, which are but the coarse setting of the diamond, or the outer walls of the castle.

Let us imagine, as I said, that there are many rooms in this castle, of which some are above, some below, others at the side; in the centre, in the very midst of them all, is the principal chamber in which God and the soul hold their most secret intercourse. Think over this comparison very carefully; God grant it may enlighten you about the different kinds of graces He is pleased to bestow upon the soul. No one can know all about them, much less a person so ignorant as I am. The knowledge that such things are possible will console you greatly should our Lord ever grant you.

St. Teresa of Ávila.
The Interior Castle. First
Mansions, Chapter 1.

Additional Biblical Reflections: Psalm 51:10-19, John 14:2, 1 Corinthians 6:19-20.

Prayer

Lord, your majesty is greater than we can possibly comprehend. An entire life of devotion is not enough to know you fully. Grant us, Lord, your Holy Spirit that we might be drawn to you more intimately, that our lives might reflect your glory, and that we would receive your mercy and blessings. Amen.

DAY 2

Nothing can be so perilous in our quest for greater intimacy with God than the tendency we all have to compare our progress to that of others. Truth be told, God does not bestow the same gifts on all of us in the same way. When we allow such comparisons between ourselves and others to creep in, however, we become quickly distracted, consumed with envy, and lose sight of our own spiritual journey. Here, Teresa bids we give thanks to God when He shows special graces to our fellow believers. Rather than being jealous of them, we should take encouragement from the fact that God does, indeed, glorify Himself in His creatures!

Meditations from St. Teresa

I feel sure that vexation at thinking that during our life on Earth God can bestow these graces on the souls of others shows a want of humility and charity for one's neighbour, for why should we not feel glad at a brother's receiving divine favours which do not deprive us of our own share? Should we not rather rejoice at His Majesty's thus manifesting His greatness wherever He chooses? Sometimes our Lord acts thus solely for the sake of showing His power, as He declared when the Apostles questioned whether the blind man whom He cured had been suffering for his own or his parents' sins. God does not bestow these favours on certain souls because they are more holy than others who do not receive them, but to manifest His greatness, as in the case of St. Paul and St. Mary Magdalen, and that we may glorify Him in His creatures.

St. Teresa of Ávila.
The Interior Castle. First
Mansions, Chapter 1.

Additional Biblical Reflections: Job 5:2, Proverbs 23:17-18, James 3:14-16.

Prayer

Dearest Lord, you are the gracious giver of every good gift. You bestow blessings on your humble creatures according to your infinite well. Grant me a spirit of gratitude for the blessings you show others and spare me from the temptation to grow jealous of how you have chosen to show yourself to others. For you, Lord, are a gracious God who gives to each of us according to your infinite knowledge precisely what is required that we might grow closer to you. Amen.

DAY 3

oday, Teresa warns us against the perils of complacency. Often, when pursuing God, we are tempted to think we have arrived. We have fleeting moments of intimacy and believe the journey is complete. When that happens, Teresa warns, several temptations arise that can destroy our spiritual progress. While we should be content in the graces God has given us, we should never remain complacent or stagnant in our quest toward greater intimacy with the Lord.

Meditations from St. Teresa

This is the deception by which the Devil wins his prey. When a soul finds itself very near to God and sees what a difference there is between the good things of Heaven and those of Earth, and what love the Lord is showing it, there is born of this love a confidence and security that there will be no falling away from what it is now enjoying. It seems to have a clear vision of the reward and believes that it cannot now possibly leave something which even in this life is so sweet and delectable for anything as base and soiled as earthly pleasure. Because it has this confidence, the Devil is able to deprive it of the misgivings which it ought to have about itself; and, as I say, it runs into many dangers, and in its zeal begins to give away its fruit without stint, thinking that it has now nothing to fear. This condition is not a concomitant of pride, for the soul clearly understands that of itself it can do nothing; it is the result of its extreme confidence in God, which knows no discretion. The soul does not realize that it is like a bird still unfledged. It is able to come out of the nest, and God is taking it out, but it is not yet ready to fly, for its virtues are not yet strong and it has no experience which will warn it of dangers, nor is it aware of the harm done by self-confidence.

St. Teresa of Ávila. *A Life.* Chapter 19.

Additional Biblical Reflections: Amos 6:1, Hebrews 6:11-12, Revelation 3:15-17.

Prayer

Lord, you are the great giver of life. As such, you are the giver of growth. Lead us Lord to always seek you more fervently, to desire you more deeply, and to know you more fully. Let us never fall complacent, but make us always content with your blessings and gifts that in all we say and do, we might glorify you through our lives and not be led astray by temptation. In Jesus's name, Amen.

DAY 4

In today's meditation, Teresa bids we consider the mental connection we have to prayer. It is not enough, she says, to simply repeat prayers by rote memory—while our lips move, our minds wander elsewhere. Nor should one speak to the Lord in prayer without forethought, casually as one would to others. The mind should be united to our prayers, whether we vocalize them or not, lest our prayers become exercises in vain repetition rather than conversations with our Divine bridegroom.

Meditations from St. Teresa

As far as I can understand, the gate by which to enter this castle is prayer and meditation. I do not allude more to mental than to vocal prayer, for if it is prayer at all, the mind must take part in it. If a person neither considers to Whom he is addressing himself, what he asks, nor what he is who ventures to speak to God, although his lips may utter many words, I do not call it prayer. Sometimes, indeed, one may pray devoutly without making all these considerations through having practised them at other times. The custom of speaking to God Almighty as freely as with a slave--caring nothing whether the words are suitable or not, but simply saying the first thing that comes to mind from being learnt by rote by frequent repetition – cannot be called prayer: God grant that no Christian may address Him in this manner. I trust His Majesty will prevent any of you, sisters, from doing so. Our habit in this Order of conversing about spiritual matters is a good preservative against such evil ways.

St. Teresa of Ávila.
The Interior Castle. First
Mansions, Chapter 1.

Additional Biblical Reflections: Matthew 6:6-7, Luke 11:1ff, Philippians 4:6

Prayer

Dear Lord, you know the words we would pray even before we speak because you know the groanings of our hearts. Grant that we are given not just the lips but the minds to pray. Guard us against the temptation to turn our prayers into rote repetitions where our voices speak without the concurrence of our hearts so that our prayers might be genuine, fruitful, and pleasing to you. In Jesus's name, Amen.

DAY 5

Teresa often spoke in her autobiography about her own sins. Much like St. Paul, who openly admitted his gravest sins in the first chapters he wrote to the Galatians, Teresa knew that God is glorified not when we hide our shortcomings but when we allow His glory and wisdom to shine through despite our foolishness. False displays of piety merit nothing before God. True confession, an honest assessment of one's sins, and a willingness to accept God's graces in spite of ourselves are what allows us to make spiritual progress. The Lord does not choose to bestow blessings on people solely on account of their merits. He also chooses to bless those of us with certain graces because, in his wisdom, He knows which of us need them the most.

Meditations from St. Teresa

With these few tears that I am here shedding, which are Thy gift (water, in so far as it comes from me, drawn from a well so impure), I seem to be making Thee payment for all my acts of treachery – for the evil that I have so continually wrought and for the attempts that I have made to blot out the favours Thou hast granted me. Do Thou, my Lord, make my tears of some efficacy. Purify this turbid stream, if only that I may not lead others to be tempted to judge me, as I have been tempted to judge others myself. For I used to wonder, Lord, why Thou didst pass by persons who were most holy, who had been piously brought up, who had always served Thee and laboured for Thee and who were truly religious and not, like myself, religious only in name: I could not see why Thou didst not show them the same favours as Thou showedst to me. And then, O my Good, it became clear to me that Thou art keeping their reward to give them all at once

— that my weakness needs the help Thou bestowest on me, whereas they, being strong, can serve Thee without it, and that therefore Thou dost treat them as brave souls and as souls devoid of self-seeking.

But nevertheless Thou knowest, my Lord, that I would often cry out unto Thee, and make excuses for those who spoke ill of me, for I thought they had ample reason for doing so. This, Lord, was after Thou of Thy goodness hadst kept me from so greatly offending Thee and when I was turning aside from everything which I thought could cause Thee displeasure; and as I did this, Lord, Thou didst begin to open Thy treasures for Thy servant. It seemed that Thou wert waiting for nothing else than that I should be willing and ready to receive them, and so, after a short time, Thou didst begin, not only to give them, but to be pleased that others should know Thou wert giving them, to me.

St. Teresa of Ávila. *A Life*. Chapter 19.

Additional Biblical Reflections: Luke 5:31, Galatians 1:11-24, Timothy 1:15

Prayer

Lord, you are a God of mercy and grace. In your son, we have been granted the right to approach your throne with confidence. Let us not shy away from confessing our sins, hiding our errors from neither you nor men. That it might be you and your grace rather than our false piety that we uphold before men. In Jesus's name. Amen.

DAY 6

One of the reasons many of us struggle to make any spiritual progress is that we are so *busy*. It is not that we lack the desire to grow in our relationship with the Divine; we simply don't have the time. However, everyone has twenty-four hours in their day. Is it a matter of not having the time? Or fearing that if we give up the time we have devoted to other tasks—especially work—we'll pay financial consequences, perhaps even lose our homes or go hungry? The fear of financial insecurity has bred many in our world who are addicted to work and, in turn, make little time for spiritual reflection. In today's meditation, Teresa speaks to some of her fellow nuns about this very issue.

Meditations from St. Teresa

Do not think, my sisters, that because you do not go about trying to please people in the world you will lack food. You will not, I assure you: never try to sustain yourselves by human artifices, or you will die of hunger, and rightly so. Keep your eyes fixed upon your Spouse: it is for Him to sustain you; and, if He is pleased with you, even those who like you least will give you food, if unwillingly, as you have found by experience. If you should do as I say and yet die of hunger, then happy are the nuns of Saint Joseph's! For the love of the Lord, let us not forget this: you have forgone a regular income; forgo worry about food as well, or thou will lose everything. Let those whom the Lord wishes to live on an income do so: if that is their vocation, they are perfectly justified; but for us to do so, sisters, would be inconsistent.

Worrying about getting money from other people seems to me like thinking about what other people enjoy. However much you worry, you will not make them change their minds nor will they become desirous of giving you alms. Leave these anxieties to Him Who can move everyone, Who is the Lord of all money and of all who possess money. It is by His command that we have come here and His words are true – they cannot fail: Heaven and Earth will fail first. Let us not fail Him, and let us have no fear that He will fail us; if He should ever do so it will be for our greater good, just as the saints failed to keep their lives when they were slain for the Lord's sake, and their bliss was increased through their martyrdom. We should be making a good exchange if we could have done with this life quickly and enjoy everlasting satiety.

St. Teresa of **Á**vila,
The Way of Perfection,
Chapter 2.

Additional Biblical Reflections: Matthew 6:25-34; Philippians 4:19; 1 Timothy 6:10

Prayer

Dearest Lord, you are the creator of the world and every good thing that we need to sustain us in this body and life. Grant us confidence in your provision, Lord, that we might know that we will never lack any good thing. For as you remind us, man cannot live on bread alone but requires the daily sustenance of your word. Help us in our unbelief that we might devote ourselves more fully to you. Amen.

DAY 7

It is notable that Teresa, when outlining what she believes are the most necessary habits to develop when engaging a contemplative life, focuses first on the love of one another. In today's meditation, she addresses—particularly for nuns in her convent—the tendency for human beings to find each other annoying. Annoyance with our fellow believers can be an insidious thing. We ignore it because we think a mere annoyance is no small thing. However, over time, these nuisances pile up, and we begin to form deep-seated resentments against one another that can be incredibly destructive not only to our own spiritual progress but also to the Church as a whole.

Meditations from St. Teresa

It is about prayer that you have asked me to say something to you. As an acknowledgment of what I shall say, I beg you to read frequently and with a good will what I have said about it thus far, and to put this into practice. Before speaking of the interior life – that is, of prayer – I shall speak of certain things which those who attempt to walk along the way of prayer must of necessity practise. So necessary are these that, even though not greatly given to contemplation, people who have them can advance a long way in the Lord's service, while, unless they have them, they cannot possibly be great contemplatives, and, if they think they are, they are much mistaken. May the Lord help me in this task and teach me what I must say, so that it may be to His glory. Amen.

With regard to the first – namely, love for each other – this is of very great importance; for there is nothing, however annoying, that cannot easily be borne by those who love each other, and anything which causes annoyance must be quite exceptional. If this commandment were kept in the world, as it should be, I believe it would take us a long way towards the keeping of the rest; but, what with having too much love for each other or too little, we never manage to keep it perfectly.

St. Teresa of **Á**vila,
The Way of Perfection,
Chapter 4.

Additional Biblical Reflections: John 13:34-35, 1 Corinthians 13:1-11, 1 Peter 4:8

Prayer

Lord, in your infinite patience, you bear with us and love us often despite ourselves. Help us, Lord, to have this same disposition toward our fellows and that we not allow minor differences or annoyances to tempt us to sin against each other and, therefore, against you. Teach us to bear one another patiently, in love, and that in our relationships with our fellow believers, we might also come to know you more intimately. Amen.

DAY 8

We should be cautious about wrapping our faith up too tightly with the example of our mentors. Writing to the nuns of her order, Teresa strongly urged them to imitate the Virgin Mother—not her. She is a sinner—too great a one, she says, to be worthy of imitation. This might strike us as odd—particularly when Teresa's piety is so renowned. But her piety came with recognition and acknowledgment of her own sin. We all have mentors in the faith—people whose example we would like to emulate. However, how do we respond when such people let us down, find themselves caught in sin, and fail to be worthy of imitation? Such things should never surprise us. We are all sinners. Perfection eludes even the most pious of the saints! Instead, let us fix our eyes on the Lord.

Meditations from St. Teresa

His Majesty knows that I have nothing to rely upon but His mercy; as I cannot cancel the past, I have no other remedy but to flee to Him, and to confide in the merits of His Son and of His Virgin Mother, whose habit, unworthy as I am, I wear as you do also. Praise Him, then, my daughters, for making you truly daughters of our Lady, so that you need not blush for my wickedness as you have such a good Mother. Imitate her; think how great she must be and what a blessing it is for you to have her for a patroness, since my sins and evil character have brought no tarnish on the lustre of our holy Order.

Still I must give you one warning: be not too confident because you are nuns and the daughters of such a Mother. David was very holy, yet you know what Solomon became. Therefore do not rely on your enclosure, on your penitential life, nor on your continual exercise of prayer and constant communion with God, nor trust in having left the world or in the idea that you hold its ways in horror. All this is good, but is not enough, as I have already said, to remove all fear; therefore meditate on this text and often recall it: 'Blessed is the man that feareth the Lord.'

St. Teresa of Ávila.
The Interior Castle.
Third Mansions,
Chapter 1.

Additional Biblical Reflections: 2 Samuel 12, Psalm 51:10-19, Matthew 26:75

Prayer

Lord, we thank you for the great men and women of faith whom you have given us to guide you into the truth. However, let us not turn our mentors into idols. Help us to see them through your eyes even as you look at us in mercy. Let us become imitators of Christ, rather than mimickers of men, that we might ever reflect your holiness more perfectly in our lives. Amen.

DAY 9

In today's world, we often find ourselves chasing a "spiritual high," a fleeting emotion that gives us a sense of God's presence. Teresa does not decry these feelings, but she insists that we should not make too much of them. This "sweetness," as she calls it, comes from us. However, there is a deeper sense, a "spiritual consolation," which may or may not feel sweet but nevertheless comes to us from God and persists even when the luster of the moment fades.

Meditations from St. Teresa

I will now describe, as I promised, the difference between sweetness in prayer and spiritual consolations. It appears to me that what we acquire for ourselves in meditation and petitions to our Lord may be termed 'sweetness in devotion.' It is natural, although ultimately aided by the grace of God. I must be understood to imply this in all I say, for we can do nothing without Him. This sweetness arises principally from the good work we perform, and appears to result from our *labours: well may we feel happy at having thus spent our time. We shall find, on consideration, that many temporal matters give us the same pleasure – such as unexpectedly coming into a large fortune, suddenly meeting with a dearly-loved friend, or succeeding in any important or influential affair which makes a sensation in the world. Again, it would be felt by one who had been told her husband, brother, or son was dead, and who saw him return to her alive. I have seen people weep from such happiness, as I have done myself. I consider both these joys and those we feel in religious matters to be natural ones. Although there is nothing wrong about the former, yet those produced by devotion spring from a more noble source – in short, they begin in ourselves and end in God.*

Spiritual consolations, on the contrary, arise from God, and our nature feels them and rejoices as keenly in them, and indeed far more keenly, than in the others I described.

O Jesus! how I wish I could elucidate this point! It seems to me that I can perfectly distinguish the difference between the two joys, yet I have not the skill to make myself understood; may God give it me!

St. Teresa of Ávila.
The Interior Castle.
Fourth Mansions,
Chapter 1.

Additional Biblical Reflections: 2 Corinthians 10:5, Philippians 4:5-7, Galatians 5:22-23

Prayer

Dearest Lord, we pray that you grant us genuine spiritual consolations. You made us, Lord, as creatures full of emotions. These emotions are good, and we thank you for them. However, in sin, our emotions often lead us astray. Console us through the Spirit, the great Comforter, that we might find solace in you and not in the pursuit of vain and temporary feelings. Amen.

DAY 10

In today's meditation, Teresa considers how to manage our human tendency to quarrel with one another. First, she emphasizes the importance of refraining from quarrels and taking such matters to prayer. Second, she speaks quite harshly about how quarrelsome individuals must be dealt with. While she is speaking in the context of convents, in truth, the severity of her remedies should give us some pause about how long we are willing to tolerate unnecessary quarrels. Such divisions should be resolved as soon as possible, lest the divide drives a wedge between the members of the body of Christ and deprive all of His presence. Many people are seemingly addicted to conflict. While we should bear with our brothers and sisters who are tempted to quarrel, this tendency must also be addressed.

Meditations from St. Teresa

If one of you should be cross with another because of some hasty word, the matter must at once be put right and you must betake yourselves to earnest prayer. The same applies to the harbouring of any grudge, or to party strife, or to the desire to be greatest, or to any nice point concerning your honour. (My blood seems to run cold, as I write this, at the very idea that this can ever happen, but I know it is the chief trouble in convents.) If it should happen to you, consider yourselves lost. Just reflect and realize that you have driven your Spouse from His home: He will have to go and seek another abode, since you are driving Him from His own house. Cry aloud to His Majesty and try to put things right; and if frequent confessions and communions do not mend them, you may well fear that there is some Judas among you.

For the love of God, let the prioress be most careful not to allow this to occur. She must put a stop to it from the very outset, and, if love will not suffice, she must use heavy punishments, for here we have the whole of the mischief and the remedy. If you gather that any of the nuns is making trouble, see that she is sent to some other convent and God will provide them with a dowry for her. Drive away this plague; cut off the branches as well as you can; and, if that is not sufficient, pull up the roots. If you cannot do this, shut up anyone who is guilty of such things and forbid her to leave her cell; far better this than that all the nuns should catch so incurable a plague. Oh, what a great evil is this! God deliver us from a convent into which it enters: I would rather our convent caught fire and we were all burned alive. As this is so important I think I shall say a little more about it elsewhere, so I will not write at greater length here, except to say that, provided they treat each other equally, I would rather that the nuns showed a tender and affectionate love and regard for each other, even though there is less perfection in this than in the love I have described, than that there were a single note of discord to be heard among them. May the Lord forbid this, for His own sake. Amen.

St. Teresa of Ávila,
The Way of Perfection,
Chapter 7.

Additional Biblical Reflections: Proverbs 15:18, 26:21-28, Mathew 5:22, 2 Timothy 2:23-24

Prayer

Lord, you are a lover of peace and concord. There should never be unsavory divisions in your body. Grant us your Spirit of peace and understanding that we would always be led to view one another with charity, and our Church would be built up through profitable dispute rather than damaged through unnecessary division. Amen.

DAY 11

The pursuit of worldly things can be all-consuming. If this was true in Teresa's day, it is likely an even greater problem now. Some of us pursue material wealth, the latest gadgets and devices, with an unhealthy obsession. Others pursue reputations before men, which leads us to compromise and engender a sense that our "worth" hinges on men's opinions. Still others pursue "success" at all costs and imagine that if we finally achieve a promotion or status, we will find happiness. In today's meditation, Teresa challenges us to reconsider our priorities.

Meditations from St. Teresa

What is there that can be bought with this money which people desire? Is there anything valuable? Is there anything lasting? If not, why do we desire it? It is but a miserable ease with which it provides us and one that costs us very dear. Very often it provides hell for us; it buys us eternal fire and endless affliction. Oh, if all would agree to consider it as useless dross, how well the world would get on, and how little trafficking there would be! How friendly we should all be with one another if nobody were interested in money and honour! I really believe this would be a remedy for everything. The soul sees what blindness there is in the world where pleasures are concerned and how even in this life they purchase only trials and unrest. What disquiet! What discontent! What useless labour! Not only does the soul perceive the cobwebs which disfigure it and its own great faults, but so bright is the sunlight that it sees every little speck of dust, however small; and so, however hard a soul may have laboured to perfect itself, once this Sun really strikes it, it sees that it is wholly unclean. Just so the water in a vessel seems quite clear when the sun is not shining upon it; but the sun shows it to be full of specks. This comparison is literally exact. Before the soul had experienced that state of ecstasy, it thought it was being careful not to offend God and doing all that it could so far as its strength permitted. But once it reaches this stage, the Sun of Justice strikes it and forces it to open its eyes, whereupon it sees so many of these specks that it would fain close them again. For it is not yet so completely the child of that mighty eagle that it can look this Sun full in the face; nevertheless, during the short time that it can keep them open, it sees that it is wholly unclean. It remembers the verse which says: Who shall be just in Thy presence?

St. Teresa of Ávila, *A Life*, Chapter 20.

Additional Biblical Reflections: John 12:42-43, Galatians 1:10, 1 Timothy 6:10

Prayer

Lord, all good things come from you. Help us to have the eyes to see your greater blessings—the treasures you have stored for us in Heaven—without fixating on the treasures of this life. Grant us priorities that mirror your heart that we might always pursue you above worldly wealth, success, or the praises of men. Amen.

DAY 12

Fear is a powerful emotion. When we read about the Devil in the Scriptures, we might be struck with fear. But fear like this proceeds from unbelief. After all, if God is for us, not even the Devil can stand against us. Nevertheless, many are consumed with this kind of fear. The fear of the Devil, or the fear of men, has led many away from God. Teresa here encourages us to take courage in our spiritual battle against the Devil because we have a Champion—our Lord—who fights on our behalf.

Meditations from St. Teresa

This courage which the Lord gave me for my fight with the devils I look upon as one of the great favours He has bestowed upon me; for it is most unseemly that a soul should act like a coward, or be afraid of anything, save of offending God, since we have a King Who is all-powerful and a Lord so great that He can do everything and makes everyone subject to Him. There is no need for us to fear if, as I have said, we walk truthfully in His Majesty's presence with a pure conscience. For this reason, as I have said, I should desire always to be fearful so that I may not for a moment offend Him Who in that very moment may destroy us. If His Majesty is pleased with us, there is none of our adversaries who will not wring his hands in despair. This, it may be said, is quite true, but what soul is upright enough to please Him altogether? It is for this reason, it will be said, that we are afraid. Certainly there is nothing upright about my own soul: it is most wretched, useless and full of a thousand miseries. But the ways of God are not like the ways of men. He understands our weaknesses and by means of strong inward instincts the soul is made aware if it truly loves Him; for the love of those who reach this state is no longer hidden, as it was when they were beginners, but is accompanied by the most vehement impulses and the desire to see God, which I shall describe later and have described already. Everything wearies such a soul; everything fatigues it; everything torments it. There is no rest, save that which is in God, or comes through God, which does not weary it, for it feels its true rest to be far away, and so its love is a thing most evident, which, as I say, cannot be hidden.

St. Teresa of Ávila, *A Life*, Chapter 26.

Additional Biblical Reflections: Isaiah 51:12, Matthew 10:26-28, Hebrews 13:6

Prayer

Dear Lord, you have defeated every enemy—sin, death, and the Devil. Give us not a spirit of fear but a spirit of courage knowing that you have already achieved for us a victory over all forces of evil. Give us the confidence to trek forward in our pursuits of you, despite any threat that might come, and that we might not be dissuaded on our journey toward greater intimacy with you. In Jesus's name. Amen.

DAY 13

Today, there is much discussion about human rights. We see the rights of many violated or feel our own rights have been infringed upon, and rightly sense that an injustice has occurred. However, Teresa bids we reconsider how we approach the question of "rights." In this world, we should expect injustices. This is a broken world. Despite this, though, we have a great example. Our Lord set aside every right that was his by virtue of His Divinity and even had his human rights violated when he was arrested, tortured, and crucified. From Him, we can take comfort in a world where justice is often fleeting.

Meditations from St. Teresa

I often tell you, sisters, and now I want it to be set down in writing, not to forget that we in this house, and for that matter anyone who would be perfect, must flee a thousand leagues from such phrases as: "I had right on my side"; "They had no right to do this to me"; "The person who treated me like this was not right". God deliver us from such a false idea of right as that! Do you think that it was right for our good Jesus to have to suffer so many insults, and that those who heaped them on Him[1] were right, and that they had any right to do Him those wrongs? I do not know why anyone is in a convent who is willing to bear only the crosses that she has a perfect right to expect: such a person should return to the world, though even there such rights will not be safeguarded. Do you think you can ever possibly have

---

[1] Lit.: "did them to Him."

25

to bear so much that you ought not to have to bear any more? How does right enter into the matter at all? I really do not know.

St. Teresa of Ávila,
The Way of Perfection,
Chapter 13.

Additional Biblical Reflections: Jeremiah 22:3-5, Ecclesiastes 5:8, Romans 12:1-7

Prayer

Dear Lord, you grant us many gifts that the world does not. Send your spirit on all who are oppressed that they might endure in the faith. Give us a heart of gratitude for your gifts rather than a spirit of entitlement for the rights that, while ours, are often denied us. And give us a spirit of patience and confidence in the full knowledge that you will eventually rule over the Earth in perfect justice. In Jesus's name. Amen.

DAY 14

Upon recognizing that we are saved by grace, we may often be tempted to minimize the severity of sin. However, as Teresa points out, while we might be saved despite our sins, the ongoing pursuit of sin can be devastating in our pursuit of God. One cannot expect the Holy Spirit to dwell within us while in the throes of a mortal sin.

Meditations from St. Teresa

While the soul is in mortal sin nothing can profit it; none of its good works merit an eternal reward, since they do not proceed from God as their first principle, and by Him alone is our virtue real virtue. The soul separated from Him is no longer pleasing in His eyes, because by committing a mortal sin, instead of seeking to please God, it prefers to gratify the Devil, the prince of darkness, and so comes to share his blackness. I knew a person to whom our Lord revealed the result of a mortal sin and who said she thought no one who realized its effects could ever commit it, but would suffer unimaginable torments to avoid it. This vision made her very desirous for all to grasp this truth, therefore I beg you, my daughters, to pray fervently to God for sinners, who live in blindness and do deeds of darkness.

In a state of grace the soul is like a well of limpid water, from which flow only streams of clearest crystal. Its works are pleasing both to God and man, rising from the River of Life, beside which it is rooted like a tree. Otherwise it would produce neither leaves nor fruit, for the waters of grace nourish it, keep it from withering from drought, and cause it to bring forth good fruit. But the soul by sinning withdraws from this stream of life, and growing beside a black and fetid pool, can produce nothing but disgusting and unwholesome fruit.

Notice that it is not the fountain and the brilliant sun which lose their splendour and beauty, for they are placed in the very centre of the soul and cannot be deprived of their lustre. The soul is like a crystal in the sunshine over which a thick black cloth has been thrown, so that however brightly the sun may shine the crystal can never reflect it.

O souls, redeemed by the Blood of Jesus Christ, take these things to heart; have mercy on yourselves! If you realize your pitiable condition, how can you refrain from trying to remove the darkness from the crystal of your souls.

St. Teresa of Ávila.
The Interior Castle. First
Mansions, Chapter 2.

Additional Biblical Reflections: 1 Samuel 16:15, John 16:7, 1 Corinthians 3:16, Ephesians 4:30

Prayer

Your Spirit, Lord, is greater than any possession and more satisfying than any sin. Cleanse our hearts, O Lord, and give us strength in temptation that we would not grieve the Spirit but grow ever more deeply in our relationship with you through Your Spirit's indwelling. Amen.

DAY 15

Christianity often gets a "bad rap" for restricting us in our freedom. However, freedom to sin is not genuine freedom; it is bondage. Teresa encourages us to explore within the confines of the great "interior castle" of our prayer lives. We should not restrict God's willingness to show us new blessings and revelations by imposing strict regulations on our forms and habits of prayer.

Meditations from St. Teresa

A soul which gives itself to prayer, either much or little, should on no account be kept within narrow bounds. Since God has given it such great dignity, permit it to wander at will through the rooms of the castle, from the lowest to the highest. Let it not force itself to remain for very long in the same mansion, even that of self-knowledge. Mark well, however, that self-knowledge is indispensable, even for those whom God takes to dwell in the same mansion with Himself. Nothing else, however elevated, perfects the soul which must never seek to forget its own nothingness. Let humility be always at work, like the bee at the honeycomb, or all will be lost. But, remember, the bee leaves its hive to fly in search of flowers and the soul should sometimes cease thinking of itself to rise in meditation on the grandeur and majesty of its God. It will learn its own baseness better thus than by self-contemplation, and will be freer from the reptiles which enter the first room where self-knowledge is acquired. Although it is a great grace from God to practise self-examination, yet 'too much is as bad as too little,' as they say; believe me, by God's help, we shall advance more by contemplating the divinity than by keeping our eyes fixed on ourselves, poor creatures of Earth that we are.

St. Teresa of Ávila.
The Interior Castle. First
Mansions, Chapter 2.

Additional Biblical Reflections: Psalm 119:45, John 8:36, 2 Corinthians 3:17

Prayer

Lord, you are the true source of genuine freedom. Let us not be enslaved to a habit or pattern that leads us to approach you with trepidation or terror. Instead, grant us the freedom to explore your graces in the great Castle of our faith. Amen.

DAY 16

It can often seem like the world is stacked against us, making greater pursuits of God impossible. However, as Teresa reminds us in today's meditation, God often works through human error and even persecution to show us Himself more clearly. In what ways has God used unfortunate circumstances, sorrow, suffering, or even bad advice to accomplish something great in your life?

Meditations from St. Teresa

Whenever the Lord gave me some command in prayer and the confessor told me to do something different, the Lord Himself would speak to me again and tell me to obey Him; and His Majesty would then change the confessor's mind so that he came back and ordered me to do the same thing. When a great many books written in Spanish were taken from us and we were forbidden to read them, I was very sorry, for the reading of some of them gave me pleasure and I could no longer continue this as I had them only in Latin. Then the Lord said to me: "Be not distressed, for I will give thee a living book." I could not understand why this had been said to me, for I had not then had any visions. But a very few days afterwards, I came to understand it very well, for what I saw before me gave me so much to think about and so much opportunity for recollection, and the Lord showed me so much love and taught me by so many methods, that I have had very little need of books – indeed, hardly any. His Majesty Himself has been to me the Book in which I have seen what is true. Blessed be such a Book, which leaves impressed upon us what we are to read and do, in a way that is unforgettable! Who can see the Lord covered with wounds and afflicted with persecutions without embracing them, loving them and desiring them for

31

himself? Who can see any of the glory which He gives to those who serve Him without recognizing that anything he himself can do and suffer is absolutely nothing compared with the hope of such a reward? Who can behold the torments suffered by the damned without feeling that the torments of Earth are by comparison pure joy and realizing how much we owe to the Lord for having so often delivered us from damnation?

St. Teresa of Ávila, *A Life,* Chapter 26.

Additional Biblical Reflections: Matthew 5:10, Luke 6:22, 2 Corinthians 12:10, 2 Timothy 3:12

Prayer

Dear Lord, you told us that those who follow you would invariably bear their crosses after you. Sustain us, Lord, in confidence and in imitation of your Son that with Him, we might pass through the fiery trials of this life and live with You in His resurrection. Amen.

DAY 17

Often, we do not see the fruit of our virtues blossom immediately. Many find this discouraging. In today's meditation St. Therese reminds her novice that in God's time the fruit of virtue will be born in the proper time—if not in this life, in the next. Thus, we should not be discouraged if we do not see an immediate improvement in our lives when we pursue virtue. Rather, we must persist in faith and trust that God will bring these rewards to fruition in the proper time.

Perspective is important. When we begin complaining to God about how things might not be as we wish, we could do well to heed Teresa's words. Here, Teresa reminds us how incredible it is that God would look upon us in favor after he, too, has seen the depths of our hearts in sin. What a marvel it is, in fact, that God has shown us grace!

Meditations from St. Teresa

O wondrous loving-kindness of God, Who permittest Thyself to be looked upon by eyes which have looked on things as sinfully as have the eyes of my soul! After this sight, Lord, may they never more accustom themselves to look on base things and may nothing content them but Thee. O ingratitude of mortal men! How far will it go? I know by experience that all I am saying now is true and that what it is possible to say is the smallest part of what Thou doest with a soul that Thou leadest to such heights as this. O souls that have begun to pray and that possess true faith, what blessings can you find in this life to equal the least of these, to say nothing of the blessings you may gain in eternity? Reflect – for this is the truth – that to those who give up everything for Him God gives Himself. He is not a respecter of persons He loves us all: no one, however wicked, can be excluded from His love since He has dealt in such a way with me and brought me to so high a state. Reflect that what I am saying is barely a fraction of what there is to say.

St Teresa of Ávila, *A Life,* Chapter 27.

Additional Biblical Reflections: Psalm 103:10-12, Micah 7:18-19, Luke 7:47-48

Prayer

Dear Lord, you bestow many blessings on us in our lives. However, most of all, the greatest wonder and marvel of our faith is that you accept us through the forgiveness merited by Jesus Christ. Help us always to cherish this reality near to our hearts. In Jesus's name. Amen.

DAY 18

We are fickle creatures. How easily do we get distracted by worldly things? Without even realizing it, we often come to realize that somehow, we put our faith on the backburner. Teresa urges us to maintain focus. At the same time, she bids us not to make too much of our sinfulness. We must be repentant but also approach God with what she calls a "holy boldness" that can approach Him in confidence on account of Jesus.

Meditations from St. Teresa

O Lord! All our trouble comes to us from not having our eyes fixed upon Thee. If we only looked at the way along which we are walking, we should soon arrive; but we stumble and fall a thousand times and stray from the way because, as I say, we do not set our eyes on the true Way. One would think that no one had ever trodden it before, so new is it to us. It is indeed a pity that this should sometimes happen. I mean, it hardly seems that we are Christians at all or that we have ever in our lives read about the Passion. Lord help us – that we should be hurt about some small point of honour! And then, when someone tells us not to worry about it, we think he is no Christian. I used to laugh – or sometimes I used to be distressed – at the things I heard in the world, and sometimes, for my sins, in religious Orders. We refuse to be thwarted over the very smallest matter of precedence: apparently such a thing is quite intolerable. We cry out at once: "Well, I'm no saint"; I used to say that myself.

God deliver us, sisters, from saying "We are not angels", or "We are not saints", whenever we commit some imperfection. We may not be; but what a good thing it is for us to reflect that we can be if we will only try and if

God gives us His hand! Do not be afraid that He will fail to do His part if we do not fail to do ours. And since we come here for no other reason, let us put our hands to the plough, as they say. Let there be nothing we know of which it would be a service to the Lord for us to do, and which, with His help, we would not venture to take in hand. I should like that kind of venturesomeness to be found in this house, as it always increases humility. We must have a holy boldness, for God helps the strong, being no respecter of persons; and He will give courage to you and to me.

St. Teresa of **Á**vila,
The Way of Perfection,
Chapter 16.

Additional Biblical Reflections: Proverbs 4:25, Colossians 3:2, Hebrews 12:2

Prayer

Lord, keep our eyes ever fixed on you. We live in a world full of shiny things that often distract us and send us astray. May your presence always be a reminder of the wonder and luster of your true nature and grace. In Jesus's name. Amen.

DAY 19

It is almost like we look at the world and our lives through distorted lenses. We often amplify the seriousness of earthly matters while minimizing the true impact that God's presence can have on our lives. It is like examining life through the convex side of a spoon, and everything is inverted. Here, Teresa encourages us to recognize that the trivial matters that stress us out in this life mean very little compared to God's glory.

Meditations from St. Teresa

On various occasions it happened that I found myself greatly tried and maligned about a certain matter, to which I shall refer later, by almost everyone in the place where I am living and by my Order. I was greatly distressed by the numerous things which arose to take away my peace of mind. But the Lord said to me: "Why dost thou fear? Knowest thou not that I am all-powerful? I will fulfil what I have promised thee." And shortly afterwards this promise was in fact completely fulfilled. But even at that time I began at once to feel so strong that I believe I could have set out on fresh undertakings, even if serving Him had cost me further trials and I had had to begin to suffer afresh. This has happened so many times that I could not count them. Often He has uttered words of reproof to me in this way, and He does so still when I commit imperfections, which are sufficient to bring about a soul's destruction. And His words always help me to amend my life, for, as I have said, His Majesty supplies both counsel and remedy. At other times the Lord recalls my past sins to me, especially when He wishes to grant me some outstanding favour, so that my soul feels as if it is really at the Judgment; with such complete knowledge is the truth presented to it that it knows not where to hide. Sometimes these locutions warn me against perils to myself and to others, or tell me of things which are to happen three or four years hence: there have been many of these and they have all come true – it would be possible to detail some of them. There are so many signs, then, which indicate that these locutions come from God that I think the fact cannot be doubted.

St. Teresa of Ávila, *A Life,* Chapter 26.

Additional Biblical Reflections: Isaiah 26:3, John 16:33, 2 Thessalonians 3:16

Prayer

Dearest Lord, you are a God of peace. You desire not only peace in the world but also peace within our hearts. May your presence give us such a sense of peace that we cannot be unsettled by the concerns of this life. In Jesus's name. Amen.

DAY 20

Teresa reminds us, here, that there is no single way to pray that is necessarily guaranteed to produce the same results no matter who prays it. We are all unique, and our relationships with God—while universally defined in terms of Christ—are likewise unique. Accordingly, we should be willing to explore different ways of praying and determine what forms are most beneficial regarding our spiritual growth.

Meditations from St. Teresa

I myself spent over fourteen years without ever being able to meditate except while reading. There must be many people like this, and others who cannot meditate even after reading, but can only recite vocal prayers, in which they chiefly occupy themselves and take a certain pleasure. Some find their thoughts wandering so much that they cannot concentrate upon the same thing, but are always restless, to such an extent that, if they try to fix their thoughts upon God, they are attacked by a thousand foolish ideas and scruples and doubts concerning the Faith. I know a very old woman, leading a most excellent life – I wish mine were like hers – a penitent and a great servant of God, who for many years has been spending hours and hours in vocal prayer, but from mental prayer can get no help at all; the most she can do is to dwell upon each of her vocal prayers as she says them. There are a great many other people just like this; if they are humble, they will not, I think, be any the worse off in the end, but very much in the same state as those who enjoy numerous consolations. In one way they may feel safer, for we cannot tell if consolations come from God or are sent by the Devil. If they are not of God, they are the more dangerous; for the chief object of the Devil's work on Earth is to fill us with pride. If they are of God, there is no reason for fear, for they bring humility with them, as I explained in my other book at great length.

Others walk in humility, and always suspect that if they fail to receive consolations the fault is theirs, and are always most anxious to make progress. They never see a person shedding a tear without thinking themselves very backward in God's service unless they are doing the same, whereas they may perhaps be much more advanced. For tears, though good, are not invariably signs of perfection; there is always greater safety in humility, mortification, detachment and other virtues. There is no reason for fear, and you must not be afraid that you will fail to attain the perfection of the greatest contemplatives.

St. Teresa of **Á**vila,
The Way of Perfection,
Chapter 17.

Additional Biblical Reflections: Psalm 139:14, Matthew 10:30, Romans 12:1-21

Prayer

Lord, each one of us is the product of your masterful workmanship. Help us to find the ways that befit our constitution and aid us in prayer most effectively. Grant this that we might not fall into vain repetition or meaningless habits, but that our prayer lives will be rich and full as we mature in our faith. Amen.

DAY 21

There is no great sage or saint who provides for us a better model to imitate in the manner of prayer than Jesus. Here, Teresa bids we simply turn to the Gospels and examine how Jesus prayed so that we might learn from His perfect example.

Meditations from St. Teresa

It is always a great thing to base your prayer on prayers which were uttered by the very lips of the Lord. People are quite right to say this, and, were it not for our great weakness and the lukewarmness of our devotion, there would be no need for any other systems of prayer or for any other books at all. I am speaking to souls who are unable to recollect themselves by meditating upon other mysteries, and who think they need special methods of prayer; some people have such ingenious minds that nothing is good enough for them! So I think I will start to lay down some rules for each part of our prayer – beginning, middle and end – although I shall not spend long on the higher stages. They cannot take books from you, and, if you are studious and humble, you need nothing more.

I have always been fond of the words of the Gospels and have found more recollection in them than in the most carefully planned books – especially books of which the authors were not fully approved, and which I never wanted to read. If I keep close to this Master of wisdom, He may perhaps give me some thoughts which will help you. I do not say that I will explain these Divine prayers, for that I should not presume to do, and there are a great many explanations of them already. Even were there none, it would be ridiculous for me to attempt any. But I will write down a few thoughts on the words of the Paternoster; for sometimes, when we are most anxious to nurture our devotion, consulting a great many books will kill it. When a master is himself giving a lesson, he treats his pupil kindly and likes him to enjoy being taught and does his utmost to help him learn. Just so will this heavenly Master do with us.

St. Teresa of Ávila,
The Way of Perfection,
Chapter 21.

Additional Biblical Reflections: Matthew 14:23, Luke 9:28-29, John 11:41-42

Prayer

Lord, how often do we look for wisdom in worldly examples when you have already provided all that we need. Thank you for the example of your Son, Jesus Christ, who not only taught us to pray but also showed us how to pray by his example. Grant that we might follow his lead and more perfectly draw near to you in the same way. Amen.

DAY 22

Are you holding back any sins that you have not yet been willing to confess? In today's meditation, Teresa tells the story of a fellow she counseled who had done exactly that and much to his peril. However, once he confessed his sin, he experienced great freedom and finally experienced greater intimacy with God.

Meditations from St. Teresa

A person came to me who for two and a half years had been living in mortal sin – one of the most abominable sins that I had ever heard of – and during the whole of that time he neither confessed it nor amended his life, and yet went on saying Mass. And, though he confessed his other sins, when it came to that one, he would ask himself how he could possibly confess such a dreadful thing. He had a great desire to give it up but could not bring himself to do so. I was terribly sorry for him and very much distressed to find that God was being offended in such a way. I promised him that I would pray earnestly to God that He would help him and that I would get other people better than myself to do so too, and I wrote to a certain person who, he said, would be able to distribute the letters. And, lo and behold, at the first possible moment, he confessed; for through the many most saintly persons who at my request had prayed to Him on his behalf God was pleased to bestow this mercy upon his soul, and I, miserable though I am, had done what I could and taken the greatest pains about it. He wrote to me and said that he was now so much better that days passed without his falling into this sin, but he was suffering such tortures from temptation that his distress made him feel as if he were already in hell; and he asked me to commend him to God. I spoke about it again to my sisters, through whose prayers the Lord must have granted me this favour, and they took it very much to heart.

St. Teresa of Ávila, *A Life,* Chapter 31.

Additional Biblical Reflections: Proverbs 28:13, 1 John 1:9, James 5:16

Prayer

Lord, there is no such thing as a secret sin in your sight. May we never withhold sins from confession. Instead, lead us to approach you in both humility and repentance but in the confidence of your grace. For you desire not that we would remain burdened by our sins but freed to live lives in greater pursuit of you. Amen.

DAY 23

There are two main thoughts in today's meditation. First, Teresa encourages us to spend time with persons who are more mature in the faith to benefit from their example. Second, she encourages us not to turn our prayer life into a mere "means to an end" of what we have imagined for ourselves. Prayer is not just a "tool" to use to get something better; it is, itself, the great prize.

Meditations from St. Teresa

It is of the utmost importance for the beginner to associate with those who lead a spiritual life, and not only with those in the same mansion as herself, but with others who have travelled farther into the castle, who will aid her greatly and draw her to join them. The soul should firmly resolve never to submit to defeat, for if the devil sees it staunchly determined to lose life and comfort and all that he can offer, rather than return to the first mansion, he will the sooner leave it alone.

Let the Christian be valiant; let him not be like those who lay down to drink from the brook when they went to battle (I do not remember when). Let him resolve to go forth to combat with the host of demons, and be convinced that there is no better weapon than the cross. I have already *said, yet it is of such importance that I repeat it here: let no one think on starting of the reward to be reaped: this would be a very ignoble way of commencing such a large and stately building. If built on sand it would soon fall down. Souls who acted thus would continually suffer from discouragement and temptations, for in these mansions no manna rains;*

farther on, the soul is pleased with all that comes, because it desires nothing but what God wills.

St. Teresa of Ávila.
The Interior Castle.
Second Mansions.

Additional Biblical Reflections: Psalm 5:1-12; Jeremiah 13:23-37; Philippians 4:6-8

Prayer

Lord, surround us with giants of faith who might encourage us in our pursuits of you. While we know we should never forget that these men and women are sinners, too, you nonetheless bless our fellow Christians with many gifts from which we might learn and grow. Fill our lives with such people so that we might pray unto you more—not so that we might achieve a particular goal, but because, in prayer, we come to relish in your presence. Amen.

DAY 24

In today's meditation, Teresa encourages proper reverence when we pray. There is a fine balance. We do not want to be so fearful that we worry about the missteps we might make or our choice of words. However, neither do we want to approach God as if he were any man.

Meditations from St. Teresa

When you approach God, then, try to think and realize Whom you are about to address and continue to do so while you are addressing Him. If we had a thousand lives, we should never fully understand how this Lord merits that we behave toward Him, before Whom even the angels tremble. He orders all things and He can do all things: with Him to will is to perform. It will be right, then, daughters, for us to endeavour to rejoice in these wondrous qualities of our Spouse and to know Whom we have wedded and what our lives should be. Why, God save us, when a woman in this world is about to marry, she knows beforehand whom she is to marry, what sort of a person he is and what property he possesses. Shall not we, then, who are already betrothed, think about our Spouse, before we are wedded to Him and He takes us home to be with Him? If these thoughts are not forbidden to those who are betrothed to men on Earth, how can we be forbidden to discover Who this Man is, Who is His Father, what is the country to which He will take me, what are the riches with which He promises to endow me, what is His rank, how I can best make Him happy, what I can do that will give Him pleasure, and how I can bring my rank into line with His.

If a woman is to be happy in her marriage, it is just those things that she is advised to see about, even though her husband be a man of very low station.

St. Teresa of **Á**vila,
The Way of Perfection,
Chapter 22.

Additional Biblical Reflections: Exodus 3:5, Proverbs 1:7, Hebrews 12:28

Prayer

Lord, we revere your Holy name. For while you desire greater intimacy with us, let us never grow arrogant in our disposition toward you. Grant that we might ever keep your name Holy in all that we say and do. Amen.

DAY 25

W hen it comes to new Christians or beginners in the habit of prayer, there is a great danger that we might imagine our initial excitement to be regularly expected. In truth, a life in prayer and contemplation—as a way of pursuing Christ—is bound to be accompanied by trials and feelings of "dryness." Teresa encourages us in today's meditation to find Christ precisely in such moments.

Meditations from St. Teresa

What a farce it is! Here are we, with a thousand obstacles, drawbacks, and imperfections within ourselves, our virtues so newly born that they have scarcely the strength to act (and God grant that they exist at all!) yet we are not ashamed to expect sweetness in prayer and to complain of feeling dryness.

Do not act thus, sisters; embrace the cross your Spouse bore on His shoulders; know that your motto should be: 'Most happy she who suffers most if it be for Christ!' All else should be looked upon as secondary: if our Lord give it you, render Him grateful thanks. You may imagine you would be resolute in enduring external trials if God gave you interior consolations: His Majesty knows best what is good for us; it is not for us to advise Him how to treat us, for He has the right to tell us that we know not what we ask. Remember, it is of the greatest importance – the sole aim of one beginning to practise prayer should be to endure trials, and to resolve and strive to the utmost of her power to conform her own will to the will of God. Be certain that in this consists all the greatest perfection to be attained in the spiritual life, as I will explain later. She who practises this most perfectly will receive from God the highest reward and is the farthest advanced on the right road. Do not imagine that we have need of a cabalistic formula or any other occult or mysterious thing to attain it our whole welfare consists in doing the will of God. If we start with the false principle of wishing God to follow our will and to lead us in the way we think best, upon what firm foundation can this spiritual edifice rest?

St Teresa of Ávila,
The Interior Castle,
Second Mansions.

Additional Biblical Reflections: John 16:33, Romans 5:3-5, James 1:2-4

Prayer

Lord, you endured suffering and the cross on our behalf. Now, when we engage in trials and suffering of any kind, we can be sure that we will find you in the midst of it. Gather us unto you in your suffering so that we might also be born again with you in your resurrection life. Amen.

DAY 26

Like Jesus, Teresa warns against the spiritual entrapping associated with wealth. She encourages us, who have been blessed, to show charity toward others and give out of our abundance.

Meditations from St. Teresa

A rich man, without son or heir, loses part of his property, but still has more than enough to keep himself and his household. If this misfortune grieves and disquiets him as though he were left to beg his bread, how can our Lord ask him to give up all things for His sake? This man will tell you he regrets losing his money because he wished to bestow it on the poor.

I believe His Majesty would prefer me to conform to His will, and keep peace of soul while attending to my interests, to such charity as this. If this person cannot resign himself because God has not raised him so high in virtue, well and good: let him know that he is wanting in liberty of spirit; let him beg our Lord to grant it him, and be rightly disposed to receive it. Another person has more than sufficient means to live on, when an opportunity occurs for acquiring more property: if it is offered him, by all means let him accept it; but if he must go out of his way to obtain it and then continues working to gain more and more – however good his intention may be (and it must be good, for I am speaking of people who lead prayerful and good lives), he cannot possibly enter the mansions near the King.

St Teresa of Ávila,
The Interior Castle,
Third Mansions,
Chapter 2.

Additional Biblical Reflections: Matthew 25:40, Philippians 2:4-8, 1 John 3:17

Prayer

Lord, you bless many of us with material goods and abundance. Protect us from turning these things, which come from you, into false gods. Grant us opportunities to share with others the blessings you have given us. Introduce us to those in need so that we might become your vessel of provision to others you love. In Jesus's name. Amen.

DAY 27

How one spends his or her time shows much about where one's heart is. What is "time," though to God, who is eternal? Does God covet our time? Teresa bids we consider the time we offer to God much like a husband might view his ring. While it might be worth relatively little, its worth comes in what it stands for and represents. Our time, likewise, does not add anything to God's character since he lacks nothing. Rather, by giving Him our time in prayer and devotion, we memorialize and live out our relationship with Him.

Meditations from St. Teresa

What wife is there who, after receiving many valuable jewels from her husband, will not give him so much as a ring – which he wants, not because of its value, for all she has is his, but as a sign of love and a token that she will be his until she dies? Does the Lord deserve less than this that we should mock Him by taking away the worthless gift which we have given Him? Since we have resolved to devote to Him this very brief period of time – only a small part of what we spend upon ourselves and upon people who are not particularly grateful to us for it – let us give it Him freely, with our minds unoccupied by other things and entirely resolved never to take it back again, whatever we may suffer through trials, annoyances or aridities. Let me realize that this time is being lent to me and is not my own, and feel that I can rightly be called to account for it if I am not prepared to devote it wholly to God.

St. Teresa of **Á**vila,
The Way of Perfection,
Chapter 23.

Additional Biblical Reflections: Mark 7:6, Ephesians 1-33, 2 Thessalonians 3:6

Prayer

Dear Lord, you lack nothing, and there is nothing we can add to improve upon your glory. Let us see our gifts and our time, which we offer unto you, not as a gift you require but as a token of our love. Return these offerings, and we bid you with an abundance of your Spirit and presence. Amen.

DAY 28

We are often blind to our faults while we seem to see the faults of others magnified as if through binoculars. Today, Teresa bids we first consider our own faults and sins before we fixate on the flaws and faults of others.

Meditations from St. Teresa

Let us look at our own faults, and not at other persons'. People who are extremely correct themselves are often shocked at everything they see; however, we might often learn a great deal that is essential from the very persons whom we censure. Our exterior comportment and manners may be better--this is well enough, but not of the first importance. We ought not to insist on every one following in our footsteps, nor to take upon ourselves to give instructions in spirituality when, perhaps, we do not even know what it is. Zeal for the good of souls, though given us by God, may often lead us astray, sisters; it is best to keep our rule, which bids us ever to live in silence and in hope. Our Lord will care for the souls belonging to Him; and if we beg His Majesty to do so, by His grace we shall be able to aid them greatly. May He be for ever blessed!

St. Teresa of Ávila,
The Interior Castle,
Third Mansions,
Chapter 2.

Additional Biblical Reflections: Isaiah 53:5-6, Matthew 7:1-5, James 4:11-12

Prayer

Lord, we know that all have sinned and fall short of our glory. Grant that we might always have the eyes to see our sins and the confidence to confess them before God and men so that we might be assured of your absolution. Let us not judge others, for it is not our place to judge, but grant us the patience to bear with our fellow brothers and sisters after the pattern of patience you first demonstrated to us. Amen.

DAY 29

In today's meditation, Teresa not only reminds us that persecution and martyrdom are likely in this world, but she also encourages us to pray for others who might be weaker in the faith, so they might stand firm under the pressures of toil and tribulation.

Meditations from St. Teresa

For a soul which God allows to walk in this way in the sight of the whole world may well prepare itself to be martyred by the world, for, if it will not die to the world of its own free will, the world itself will kill it. Really, I can see nothing in the world that seems to me good save its refusal to allow that good people can ever do wrong and the way it perfects them by speaking ill of them. I mean that more courage is necessary for following the way of perfection, if one is not perfect, than for suddenly becoming a martyr; for perfection cannot be acquired quickly, except by one to whom by some particular privilege the Lord is pleased to grant this favour. When the world sees anyone setting out on that road it expects him to be perfect all at once and detects a fault in him from a thousand leagues' distance; yet in that particular person the fault may be a virtue, and his critic, in whom it is a vice, may be judging him by himself. They will not allow him to eat or sleep – they will hardly let him breathe, as we say: the more highly they think of him, the more they seem to forget that he is still in the body. For, however perfect his soul may be, he is still living on Earth, and however resolutely he may trample Earth's miserable limitations beneath his feet, he is still subject to them. And so, as I say, he needs great courage. His poor soul has not yet begun to walk, and men expect it to fly. He has not yet conquered his passions, and men expect him to rise to great occasions and be as brave as they read the saints were after they had been confirmed in grace. What happens here gives us cause for praising the Lord and also for great sorrow of heart, since so many poor souls turn back because they have no idea what to do to help themselves. And I believe my soul would have been like them had not the Lord Himself had such compassion on me and done everything for me. Until He of His goodness had done everything, I myself did nothing, as Your Reverence will know, but fall and rise again.

St. Teresa of Ávila, *A Life*, Chapter 31.

Additional Biblical Reflections: John 15:19, Acts 14:22, Romans 8:35, 1 Peter 3:16

Prayer

Lord, be with all those who are persecuted in both our communities and around the world. Sustain them with the consolations of your Spirit so that their sufferings might also bear witness to you and your glory. In Jesus's name. Amen.

DAY 30

In today's mediation, Teresa offers a prayer unto the Lord, honoring his faithfulness despite our faithlessness. We would do well to imitate Teresa in this way—praising Christ's virtues while recognizing our needs in His presence.

Meditations from St. Teresa

Behold, my Lord, with the love that Thou hast for us and with Thy humility, nothing can be an obstacle to Thee. And then, Lord, Thou hast been upon Earth and by taking our nature upon Thee hast clothed Thyself with humanity: Thou hast therefore some reason to care for our advantage. But behold, Thy Father is in Heaven, as Thou hast told us, and it is right that Thou shouldst consider His honour. Since Thou hast offered Thyself to be dishonoured by us, leave Thy Father free. Oblige Him not to do so much for people as wicked as I, who will make Him such poor acknowledgment.

O good Jesus! How clearly hast Thou shown that Thou art One with Him and that Thy will is His and His is Thine! How open a confession is this, my Lord! What is this love that Thou hast for us? Thou didst deceive the Devil, and conceal from him that Thou art the Son of God, but Thy great desire for our welfare overcomes all obstacles to Thy granting us this greatest of favours. Who but Thou could do this, Lord? I cannot think how the Devil failed to understand from that word of Thine Who Thou wert, beyond any doubt. I, at least, my Jesus, see clearly that Thou didst speak as a dearly beloved son both for Thyself and for us, and Thou hast such power that what Thou sayest in Heaven shall be done on Earth. Blessed be Thou for ever, my Lord, Who lovest so much to give that no obstacle can stay Thee.

St. Teresa of **Á**vila,
The Way of Perfection,
Chapter 27.

Additional Biblical Reflections: Proverbs 22:4, Matthew 5:2-11, Luke 14:11.

Prayer

Dear Lord, we thank you for the many blessings and graces you have poured upon our lives. Continue to nurture us in your Word that we might come to know you more, pray to you more frequently, and represent your Son more faithfully. In His name. Amen.

DAY 31

We do not earn God's love any more than a child straight from the womb earns the love of their mother. God's love for His creatures is on account of that very fact—we are *his* creatures. Thus, St. Therese reflects on how God bestows His love on the simplest of us and the holy Doctors. He cares even for the "poor savage" just as much as He loves the refined and the wealthy. The basis of God's love is not in those whom He loves but in the character of His divine heart. Thus, we can take great comfort in how no matter our estate, our place in the world, our rank, or our past mistakes, God still "deigns to stoop" to our level and show us His love.

Meditations from St. Therese

The love of God reveals itself in the very simplest soul who resists His grace in nothing, as well as in the most sublime. Indeed, the characteristic of love being to humble itself, if all souls resembled those of the holy Doctors who have enlightened the Church, the good God would not seem to descend low enough in coming to them. But He has created the infant who knows nothing and can only wail; He has created the poor savage who has but the natural law for guidance, and it is even unto their hearts that He deigns to stoop.

HIST. D'UNE
AME, CH. I

Additional Biblical Reflections: 1 Kings 8:23; Psalm 6:4; John 15:12-13.

Prayer

Lord, though we might be loved or unloved, welcomed or rejected, by the world, you are our maker and redeemer. We give thanks for your great love that considers not our worth, status, or merit, but only the merits of Christ in whom we are all adopted as your beloved children. Let us draw nearer to you in your love that we might within your embrace demonstrate your unwavering love to one another. Amen.

DAY 32

The path of holiness is not complicated. All the rites, prayers, and practices embraced by the saints boil down to a basic but fundamental Biblical principle—love. However, to say that the path of holiness is *simple* does not mean that it is easy. The demonstration of God's love, through Jesus, was simple, but the journey to the cross was arduous and costly. To follow the saints' path does not require a special insight or revelation, but rather, a heart willing to follow the path of the cross, the path of love.

Meditations from St. Therese

I know of one means only by which to attain to perfection: LOVE. Let us love, since our heart is made for nothing else. Sometimes I seek another word to express Love, but in this land of exile the word which begins and ends is quite incapable of rendering the vibrations of the soul; we must then adhere to this simple and only word: TO LOVE. But on whom shall our poor heart lavish its love? Who shall be found that is great enough to be the recipient of its treasures? Will a human being know how to comprehend them, and above all will he be able to repay? There exists but one Being capable of comprehending love; it is Jesus; He alone can give us back infinitely more than we shall ever give to Him.

LETTER TO HER
COUSIN MARIE
GUÉRIN

Additional Biblical Reflections: Micah 7:18; 1 Corinthians 13:13; Luke 9:23.

Prayer

Lord, the path toward intimacy with you was revealed to us clearly. Yet, too often, we resist the path of love. Soften our hearts, Lord, and give us the endurance and willingness to take up our crosses in the image of your Son's love for the world that we, too, might offer ourselves to as living sacrifices. Amen.

DAY 33

God is liberal in His love. However, embracing His love requires self-surrender and gratitude. It is not enough to surrender ourselves to His love while imagining we are entitled to it. Gratitude and thanksgiving are more than good manners. It is how we take hold of God's love and embrace it not as something we merit but as a gift merited only by Christ on our behalf.

Meditations from St. Therese

Oh! if souls weak and imperfect as mine, felt what I feel, not one would despair of reaching the summit of the mountain of Love, since Jesus does not demand from us great deeds, but only self-surrender and gratitude. I have no need, saith He, of the goats of thy flocks . . . If I were hungry I would not tell thee . . . Offer unto God the sacrifice of praise and thanksgiving. See then, all that Jesus asks of us! He has not need of our works but only of our love. This very God who declares that He needs not to tell us if He were hungry, did not hesitate to beg of the Samaritan woman a little water . . . He thirsted!!! But in saying: "Give me to drink," it was the love of His poor creature that the Creator of the universe besought. He thirsted for Love! And now, more than ever is Jesus athirst. He meets with none but the ungrateful and the indifferent among the disciples of the world; and amongst His own disciples He finds, alas! very few hearts that surrender themselves without any reserve to the tenderness of His infinite Love.

HIST. D'UNE
AME, CH. XI

Additional Biblical Reflections: 1 Chronicles 16:8; Psalm 49; John 4:7.

Prayer

Lord, all things we have come to us out of your open heart. Engender within us hearts of gratitude that we might not boast of our status as your children but cherish every good gift that comes from your hand. Amen.

DAY 34

We are people who have been given much. We have even been given callings. This pattern of having received takes new shape in the form of charity as we serve others through the callings and tasks the Lord has given us in love. Thus. St. Therese reminds us that love "comprises all vocations," and no matter how humble a work we might do, whether it be serving kings and presidents or waiting on tables, in all things we are called to serve.

Meditations from St. Therese

Charity gave me the key to my vocation. I understood that the Church being a body composed of different members, the most essential, the most noble of all the organs would not be wanting to her; I understood that the Church has a heart and that this heart is burning with love; that it is love alone which makes the members work, that if love were to die away apostles would no longer preach the Gospel, martyrs would refuse to shed their blood. I understood that love comprises all vocations, that love is everything, that it embraces all times and all places because it is eternal!

HIST. D'UNE
AME, CH. XI

Additional Biblical Reflections: Proverbs 19:13; Luke 21:1-4; 1 John 3:17.

Prayer

Lord, if anyone ever had reason to boast, it was you. Still, you humbled yourself to dwell among us—even accepting a death befitting a common criminal in our place. Let us not boast of our status and rights but, rather, let us live lives that consider others first, lives shaped by charity. Amen.

DAY 35

One of the temptations that can befall us when we are charitable is that we begin to take credit and pride in our benevolence. We might also be tempted to judge those who appear less virtuous than us. However, St. Therese reminds us that even when we act in a godly way, it is on account of Jesus who acts through us. Because it is Jesus who works through us, we know that Jesus is the one who works—and is constantly working—through our fellow believers. Thus, there is no room for pride. It is the same Lord who works through us all.

Meditations from St. Therese

I feel that when I am charitable it is Jesus alone who acts in me; the more I am united to Him the more do I love all my Sisters. If, when I desire to increase this love in my heart, the demon tries to set before my eyes the faults of one or other of the Sisters, I hasten to call to mind her virtues, her good desires; I say to myself that if I have seen her fall once, she may well have gained many victories which she conceals through humility; and that even what appears to me a fault may in truth be an act of virtue by reason of the intention.

HIST. D'UNE
AME, CH. IX

Additional Biblical Reflections: Colossians 3:12-14; Roman 7:17-20; Philippians 2:1-5.

Prayer

Lord, every move we make is on account of you and your Spirit, who dwells in us. Let us not grow prideful in our virtue that your goodness might become an occasion for vice. Rather, let us celebrate the ways you choose to work through others and give thanks for however you have chosen to work in our hearts. Amen.

DAY 36

Today's meditation is brief but profound. While we are to be mindful of the company we keep—that we not be lured into sin—we are also called to humble ourselves, love our enemies, and do as Jesus did when he ate with sinners, much to the chagrin of the Pharisees. When we only seek company with those we like, it is ultimately a symptom of our pride—we are using those with whom we keep company to satisfy our own needs, our desire for companionship that satisfies our emotions, and the like. When we seek the companies of even those whom we do not particularly like or appreciate, the Lord can open our eyes to see past our shallow judgments and demonstrate that on account of Christ, we are all one body and members of His church.

Meditations from St. Therese

I ought to seek the company of those Sisters who according to nature please me least. I ought to fulfil in their regard the office of the Good Samaritan. A word, a kindly smile, will often suffice to gladden a wounded and sorrowful heart.

HIST. D'UNE
AME, CH. X

Additional Biblical Reflections: 1 Corinthians 5:11; Mark 2:13-17; Luke 15:7.

Prayer

Lord, while we are called out of the world and should not keep unsavory company, we are also called to embrace the lowly and rejected. Let us not be prideful about the company we keep but give us hearts for the outcasts and the despised that we might be ever mindful of the fact that we, too, were outcasts and despised on account of our sin when Jesus came to die for us. Amen.

DAY 37

In today's meditation, St. Therese addresses Jesus's controversial teaching that he should gladly give the cloak off his back if one comes to contend with him. In our world, we become quite attached to our property and material goods. But here, St. Therese reminds us that, for our Lord, the reward of being a servant to others is greater than that of any material benefit. Rather than asking how I can protect what is mine, she suggests, the question one should ask is how I can render service to others with all that God has given me.

Meditations from St. Therese

Oh! what peace inundates the soul when she rises above natural sentiment. No joy can compare with that known to one who is truly poor in spirit. If he ask with detachment for some necessary thing, and it is not only refused him, but an attempt made besides to deprive him of what he already has, he follows the counsel of our Lord: "And if a man will contend with thee in judgment and take away thy coat, let go thy cloak also unto him." To yield up our cloak means, I think, to renounce our last rights, to consider oneself as the servant, the slave of others. When we have abandoned our mantle it is easier to walk, to run; therefore Jesus adds: "And whosoever will force thee one mile, go with him other two." It is not enough that I should give to whosoever may ask of me, I must forestall their desires, and show that I feel much gratified, much honored in rendering service; and if they take a thing that I use, I must seem as though glad to be relieved of it.

HIST. D'UNE
AME, CH. IX

Additional Biblical Reflections: Proverbs 19:17; Matthew 5:40-42; Luke 3:10-11.

Prayer

You are both Lord and servant of all. While you rule over the earth, you also open your hand to satisfy all your creatures' needs. Grant us hearts for service that we might find more gratification in giving unto others than in acquiring material goods and wealth. Amen.

DAY 38

St. Therese here observes that, particularly for his close friends and family, Jesus only worked miracles after he put their faith to the test. Faith is not a disposition of the heart but a fervent belief that takes root in action when tested. While we often pray for miracles, we do well to remember that such prayers are only granted after our faith, too, has been tested. However, what reward there is for those whose faith is steadfast.

Meditations from St. Therese

He whose Heart ever watcheth, taught me, that while for a soul whose faith equals but a tiny grain of mustard seed, he works miracles, in order that this faith which is so weak may be fortified; yet for His intimate friends, for His Mother, He did not work miracles until He had put their faith to the test. Did He not let Lazarus die though Martha and Mary had sent to tell Him that he was sick? At the marriage at Cana, the Blessed Virgin having asked Him to come to the assistance of the Master of the house, did He not reply that His hour was not yet come? But after the trial, what a recompense! Water changed to wine, Lazarus restored to life.

HIST. D'UNE
AME, CH. VI

Additional Biblical Reflections: John 2:1-12; John 11; 1 Peter 1:7.

Prayer

Lord, how often we ask you for great things but lack the patience and faith to endure through the trial. Let us embrace times of testing in our lives, and that through such things, our faith might be made pure and genuine, and that we might be properly disposed to receive your good gifts. Amen.

DAY 39

Today, St. Therese reminds us of the promise of eternal life. While it sometimes seems that life struggles are never-ending, the only thing, in truth, that is eternal is God and His plans for us. Thus, even if we endure life-long hardships, we can take great comfort in knowing that with God, the best is yet to come.

Meditations from St. Therese

Life is passing, Eternity draws nigh; soon shall we live the very life of God. After having drunk deep at the fount of bitterness, our thirst will be quenched at the very source of all sweetness. Yes, the figure of this world passeth away, soon shall we see new heavens; a more radiant sun will brighten with its splendours, ethereal seas and infinite horizons . . . We shall no longer be prisoners in a land of exile, all will be at an end and with our Heavenly Spouse we shall sail o'er boundless waters: now our harps are hung upon the willows that border the rivers of Babylon, but in the day of our deliverance what harmonies will then be heard! With what joy shall we not make every chord of our instruments to vibrate! Today, we weep remembering Sion . . . how shall we sing the songs of the Lord in a strange land?

LETTER TO HER
SISTER CÉLINE

Additional Biblical Reflections: Psalm 136; 1 Corinthians 7:31; 1 John 2:17.

Prayer

Thank you, Lord, for revealing your plan for our eternal future with you. Make us ever mindful of your promises and the splendor you have granted us for Jesus's sake, that we might not be overwhelmed by the cares of this world but endure them for what is yet to come. Amen.

DAY 40

Again, today, St. Therese reminds us of the splendor of the life to come. Here, she likens the humblest of us by worldly standards to martyrs, saints, doctors, and virgins. Even a simple child is valued as much as an Apostle or a patriarch. In an often unfair and unjust world, we can take comfort knowing that these injustices are temporary.

Meditations from St. Therese

Oh! What mysteries will be revealed to us later . . . How often have I thought that I perhaps owe all the graces showered upon me to the earnest prayer of a little soul whom I shall know only in Heaven. It is God's will that in this world by means of prayer Heavenly treasures should be imparted by souls one to another, so that when they reach the Fatherland they may love one another with a love born of gratitude, with an affection far, far exceeding the most ideal family affection upon earth. There, we shall meet with no indifferent looks, because all the Saints will be indebted to each other. No envious glances will be seen; the happiness of every one of the elect will be the happiness of all. With the Martyrs we shall be like the Martyrs; with the Doctors we shall be as the Doctors; with the Virgins, as the Virgins; and just as the members of a family are proud of one another, so shall we be of our brethren, without the least jealousy.

Who knows even if the joy we shall experience in beholding the glory of the great Saints, and knowing that by a secret dispensation of Providence we have contributed thereunto, who knows if this joy will not be as intense and sweeter perhaps, than the happiness they will themselves possess. And do you not think that on their side the great Saints, seeing what they owe to quite little souls, will love them with an incomparable love? Delightful and surprising will be the friendships found there—I am sure of it. The favoured companion of an Apostle or a great Doctor of the Church, will perhaps be a young shepherd lad; and a simple little child may be the intimate friend of a Patriarch. Oh! how I long to dwell in that Kingdom of Love . . .

COUNSELS AND
REMINISCENCES

Additional Biblical Reflections: Psalm 89:14; Galatians 3:28; 2 Timothy 4:8.

Prayer

Lord, in this world, we are esteemed and often despised without just cause. However, your justice is wrapped in mercy. Let us take comfort in the fact that you heed the prayers of even sinners and the weak of faith, as you hear those of saints and martyrs. Let us pray "thy kingdom come" that your justice will prevail in this world and in the life to come. Amen.

DAY 41

One of the difficulties with doing good deeds is that the moment we do them, pride begins to well up within us, and we spoil it by allowing our piety to puff us up. Even worse, we often take additional pride in our appearance of piety before others. St. Therese offers us simple advice: Draw near to the heart of Christ and allow His deeds to flow through us without notice or care. Only in this way do deeds become truly "good deeds," when we find ourselves serving others not because we must, but because of who we are in Christ.

Meditations from St. Therese

Jesus made me understand that the true, the only glory is that which will last forever; that to attain to it we need not perform wonderful deeds, but rather, those hidden from the eyes of others and from self, so that the left hand knoweth not what the right hand doth.

HIST. D'UNE
AME, CH. IV

Additional Biblical Reflections: Jeremiah 9:23-24; Ephesians 2:8-9; Matthew 6:1-3.

Prayer

Lord, you need not think about doing good to us but do so out of the abundance of your heart. Grant us hearts in your image that we might be spared from pride or boasting in our deeds, and instead, might serve all in love, and you alone might receive the glory. Amen.

DAY 42

Even the disciples lamented for a moment when Jesus told them he had to return to the Father. But Jesus declared it was necessary that he go away, and that he might send the Holy Spirit, a comforter, to guide us. The role of the Holy Spirit is to connect us with Christ in an ever-present way. While the Spirit is with us always, as Jesus himself promised, if we feel like we are lost or have wandered from the path, we need only contemplate the Gospels.

Meditations from St. Therese

Since Jesus has gone back to Heaven I can follow Him only by the path He has traced. Oh how luminous are His footprints—diffusing a divine sweetness. I have but to glance at the holy Gospels and immediately I inhale the fragrance of the life of Jesus, and I know aspire to be little and unknown.

LETTER TO HER
SISTER CÉLINE

Additional Biblical Reflections: 1 Kings 18:12; Matthew 29:19-20; John 16:7.

Prayer

Lord, we do not always feel your presence in our lives. Nonetheless, you have promised you would be with us no less. Help us cling to your word of promise as we navigate our lives and that in all things, we might follow your path and give glory to you alone. Amen.

DAY 43

St. Therese recognizes that her example and words often cause struggle for the novices in her order, who would hope to follow her path. That her piety elicits a struggle in these young sisters is, to her, more than satisfying. This is an insight that comes from experience. Without trying, has the way we lived out our faith inadvertently challenged others and unsettled them? If so, St. Therese suggests that we should cherish it because God works through trials like these.

Meditations from St. Therese

With a simplicity that delights me my little Sisters, the novices, tell me of the interior combats I arouse in them, in what way they find me trying; they are no more embarrassed than if it were question of someone else, knowing that by acting thus, they greatly please me. Ah! truly it is more than a pleasure, it is a delicious feast which replenishes my soul with joy. How can a thing so disagreeable to nature give such happiness? Had I not experienced it I could not have believed it. One day when I had an ardent desire for humiliation, it happened that a young postulant so fully satisfied it, that the thought of Semei cursing David came to my mind and I repeated interiorly with the holy King: Yes, it is indeed the Lord who has commanded him to say all these things to me. Thus the good God takes care of me. He cannot always offer me the strength—giving bread of exterior humiliation, but from time to time He permits me to feast upon the crumbs that fall from the table of the children. How great is His Mercy!

HIST. D'UNE
AME, CH. X

Additional Biblical Reflections: Jeremiah 22:3-5, Ecclesiastes 5:8, Romans 12:1-7.

Prayer

Lord, you showed us the art of suffering as you persisted through the cross. So, too, let us recognize that you work new life in us as we follow in your path and struggle with the principles of our faith. May these struggles be like the one who labors a field with toil, and the blessed struggles in our lives might bear the sweetest fruit. Amen.

DAY 44

Seeking the lowest of places rather than places of esteem is—St. Therese tells us—good for our souls. In lofty places, we tend to find vanity and "affliction of spirit," but when we humble ourselves, confess that we have "slipped" and cannot stand on our own, the Lord reaches out His hand to steady us. In His embrace, in the lowest place, is where we find holiness.

Meditations from St. Therese

The only thing not subject to be envied is the lowest place, it is therefore this lowest place alone which is without vanity and affliction of spirit. Still, the way of a man is not always in his power and sometimes we are surprised by a desire for that which glitters. Then, let us take our place humbly amongst the imperfect, deeming ourselves little souls whom the good God must sustain at each moment. As soon as He sees us truly convinced of our nothingness and we say to Him: My foot hath slipped: Thy mercy, O Lord, hath held me up, He stretches out His Hand to us; but if we will attempt to do something grand, even under pretext of zeal, He leaves us alone. It is enough therefore that we humble ourselves, and bear our imperfections with sweetness: there, for us, lies true sanctity.

COUNSELS AND
REMINISCENCES

Additional Biblical Reflections: Jeremiah 10:23; Psalm 93; Luke 14:7-10.

Prayer

Your ways, Oh Lord, are not ours. You are not found in the lofty places but the lowest. Pray, Lord, that we have hearts to seek you in our humble estate, and thereby draw nearer to you and know you more. Amen.

DAY 45

God's grace and His gifts are all around us. Today, St. Therese bids us to consider the sweetness of a rose-tinted peach. This peach, she says, was made sweet for our sake. Our Lord does not only grant us gifts to sustain our lives in the world, but He gives us "lavish" things that we might enjoy the gift of life. So, as long as we recognize that these good things come from the great Giver, we need not be tempted to idolize the things of this world. Indeed, He desires that we would enjoy the gifts of the world all the more as we accept these things as His gifts.

Meditations from St. Therese

The most eloquent discourses would be incapable of inspiring one act of love without the grace that moves the heart. See a beautiful, rose-tinted peach, of so sweet a savor that no craft of confectioner could produce nectar like it. Is it for the peach itself that God has created this lovely color and delicate velvety surface? Is it for the sake of the peach that He has given it so delicious a flavor? No, it is for us; what alone belongs to it and forms the essence of its existence is its stone; it possesses nothing more. Thus is Jesus pleased to lavish His gifts on some of His creatures, that through them He may draw to Himself other souls; but in His mercy He humiliates them interiorly, and gently constrains them to recognize their nothingness and His Omnipotence. These sentiments form in them, as it were, a kernel of grace, which Jesus hastens to develop for that blessed day when clothed with a beauty, immortal, imperishable, they shall without danger have place at the Celestial banquet.

LETTER TO HER
SISTER CÉLINE

Additional Biblical Reflections: Genesis 1:31; Psalm 40:5; Matthew 6:25-34.

Prayer

Lord, every good gift in this world comes from you. Yet too often, we seize what this world has to offer without giving thought to the fact that it was given to us by your hand. Let us always be thankful for the many blessings you have given us, and might we cherish our lives as your greatest gift and this world as the wondrous result of your handiwork. Amen.

DAY 46

It must have been embarrassing and frustrating for a professional fisherman to admit to Jesus that he had caught nothing through his night's labors. Still, when we recognize our humility and helplessness, our Lord is moved by compassion and goodness to act and intervene. In this way, Jesus demonstrates his character and goodness—the one who made all things also grants us all things. However, we must confess our helplessness and trust in His provision.

Meditations from St. Therese

The Apostles, without Jesus, labored long—a whole night—without taking any fish; their toil was pleasing to Him but He wished to show that He alone can give anything. He asked only an act of humility: "Children, have you any meat?" and St. Peter confesses his helplessness: "Lord we have labored all night and have taken nothing." It is enough! The Heart of Jesus is touched. Perhaps if the Apostle had taken a few little fishes the Divine Master would not have worked a miracle; but he had nothing, and so through God's power and goodness his nets were soon filled with great fishes. That is just our Lord's way. He gives as God, but He will have humility of heart.

LETTER TO HER
SISTER CÉLINE

Additional Biblical Reflections: Psalm 116:6-16; Luke 5:5; John 21:5.

Prayer

Lord, your compassion exceeds even our needs and desire. Help us always to be mindful of our dependence on you and that we might not think ourselves self-sufficient but needy. For in such a poverty of spirit, your graces are magnified, and your name is glorified. Amen.

DAY 47

Meditations from St. Therese

A novice confided to her that she made no progress and felt quite discouraged. "Till the age of fourteen," said Therese, "I practiced virtue without feeling its sweetness. I wished for suffering but had no thought of finding my joy therein; that is a grace which has been granted me later. My soul was like a beautiful tree whose blossoms no sooner opened than they fell. "Offer to the good God the sacrifice of never gathering the fruits of your labors. If He so will that during your whole life you feel a repugnance to suffer and to be humiliated, if He permit that all the flowers of your desires and of your good-will fall to earth without fruit, be not troubled. At the moment of your death He will know well how to bring to perfection, in the twinkling of an eye, beautiful fruits on the tree of your soul. "We read in the Book of Ecclesiasticus: 'There is an inactive man that wanteth help, is very weak in ability, and full of poverty: yet the eye of God hath looked upon him for good, and hath lifted him up from his low estate, and hath exalted his head: and many have wondered at him and have glorified God.

'Trust in God, and stay in thy place. For it is easy in the eyes of God, on a sudden to make the poor man rich. The blessing of God maketh haste to reward the just, and in a swift hour His blessing beareth fruit!'"

COUNSELS AND
REMINISCENCES

Additional Biblical Reflections: Exodus 18:23; Ecclesiasticus 11; 1 Timothy 6:12.

91

Prayer

Dear Lord, for you, a day is like a thousand years. However, we often treat every minute as if we had endured a thousand years in waiting. Grant us perseverance, Lord, and that the seeds of faith granted us might sprout and bear fruit in their due season. Let us not grow weary in waiting, but grant us the patience to see the fruit you have in store for us when we endure in faith. Amen.

DAY 48

Most of us do not like being corrected. If an unrepentant sinner challenges us, it makes sense that we might be ashamed. However, in truth, we rarely take the rebuke of even a just or righteous person well. In such moments, we should give thanks—rather than take offense—that the Lord has given us others who might lead us toward greater godliness.

Meditations from St. Therese

In a moment of temptation and combat a novice received this note: "The just man shall correct me in mercy and reprove me; but let not the oil of the sinner anoint my head. I cannot be corrected or tried except by the just, inasmuch as all my Sisters are pleasing to God. It is less bitter to be reproved by a sinner than by the just; but through compassion for sinners, to obtain their conversion, I pray Thee, O my God, that I may be bruised by the just souls who are round about me. Again, I beg that the oil of praise, so sweet to nature, anoint not my head, that is to say, enervate not my mind, by making me believe that I possess virtues which I have only with difficulty practiced several times.

"O my Jesus! Thy Name is as oil poured out; it is in this divine perfume that I wish to be wholly bathed, far away from the notice of creatures."

COUNSELS AND
REMINISCENCES

Additional Biblical Reflections: Proverbs 9:8; Psalm 140; Luke 17:3-4.

Prayer

Lord, send us godly men and women who are willing to speak the truth to us in love. Let us not rear back in wounded pride when corrected but embrace a rebuke with gratitude. You have not sent us fellow believers to coddle us in our sin but to speak a harsh word, out of love, when warranted. Let us respond with appropriate penitence when called to account and give thanks that you have provided others to steer us toward godliness. Amen.

DAY 49

One of the trappings of spiritual progress is arrogance. Today, St. Therese reminds us that honors are always dangerous, and men's praises can be poison. Still, when we progress in piety, others will notice and praise us for it. In such instances, we dare never accept these praises as if they are due, but always direct such praises to the Lord who sanctifies us.

Meditations from St. Therese

"GOD has a special love for you," remarked a young Sister, "since to you He entrusts other souls." "That does not add anything to me, and I am only really just what I am in God's sight . . . It does not follow that He loves me more, because He wills that I should be His interpreter to you; rather, He makes me your little servant. It is for you and not for me that He has given me the charms and virtues apparent to you. "Often I compare myself to a little bowl which God fills with good things of every kind. All the kittens come to it to take their share, and sometimes there is a contest as to which shall have most. But the Child Jesus is there, keeping watch: 'I am very willing that you drink from my little bowl' saith He, 'but take care lest you overturn it and break it.' "Truth to tell, the danger is not great, because I am placed on the ground. It is otherwise with Prioresses: they, being set on tables run many more risks. Honors are always dangerous. "Oh! how poisonous the praises served up day by day to those who hold high places.

What baneful incense! And how necessary it is that the soul be detached from self, that so she may escape unharmed."

COUNSELS AND
REMINISCENCES

Additional Biblical Reflections: 1 Samuel 16:7; John 5:44; Galatians 1:10.

Prayer

Lord, help us always to be mindful that any progress we have experienced in our walk toward you has come through your efforts in our hearts. Let us not become prideful when others observe our progress and, even more, let us not become content or imagine that we have attained the fullness of spiritual life. Rather, let us always give you the glory that we might not inadvertently wander from your path. Amen.

DAY 50

The esteem of other people is highly prized in the world. Without a good name, one can hardly experience success, and a name that has been ill-considered can cause great hardship. But for the Lord, we all have one name—the name in which we were Baptized—and what we seek should not be the greatness of our names but the consolation of our souls, wherein we find the great name of Christ sealed upon us.

Meditations from St. Therese

Far from dazzling me all the titles of nobility appear to me but empty vanity. I have understood those words of the Imitation: "Be not solicitous for the shadow of a great name." I have understood that true greatness is found not in the name but in the soul. The Prophet tells us that the Lord God shall call His servants by another name; and we read in St. John: "To him that overcometh, I will give . . . a white counter, and in the counter a new name written, which no man knoweth but he that receiveth." It is in Heaven, therefore, that we shall know our titles of nobility. Then shall each one receive from God the praise that he merits, and he who upon earth will have made choice of being the poorest and the most unknown for love of our Lord, he will be the first, the noblest and the richest.

HIST. D'UNE
AME, CH. VI

Additional Biblical Reflections: Isaiah 65:15; 1 Corinthians 4:5.

Prayer

Dear Lord, you have placed your triune name upon each of us and thereby called us your children. Let us seek no glory in our own names nor let the esteem or ill repute of our name determine our worth. Rather, let us be ever mindful that our worth is measured in the cost you paid for our souls. Amen.

DAY 51

In today's meditation, St. Therese shares a moment from her childhood wherein she grew temporarily jealous of her sister. However, as such sentiments boiled up within her, she decided to remain silent and instead turned to Jesus. Yet here, she teaches us that taming the tongue when our pride is wounded can direct us to ponder the Lord, for when we speak up to defend ourselves, we often give voice to our envy and arrogance.

Meditations from St. Therese

I was ten years old the day that my Father told Céline he was going to let her have lessons in painting; I was by, and envied her. Then Papa said to me: "And you, my little queen, would it give you pleasure too to learn drawing?" I was just going to respond with a very gladsome yes, when Marie made the remark that I had not the same taste for it as Céline. At once she gained the day; and I, thinking that here was a good opportunity of offering a grand sacrifice to Jesus, said not a word. So eager was my desire to learn drawing that now I still wonder how I had the fortitude to remain silent.

HIST. D'UNE
AME, CH. VIII

Additional Biblical Reflections: Romans 12:6-8; 1 Corinthians 12:12-27; James 3:1-12.

Prayer

Lord, you often speak to us in silence. Let us be slow to speak when we feel slighted or wounded, and that rather than compound our problems, we might find peace in your presence. In Jesus's name. Amen.

DAY 52

Many of us live in fear of bad things happening. We have often grown jaded by injustices and trials we have suffered, and we worry that these things might compound upon us in our lives. In today's meditation, St. Therese shows how—as she has drawn closer to Jesus, who taught us how to suffer—we might look toward a day's troubles with a different attitude entirely.

Meditations from St. Therese

In the world, on awakening in the morning I used to think over what would probably occur either pleasing or vexatious during the day; and if I foresaw only trying events I arose dispirited. Now it is quite the other way: I think of the difficulties and the sufferings that await me, and I rise the more joyous and full of courage the more I foresee opportunities of proving my love for Jesus, and earning the living of my children—seeing that I am the mother of souls. Then I kiss my crucifix and lay it tenderly on the pillow while I dress, and I say to Him: "My Jesus, Thou hast worked enough and wept enough during the three-and-thirty years of Thy life on this poor earth. Take now Thy rest . . . My turn it is to suffer and to fight."

COUNSELS AND
REMINISCENCES

Additional Biblical Reflections: Habakkuk 3:17-19; Matthew 5:12; Hebrews 12:2.

Prayer

Lord, for the joy set before you, you endured the cross and scorned its shame. Set your cross always before our eyes so that every morning when we rise, it might be as a little resurrection with victory over the struggles that the world might throw upon us. In Jesus's name. Amen.

DAY 53

It is not always the big trials and tribulations that vex us the most. Sometimes, the small annoyances that grate upon us until we find ourselves reacting in an ungodly way. In a moment of candor, St. Therese reflects how another sister with a simple habit caused her such an annoyance that she found herself on the brink of sin. However, rather than show her irritation, she took the opportunity to accept it as an occasion to learn patience and the love of another.

Meditations from St. Therese

At prayer I was for a long time near a Sister who used to handle incessantly either her Rosary-beads or some other thing; perhaps none heard it but myself, for my hearing is extremely acute, but I cannot say how it tormented me! I should have liked to turn my head and look at the culprit so as to make her stop that noise: however in my heart I knew it was better to bear it patiently, for the love of God in the first place, and also to avoid giving pain. I kept quiet therefore, but was sometimes worked up to fever-heat and obliged to make simply a prayer of endurance. Finally I sought out the means of suffering with peace and joy, at least in my innermost soul; I tried to like the teasing little noise. Instead of endeavoring not to hear it—a thing impossible—I listened with fixed attention as if it had been a delightful concert; and my prayer, which was not the prayer of quiet, passed in offering this concert to Jesus. Another time I was in the laundry opposite a Sister who while washing handkerchiefs splashed me every minute with dirty water. My first impulse was to draw back and wipe my face, so as to show her who besprinkled me in that fashion, that she would oblige me by working more quietly; but I reflected immediately that it was very foolish

103

to refuse treasures so generously offered me, and I took good care not to show my annoyance. On the contrary, I made such successful efforts to wish for a plentiful splashing of dirty water, that at the end of half an hour I had really acquired a taste for this new sort of aspersion, and I determined to come again as often as possible to a place where happily such riches could be had gratuitously.

HIST. D'UNE
AME, CH. X

Additional Biblical Reflections:

Prayer

Lord, let us not become perplexed by the little annoyances of this life. Rather, show us the opportunity to grow, and show your love when such things vex us that we might be spared from sin and grow deeper in intimacy with you. Amen.

DAY 54

Even when we know we are guilty of sin, St. Therese urges that we should take refuge in the Lord's embrace, sure of his love and character. Despair is not a cure for sin in itself. In despair, we often fail to see the Father's loving gaze as He longs to take us into His arms. Out of desolation, we should learn to embrace the Lord and rest in His embrace.

Meditations from St. Therese

I want to make you understand by a very simple comparison how much Jesus loves souls, even the imperfect, who trust in Him. Suppose the father of two wayward and disobedient children, coming to punish them, sees one tremble and draw away from him in terror; while the other, on the contrary, throwing himself into his arms, says he is sorry, promises to be good henceforward and begs for a kiss as punishment. Do you think the delighted father will withstand the filial confidence of this child? He knows nevertheless that his son will fall again many a time into the same faults, but he is disposed to pardon him always, if always there be an appeal to his heart. I say nothing of the other child: you must understand that his father cannot love him as much or treat him with the same indulgence.

LETTER TO
HER MISSIONARY
"BROTHERS"

Additional Biblical Reflections: Joel 2:12-13; Luke 15:11-32; 1 John 4:10.

Prayer

Lord, you know we are prone to fall and sin, yet you stand very willing to embrace us when we return to you. Let us now not wallow in unnecessary despair, but in Godly penitence rest in your embrace and know your steadfast love, for you are gracious and merciful. Amen.

DAY 55

The Lord is overjoyed—as the father of the prodigal—when we return to Him after we sin. Too many people, after falling into sin, wallow in their guilt for a season. This accomplishes nothing because we cannot progress in our piety if we separate ourselves from God. Of course, we are unworthy of His love, but that has always been the case. Who are we to tell God that He should not embrace us when He desires to?

Meditations from St. Therese

Truly the Heart of Jesus is more grieved by the thousand little imperfections of His friends than by even grave faults of His enemies. But it seems to me that it is only when His own chosen ones make a habit of these infidelities, and do not ask His pardon, that He can say: "These wounds which you see in the midst of My Hands: with these was I wounded in the house of them that loved Me." For those who love Him and who come after each little fault and throw themselves into His arms, begging His forgiveness, the Heart of Jesus thrills with joy. He says to His Angels what the father of the prodigal son said to His servants: "Put a ring on his finger and let us rejoice." Oh! the goodness and the merciful love of the Heart of Jesus, how little is it known! True it is, that to share in these treasures we must humble ourselves, must acknowledge our nothingness, and that is what many souls are unwilling to do.

LETTER TO
HER MISSIONARY
"BROTHERS"

Additional Biblical Reflections: Zechariah 13:6; Luke 15:22.

Prayer

Lord, you rejoice when we return to you. Let us learn to come to you whenever we stumble, and that you might put us back on our feet again and restore us to the path of righteousness. In Jesus's name. Amen.

DAY 56

When we perceive holy men and women, we often imagine that these are people who have never fallen into mortal sin. St. Therese dispels this notion in today's meditation. Those who are made holy in piety are not so because they have been shielded from sin, but because when they have sinned, they have quickly turned to the Lord.

Meditations from St. Therese

It is not because I have been shielded from mortal sin that I lift up my heart to God in trust and love. I feel that even if there lay upon my conscience all the crimes one could commit I should lose nothing of my confidence. Brokenhearted with compunction I would go and throw myself into the arms of my Savior. I know that He cherished the Prodigal Son, I have heard His words to Mary Magdalene, to the adulteress, to the Samaritan woman. No one could frighten me, for I know what to believe concerning His Mercy and His Love. I know that in one moment all that multitude of sins would disappear—as a drop of water cast into a red-hot furnace. It is related in the Lives of the Fathers of the Desert that one of them converted a public sinner whose misdeeds scandalized the whole country. Touched by grace this sinful woman was following the saint into the desert, there to do rigorous penance, when, on the first night of her journey, before she had even reached the place of her retreat, the bonds of life were broken by the impetuosity of her loving contrition. The holy hermit at the same moment saw her soul borne by Angels into the Bosom of God. That is truly a striking instance of what I want to express, but one cannot put these things into words.

HIST. D'UNE
AME, CH. XI

Additional Biblical Reflections: Matthew 25:40, Philippians 2:4-8, 1 John 3:17.

Prayer

Lord, you know our hearts, including our weaknesses. You know when we fall and even when we are likely to fail. Yet you still bear with us in patience. Let us learn that the path to holiness is not in being sheltered from sin or the absence of failings, but in our willingness to cast our sins upon your Son, who bore them willingly for our sake. Amen.

DAY 57

In today's meditation, St. Therese uses the metaphor of a "Bank of Love," an unending deposit of good favor that God has stored up for us that we might draw upon in moments when we are discouraged. When we find ourselves lacking faith or acting out of character with what God would desire for us, we must draw upon that Bank of Love and find the strength to correct our path.

Meditations from St. Therese

I am not always faithful, but I am never discouraged; I leave myself wholly in the arms of our Divine Lord; He teaches me to draw profit from all—both good and ill that He finds in me. He teaches me to speculate in the Bank of Love, or rather it is He who acts for me without telling me how He goes to work, that is His affair and not mine; my part is complete surrender, reserving nothing to myself, not even the gratification of knowing how my credit stands with the Bank.

LETTER TO HER
SISTER CÉLINE

Additional Biblical Reflections: Mark 7:6, Ephesians:1-33, 2 Thessalonians 3:6.

Prayer

Lord, your love for us is abundant. Let us never imagine that your love for us has run thin. Rather, teach us to always return to your Bank of Love when we find ourselves going astray and that we might once again be shown the path of holiness. Amen.

DAY 58

Anxiety is not only a common experience but, in today's word, a diagnosable condition. Fearing for our future, worried about what might happen, can paralyze us in the present. In today's meditation, St. Therese bids us neither to wallow in the past nor to anticipate the future. Rather, we must always find God where we are in the moment.

Meditations from St. Therese

You are quite wrong to think of sorrows that the future may bring; it is, as it were, intermeddling with Divine Providence. We who run in the way of Love must never torment ourselves about anything. If I did not suffer minute by minute, it would be impossible for me to be patient; but I see only the present moment, I forget the past and I take good care not to anticipate the future. If we grow disheartened, if sometimes we despair, it is because we have been dwelling on the past or the future.

HIST. D'UNE
AME, CH. XII

Additional Biblical Reflections: Isaiah 35:4; Luke 12:22; 1 John 4:18.

Prayer

Lord, you are an ever-present God who redeems our past and knows our future. Let us not grow weary or anxious by worrying about the future, lest such worry causes us to sin today. Instead, let us take comfort in your presence in the present and move through each moment in godliness. Amen.

DAY 59

While the Lord will embrace us when we fall, we should also take care to note that the Lord has promised not to tempt us beyond what we can bear. The Lord has walked the path before us—like the doctor in the story St. Therese tells us in today's meditation—and cleared away any stones that might be too great for us. In this, we should have confidence that the Lord knows whatever temptations that remain we can overcome with his aid.

Meditations from St. Therese

I understand well that our Lord knew I was too weak to be exposed to temptation; without doubt I should have been wholly destroyed had I been dazzled by the deceitful glamour of the love of creatures; but never has it shone before my eyes. There, where strong souls find joy, and through fidelity detach themselves from it, I have found only affliction. Where then is my merit in not being given up to these fragile attachments, since it is only by a gracious effect of God's mercy that I was preserved from it? Without Him, I recognize that I might have fallen as low as St. Magdalene; and that word of deep meaning spoken by the Divine Master to Simon the Pharisee, re-echoes with great sweetness in my soul. Yes, I know it: "To whom less is forgiven, he loveth less." But I also know that Jesus has forgiven more to me than to St. Magdalene. Ah, how I wish I could express what I feel. Here at least is an example which will in some measure convey my thought.

Suppose the son of a skilful doctor is tripped by a stone in his path, which causes him to fall and fracture a limb. His father comes in haste, lifts him up lovingly and attends to his injuries, employing therein all the resources of his art; and the boy, very soon completely cured, testifies his gratitude.

This child has certainly good reason to love so kind a father; but here is another supposition.

The father having learnt that there lies in his son's way a dangerous stone, sets out beforehand and removes it unseen by anyone. His son, the object of this tender forethought, unaware of the misfortune from which he has been preserved by the father's hand, will of course show no gratitude, and will love him less than if he had cured him of a grievous wound. But should he come to know all, will he not love him still more? Well—I am this child, the object of the preventing love of a Father Who sent His Son not to redeem the just but sinners. He wills that I should love Him because He has forgiven me, not much, but everything. Without waiting for me to love Him much, like St. Mary Magdalene, He has made me to know how He had loved me with a preventing and ineffable love, in order that I may now love Him even unto folly!

HIST. D'UNE
AME, CH. IV

Additional Biblical Reflections: 1 Corinthians 10:13; Luke 5:32, 7:47.

Prayer

Lord, you care for us at every step of life. We thank you for going ahead of us and ensuring that no temptation greater than what we can handle has befallen us. Let us face temptation with confidence, and if we endure it with you, we will not fail. In Jesus's name. Amen.

DAY 60

S t. Therese speaks of God as the great "fulcrum" upon which we, as His saints, can uplift the world. Let us learn not to toil with anxiety to please the Lord, like Marth, but to do whatever we have been called to do with confidence, like Mary.

Meditations from St. Therese

Souls thus on fire cannot rest inactive. They may sit at the feet of Jesus, like Saint Mary Magdalene, listening to His sweet and ardent words; but, while seeming to give nothing, they do give far more than Martha who troubles herself with many things. It is not however of Martha's labors that Jesus disapproves, but only her too great anxiety; to this very same work His Blessed Mother humbly submitted herself, when she had to prepare the repasts for the Holy Family. All the Saints have understood this, and more especially perhaps those who have enlightened the world with the luminous teaching of the Gospel. Was it not from prayer that Saint Paul, Saint Augustine, Saint Thomas of Aquin, Saint John of the Cross, Saint Teresa and so many other friends of God drew that wondrous science which enraptures the greatest intellects? Archimedes said: "Give me a lever and a fulcrum, and I will raise the world." What he was unable to obtain because his request had but a material end and was not addressed to God, the Saints have obtained in full measure. For fulcrum, the Almighty has given them Himself, Himself alone! for lever, prayer, which enkindles the fire of love;

and thus it is that they have uplifted the world, thus it is that saints still militant, uplift it, and will uplift it till the end of time.

HIST. D'UNE
AME, CH. XI

Additional Biblical Reflections: Luke 10:41.

Prayer

Lord, in you, is only wisdom, but in your love, you bear with our foolishness. Help us see the great comfort and peace that comes with your presence, and may your peace cast out all anxiety and fear. On the fulcrum of your gift of love, let us all uplift the world that you might be glorified throughout creation. Amen.

DAY 61

God is love. If we are going to ask why it is important that we love God, the answer must start with God's nature and character. This is the insight that St. Bernard gave in his book, *On Loving God,* and we would do well to consider it. Often, we hear people say things like, "I couldn't love a God who allows bad things to happen," and other similar sentiments. However, God *is* love. We love because He first loved us. The cross is sufficient to demonstrate the basis of our love of God. It's there that we should look, not within the contingencies of our lives, if we are to love God properly.

Meditations from St. Bernard

You want me to tell you why God is to be loved and how much. I answer, the reason for loving God is God Himself; and the measure of love due to Him is immeasurable love. Is this plain? Doubtless, to a thoughtful man; but I am debtor to the unwise also. A word to the wise is sufficient; but I must consider simple folk too. Therefore, I set myself joyfully to explain more in detail what is meant above.

We are to love God for Himself, because of a twofold reason; nothing is more reasonable, nothing more profitable. When one asks, Why should I love God? he may mean, What is lovely in God? or What shall I gain by loving God? In either case, the same sufficient cause of love exists, namely, God Himself.

And first, of His title to our love. Could any title be greater than this, that He gave Himself for us unworthy wretches? And being God, what better gift could He offer than Himself? Hence, if one seeks for God's claim upon our love here is the chiefest: Because He first loved us (I John 4.19).

Ought He not to be loved in return, when we think who loved, whom He loved, and how much He loved? For who is He that loved? The same of whom every spirit testifies: 'Thou art my God: my goods are nothing unto Thee' (Ps. 16.2, Vulg.). And is not His love that wonderful charity which 'seeketh not her own'? (I Cor.13.5). But for whom was such unutterable love made manifest? The apostle tells us: 'When we were enemies, we were reconciled to God by the death of His Son' (Rom. 5.10). So it was God who loved us, loved us freely, and loved us while yet we were enemies. And how great was this love of His? St. John answers: 'God so loved the world that He gave His only-begotten Son, that whosoever believeth in Him should not perish, but have everlasting life' (John 3.16). St. Paul adds: 'He spared not His own Son, but delivered Him up for us all' (Rom. 8.32); and the Son says of Himself, 'Greater love hath no man than this, that a man lay down his life for his friends' (John 15.13).

St. Bernard of
Clairvaux. *On Loving God*, Ch. 1.

Additional Biblical Reflections: Deuteronomy 6:5; John 14:21; Galatians 2:20.

Prayer

Lord, your love for us is greater than we can possibly comprehend. Yet, so often, the love we have for you pales in comparison to the love you demonstrated for us on the cross. Lord, grant us hearts that conform to the image of your Son so that we might love you as you love us. Amen.

DAY 62

Even besides the cross, the Love of God is abundant and evident to believers and unbelievers alike. Despite our lack of gratitude, God continues to grant earthly blessings like food, sunlight, and food even to those who blaspheme His name. As such, life in creation testifies to our basis of love for God on several levels. If we do not see cause to love God, it is on account of the hardness of our hearts, not on account of any lack of graciousness on God's part.

Meditations from St. Bernard

Those who admit the truth of what I have said know, I am sure, why we are bound to love God. But if unbelievers will not grant it, their ingratitude is at once confounded by His innumerable benefits, lavished on our race, and plainly discerned by the senses. Who is it that gives food to all flesh, light to every eye, air to all that breathe? It would be foolish to begin a catalogue, since I have just called them innumerable: but I name, as notable instances, food, sunlight and air; not because they are God's best gifts, but because they are essential to bodily life. Man must seek in his own higher nature for the highest gifts; and these are dignity, wisdom and virtue. By dignity I mean free-will, whereby he not only excels all other earthly creatures, but has dominion over them. Wisdom is the power whereby he recognizes this dignity, and perceives also that it is no accomplishment of his own. And virtue impels man to seek eagerly for Him who is man's Source, and to lay fast hold on Him when He has been found.

Now, these three best gifts have each a twofold character. Dignity appears not only as the prerogative of human nature, but also as the cause of that fear and dread of man which is upon every beast of the earth. Wisdom perceives this distinction, but owns that though in us, it is, like all good qualities, not of us. And lastly, virtue moves us to search eagerly for an Author, and, when we have found Him, teaches us to cling to Him yet more eagerly. Consider too that dignity without wisdom is nothing worth; and wisdom is harmful without virtue, as this argument following shows: There is no glory in having a gift without knowing it. But to know only that you have it, without knowing that it is not of yourself that you have it, means self-glorying, but no true glory in God. And so the apostle says to men in such cases, 'What hast thou that thou didst not receive? Now, if thou didst receive it, why dost thou glory as if thou hadst not received it? (I Cor. 4.7). He asks, Why dost thou glory? but goes on, as if thou hadst not received it, showing that the guilt is not in glorying over a possession, but in glorying as though it had not been received. And rightly such glorying is called vain-glory, since it has not the solid foundation of truth. The apostle shows how to discern the true glory from the false, when he says, He that glorieth, let him glory in the Lord, that is, in the Truth, since our Lord is Truth (I Cor. 1.31; John 14.6).

> St. Bernard of
> Clairvaux. *On Loving
> God*, Ch. 2.

Additional Biblical Reflections: 1 Chronicles 29:12-13; Matthew 5:45; Philippians 4:19.

Prayer

Lord, you open your hand to satisfy the needs of every living thing. Your generosity is not contingent on our faith, but our faith is awakened by your graciousness. Grant us, likewise, such gratitude so that we might love you as we ought. In Jesus's name. Amen.

DAY 63

In today's meditation, St. Bernard tells us that if our love of God has fallen out of balance, it's often because the way we love ourselves—either loving ourselves too much or too little—is likewise out of balance. That is why we must examine ourselves in our pursuit of loving God. For, if we do not consider ourselves and our spiritual state properly, we will inevitably miss the mark when it comes to our disposition toward God.

Meditations from St. Bernard

We must know, then, what we are, and that it is not of ourselves that we are what we are. Unless we know this thoroughly, either we shall not glory at all, or our glorying will be vain. Finally, it is written, 'If thou know not, go thy way forth by the footsteps of the flock' (Cant. 1.8). And this is right. For man, being in honor, if he know not his own honor, may fitly be compared, because of such ignorance, to the beasts that perish. Not knowing himself as the creature that is distinguished from the irrational brutes by the possession of reason, he commences to be confounded with them because, ignorant of his own true glory which is within, he is led captive by his curiosity, and concerns himself with external, sensual things. So he is made to resemble the lower orders by not knowing that he has been more highly endowed than they.

We must be on our guard against this ignorance. We must not rank ourselves too low; and with still greater care we must see that we do not think of ourselves more highly than we ought to think, as happens when we foolishly impute to ourselves whatever good may be in us. But far more than either of these kinds of ignorance, we must hate and shun that presumption which would lead us to glory in goods not our own, knowing that they are not of ourselves but of God, and yet not fearing to rob God of the honor due unto Him. For mere ignorance, as in the first instance, does not glory at all; and mere wisdom, as in the second, while it has a kind of glory, yet does not glory in the Lord. In the third evil case, however, man sins not in ignorance but deliberately, usurping the glory which belongs to God. And this arrogance is a more grievous and deadly fault than the ignorance of the second, since it contemns God, while the other knows Him not. Ignorance is brutal, arrogance is devilish. Pride only, the chief of all iniquities, can make us treat gifts as if they were rightful attributes of our nature, and, while receiving benefits, rob our Benefactor of His due glory.

Wherefore to dignity and wisdom we must add virtue, the proper fruit of them both. Virtue seeks and finds Him who is the Author and Giver of all good, and who must be in all things glorified; otherwise, one who knows what is right yet fails to perform it, will be beaten with many stripes (Luke 12.47). Why? you may ask. Because he has failed to put his knowledge to good effect, but rather has imagined mischief upon his bed (PS. 36.4); like a wicked servant, he has turned aside to seize the glory which, his own knowledge assured him, belonged only to his good Lord and Master. It is plain, therefore, that dignity without wisdom is useless and that wisdom without virtue is accursed. But when one possesses virtue, then wisdom and dignity are not dangerous but blessed.

St. Bernard of
Clairvaux. *On Loving
God*, Ch. 2.

Additional Biblical Reflections: Matthew 7:5; 1 Corinthians 11:27-31; 2 Corinthians 13:5.

Prayer

Dear Lord, show us our own hearts so that we might be ever aware of our condition. If we think too highly of ourselves, curb our egos. If we think too low of ourselves, remind us that you loved us enough that you would exalt us should we cling to your son. Grant this so that we might be ever more aware of our need for you. Amen.

DAY 64

In today's meditation, in a letter he wrote to several monks, St. Bernard tells us that mercy is not something merited. It does not judge but *feels*. Christian love is a matter of the heart, not the mind. When we rationalize our decisions to love, it is rarely our neighbor whose interest is at heart. Rather, by rationalizing, we are bound to ask whether love is beneficial to the self, which, in turn, contradicts the very definition of love.

Meditations from St. Bernard

To the very dear Lord and Reverend father Guigues, Prior of the Grande Chartreuse, and to the holy brethren who are with him, Brother Bernard of Clairvaux offers his humble service.

In the first place, when lately I approached your parts, I was prevented by unfavourable circumstances from coming to see you and to make your acquaintance; and although my excuse may perhaps be satisfactory to you, I am not able, I confess, to pardon myself for missing the opportunity. It is a vexation to me that my occupations brought it about, not that I should neglect to come to see you, but that I was unable to do so. This I frequently have to endure, and therefore my anger is frequently excited. Would that I were worthy to receive the sympathy of all my kind friends. Otherwise I shall be doubly unhappy if my disappointment does not excite your pity. But I give you an opportunity, my brethren, of exercising brotherly compassion towards me, not that I merit it. Pity me not because I am worthy, but because I am poor and needy. Justice inquires into the merit of the suppliant, but mercy only looks to his unhappiness. True mercy does not judge, but feels; does not discuss the occasion which presents itself, but seizes it. When affection calls us, reason is silent. When Samuel wept over Saul it was by a feeling of pity, and not of approval (1 Samuel xv. 13). David shed tears over his parricidal son, and although they were profitless, yet they were pious. Therefore do ye pity me (because I need it, not because I merit it), ye who have obtained from God the grace to serve Him without fear, far from the tumults of the world from which ye are freed. Happy those whom He has hidden in His tabernacle in the day of evil men; they shall trust in the shadow of His wings until the iniquity be overpast. As for me, poor, unhappy, and miserable, labour is my portion. I seem to be as a little unfledged bird almost constantly out of the shelter of its nest, exposed to wind and tempest. I am troubled, and I stagger like a drunken man, and my whole conscience is gnawed with care. Pity me, then; for although I do not merit pity I need it, as I have said.

St. Bernard of Clairvaux. *Letter to the Monks of the Grand Chartreuse.*

Additional Biblical Reflections: John 1:16; Ephesians 4:4-9; 1 Corinthians 12:9-10.

Prayer

Lord, mercy or pity is not something we deserve, nor is it something we should withhold on account of someone else's lack of merit. For, while we did not yet deserve it, you chose to die for our sake. Let us embrace your grace so that not only might we achieve salvation for ourselves, but by grace, we might also love others. Amen.

DAY 65

Vanity—or the love of self—we hear from St. Bernard leads us to have hatred for the truth, which also leads to our spiritual blindness. Again, we hear why we must examine ourselves properly to learn to love God properly. This is why, for instance, it was not just a judgment but an act of grace when God allowed His people, in the Scriptures, to experience exile and punishment. It was not punishment for its own sake but for the sake of killing vanity and opening hearts and minds to Him and His truth.

Meditations from St. Bernard

The love of vanity is the contempt of truth, and the contempt of truth the cause of our blindness. And because they did not like, he says, to retain God in their knowledge, He gave them over unto a reprobate mind (Rom. i. 28).

From this blindness, then, it follows that we frequently love and approve that which is not for that which is; since while we are in this body we are wandering from Him who is the Fulness of Existence. And what is man, O God, except that Thou hast taken knowledge of Him? If the knowledge of God is the cause that man is anything, the want of this makes him nothing. But He who calls those things which are not as though they were, pitying those reduced in a manner to nothing, and not yet able to contemplate in its reality, and to embrace by love that hidden manna, concerning which the Apostle says: Your life is hidden with Christ in God (Cor. iii. 3). But in the meantime He has given us to taste it by faith and to seek for by strong desire. By these two we are brought for the second time from not being, to begin to be that His (new) creature, which one day shall pass into a perfect man, into the measure of the stature of the fulness of Christ. That, without doubt, shall take place, when righteousness shall be turned into judgment, that is, faith into knowledge, the righteousness which is of faith into the righteousness of full knowledge, and also the hope of this state of exile shall be changed into the fulness of love. For if faith and love begin during the exile, knowledge and love render perfect those in the Presence of God. For as faith leads to full knowledge, so hope leads to perfect love, and, as it is said, If ye will not believe ye shall not understand (Is. vii. 9, acc. to lxx.), so it may equally be said with fitness, if you have not hoped, you will not perfectly love. Knowledge then is the fruit of faith, perfect charity of hope. In the meantime the just lives by faith (Hab. ii. 4), but he is not happy except by knowledge; and he aspires towards God as the hart desires the water-brooks; but the blessed drinks with joy from the fountain of the Saviour, that is, he delights in the fulness of love.

St. Bernard of
Clairvaux. *Letter VI.*

Additional Biblical Reflections: Habakkuk 2:4; Isaiah 7:9; Romans 1:28.

Prayer

Lord, please destroy our vanity so that we might see your truth and, thereby, see you as you are. Let us not be blind by imagining we see better than we do what is good and right, but soften our hard hearts so that we might pursue what you have told us is good and salutary. In Jesus's name. Amen.

DAY 66

Apart of loving God, St. Bernard teaches us today, is to both have knowledge of the truth and delight in it. Many people, it seems, learn the faith on a mental level. They learn the Scriptures and the canons of faith, and some even pursue academic degrees. However, many such persons have little *delight* in their knowledge; others have much delight in the truth of the faith but cannot be bothered to study the truths of God. St. Bernard urges us to maintain a balance in our love of God and the truth.

Meditations from St. Bernard

Thus understanding and love, that is, the knowledge of and delight in the truth, are, perhaps, as it were, the two arms of the soul, with which it embraces and comprehends with all saints the length and breadth, the height and depth, that is the eternity, the love, the goodness, and the wisdom of God. And what are all these but Christ? He is eternity, because "this is life eternal to know Thee the true God and Jesus Christ whom Thou hast sent" (S. John xvii. 3). He is Love, because He is God, and God is Love (1 S. John iv. 16). He is both the Goodness of God and the Wisdom of God (I Cor. i. 24), but when shall these things be? When shall we see Him as He is? For the expectation of the creature waiteth for the revelation of the sons of God. For the creature was subjected unto vanity, not willingly (Rom. viii. 19, 20). It is that vanity diffused through all which makes us desire to be praised even when we are blamable, and not to be willing to praise those whom we know to be worthy of it. But this too is vain, that we, in our ignorance, frequently praise what is not, and are silent about what is.

What shall we say to this, but that the children of men are vain, the children of men are deceitful upon the weights, so that they deceive each other by vanity (Ps. lxi. 9; lxx.). We praise falsely, and are foolishly pleased, so that they are vain who are praised, and they false who praise. Some flatter and are deceptive, others praise what they think deserving, and are deceived; others pride themselves in the commendations which are addressed to them, and are vain. The only wise man is he who says with the Apostle: I forbear, lest any man should think of me above that which he seeth me to be or that he heareth of me (2 Cor. xii. 6).

St. Bernard of
Clairvaux. *Letter VI.*

Additional Biblical Reflections: Psalm 119:33-35; Proverbs 1:7; Hosea 4:6-7.

Prayer

Dearest Lord, you are the way, the truth, and the life. Grant that we who pursue your way would seek both knowledge and delight of your truth so that we might truly experience the life that you have given us on account of your Son. In Jesus's name. Amen.

DAY 67

St. Bernard tells us today that the genuine love of God is manifest when we feel pangs of the heart to the extent that we cannot love God more than we are capable of. These pangs come from our recognition and gratitude for God's love for us. That we cannot love God more than we are capable, as human beings, is a source of a holy lament not because we are insufficient—God made us as we are and declared us good—but because God's love is so magnificent.

Meditations from St. Bernard

The faithful know how much need they have of Jesus and Him crucified; but though they wonder and rejoice at the ineffable love made manifest in Him, they are not daunted at having no more than their own poor souls to give in return for such great and condescending charity. They love all the more, because they know themselves to be loved so exceedingly; but to whom little is given the same loveth little (Luke 7.47). Neither Jew nor pagan feels the pangs of love as doth the Church, which saith, 'Stay me with flagons, comfort me with apples; for I am sick of love' (Cant. 2.5). She beholds King Solomon, with the crown wherewith his mother crowned him in the day of his espousals; she sees the Sole-begotten of the Father bearing the heavy burden of His Cross; she sees the Lord of all power and might bruised and spat upon, the Author of life and glory transfixed with nails, smitten by the lance, overwhelmed with mockery, and at last laying down His precious life for His friends. Contemplating this the sword of love pierces through her own soul also and she cried aloud, 'Stay me with flagons, comfort me with apples; for I am sick of love.' The fruits which the Spouse gathers from the Tree of Life in the midst of the garden of her Beloved, are pomegranates (Cant. 4.13), borrowing their taste from the Bread of heaven, and their color from the Blood of Christ. She sees death dying and its author overthrown: she beholds captivity led captive from hell to earth, from earth to heaven, so 'that at the name of Jesus every knee should bow, of things in heaven and things in earth and things under the earth' (Phil. 2.10). The earth under the ancient curse brought forth thorns and thistles; but now the Church beholds it laughing with flowers and restored by the grace of a new benediction. Mindful of the verse, 'My heart danceth for joy, and in my song will I praise Him', she refreshes herself with the fruits of His Passion which she gathers from the Tree of the Cross, and with the flowers of His Resurrection whose fragrance invites the frequent visits of her Spouse.

Then it is that He exclaims, 'Behold thou art fair, My beloved, yea pleasant: also our bed is green' (Cant. 1.16). She shows her desire for His coming and whence she hopes to obtain it; not because of her own merits but because of the flowers of that field which God hath blessed. Christ who willed to be conceived and brought up in Nazareth, that is, the town of branches, delights in such blossoms. Pleased by such heavenly fragrance the bridegroom rejoices to revisit the heart's chamber when He finds it adorned with fruits and decked with flowers—that is, meditating on the mystery of His Passion or on the glory of His Resurrection.

St. Bernard of Clairvaux. *On Loving God*, Ch. 3.

Additional Biblical Reflections: Deuteronomy 6:5; Luke 10:27; 1 John 5:3.

Prayer

Lord, you made our hearts and all our bodies. When our hearts ache for you more than we are capable of, it is a pious sentiment that stems from the very design with which you made us. Grant us a holy longing to love you even more than we are capable of, and let us rest in the merits of Christ, whose limitless love of us and love of you is ours on account of your gracious favor. Amen.

DAY 68

The glory of God is known through both His death and resurrection—His and ours! In today's meditation, we hear how, while our flesh remains corrupt, corruption dies in the crucifixion. In the resurrection, we are granted a new body, new flesh, without corruption so that we might love God in ways we cannot yet fathom.

Meditations from St. Bernard

The tokens of the Passion we recognize as the fruitage of the ages of the past, appearing in the fullness of time during the reign of sin and death (Gal. 4.4). But it is the glory of the Resurrection, in the new springtime of regenerating grace, that the fresh flowers of the later age come forth, whose fruit shall be given without measure at the general resurrection, when time shall be no more. And so it is written, 'The winter is past, the rain is over and gone, the flowers appear on the earth' (Cant. 2.11 f); signifying that summer has come back with Him who dissolves icy death into the spring of a new life and says, 'Behold, I make all things new' (Rev. 21.5). His Body sown in the grave has blossomed in the Resurrection (I Cor. 15.42); and in like manner our valleys and fields which were barren or frozen, as if dead, glow with reviving life and warmth.

The Father of Christ who makes all things new, is well pleased with the freshness of those flowers and fruits, and the beauty of the field which breathes forth such heavenly fragrance; and He says in benediction, 'See, the smell of My Son is as the smell of a field which the Lord hath blessed' (Gen. 27.27). Blessed to overflowing, indeed, since of His fullness have all we received (John 1.16). But the Bride may come when she pleases and gather flowers and fruits therewith to adorn the inmost recesses of her conscience; that the Bridegroom when He cometh may find the chamber of her heart redolent with perfume.

So it behoves us, if we would have Christ for a frequent guest, to fill our hearts with faithful meditations on the mercy He showed in dying for us, and on His mighty power in rising again from the dead. To this David testified when he sang, 'God spake once, and twice I have also heard the same; that power belongeth unto God; and that Thou, Lord, art merciful (Ps. 62.11f). And surely there is proof enough and to spare in that Christ died for our sins and rose again for our justification, and ascended into heaven that He might protect us from on high, and sent the Holy Spirit for our comfort. Hereafter He will come again for the consummation of our bliss. In His Death He displayed His mercy, in His Resurrection His power; both combine to manifest His glory.

St. Bernard of
Clairvaux. *On Loving
God*, Ch. 3.

Additional Biblical Reflections: Isaiah 26:19; 1 Corinthians 6:14; John 11:25.

Prayer

Lord, your love for us is manifest in both your death and resurrection. Let us embrace, likewise, our death and resurrection, so our death might not be a cause to lament, and our resurrection might grant us hope in your image. Together, may the cross and resurrection pattern revive our hearts so that we might love you and love one another as you first loved us. Amen.

DAY 69

In today's meditation, St. Bernard expounds on the many ways that the Lord has demonstrated His love for us—ways that we cannot possibly reciprocate. Yet, by simply recognizing this fact, we are driven to a holy posture of gratitude, which is pious, noble, and good.

Meditations from St. Bernard

What shall I render unto the Lord for all His benefits towards me?' (Ps. 116.12). Reason and natural justice alike move me to give up myself wholly to loving Him to whom I owe all that I have and am. But faith shows me that I should love Him far more than I love myself, as I come to realize that He hath given me not my own life only, but even Himself. Yet, before the time of full revelation had come, before the Word was made flesh, died on the Cross, came forth from the grave, and returned to His Father; before God had shown us how much He loved us by all this plenitude of grace, the commandment had been uttered, 'Thou shalt love the Lord thy God with all thine heart, and with all thy soul and with all thy might' (Deut. 6.5), that is, with all thy being, all thy knowledge, all thy powers. And it was not unjust for God to claim this from His own work and gifts. Why should not the creature love his Creator, who gave him the power to love? Why should he not love Him with all his being, since it is by His gift alone that he can do anything that is good? It was God's creative grace that out of nothingness raised us to the dignity of manhood; and from this appears our duty to love Him, and the justice of His claim to that love. But how infinitely is the benefit increased when we bethink ourselves of His fulfillment of the promise, 'thou, Lord, shalt save both man and beast: how excellent is Thy mercy, O Lord!' (Ps. 36.6f.). For we, who 'turned our glory into the similitude of a calf that eateth hay' (Ps. 106.20), by our evil deeds debased ourselves so that we might be compared unto the beasts that perish. I owe all that I am to Him who made me: but how can I pay my debt to Him who redeemed me, and in such wondrous wise? Creation was not so vast a work as redemption; for it is written of man and of all things that were made, 'He spake the word, and they were made' (Ps. 148.5). But to redeem that creation which sprang into being at His word, how much He spake, what wonders He wrought, what hardships He endured, what shames He suffered! Therefore what reward shall I give unto the Lord for all the benefits which He hath done unto me? In the first creation He gave me myself; but in His new creation He gave me Himself, and by that gift restored to me the self that I had lost. Created first and then restored, I owe Him myself twice over in return for myself. But what have I to offer Him for the gift of Himself? Could I multiply myself a thousand-fold and then give Him all, what would that be in comparison with God?

St. Bernard of
Clairvaux. *On Loving
God*, Ch. 5.

Additional Biblical Reflections: Psalm 51:17; Psalm 116:12; Hebrews 10:1-39.

Prayer

Lord, what could we possibly give to you that compares to what you have given us? Still, like the widow, who gave a greater portion of herself than the rich man, who gave greater quantities but less by comparison of his heart, you graciously accept our lives as living sacrifices—offerings greater than that of calves and bulls. Let us live gratefully and be so moved to dedicate our lives to you, the giver of life itself. Amen.

DAY 70

In today's meditation, we take a break from considering the primary topic in St. Bernard's writings and consider, rather, how we might better follow God by looking to the pious lives of the saints as an example. When we struggle to know how to love God, though our heart longs to love Him more, we can do no better than consider the examples of saints who loved God before us.

Meditations from St. Bernard

It is indeed always worth while to portray the illustrious lives of the saints, that they may serve as a mirror and an example, and give, as it were, a relish to the life of men on earth. For by this means in some sort they live among us, even after death, and many of those who are dead while they live are challenged and recalled by them to true life. But now especially is there need for it because holiness is rare, and it is plain that our age is lacking in men. So greatly, in truth, do we perceive that lack to have increased in our day that none can doubt that we are smitten by that saying, Because iniquity shall abound the love of many shall wax cold; and, as I suppose, he has come or is at hand of whom it is written, Want shall go before his face. If I mistake not, Antichrist is he whom famine and sterility of all good both precedes and accompanies. Whether therefore it is the herald of one now present or the harbinger of one who shall come immediately, the want is evident. I speak not of the crowd, I speak not of the vile multitude of the children of this world: I would have you lift up your eyes upon the very pillars of the Church.

St. Bernard of
Clairvaux, *Life of St.
Malachy of Armagh,*
Preface.

Additional Biblical Reflections: 1 Corinthians 11:1-34; 1 Thessalonians 1:6; Revelation 20:11-15.

Prayer

Lord, you have worked marvels in the hearts of your saints who, though born of earthly mothers, as we have been, became pious exemplars of the faith. Lift up such examples so that, like patterns, we might follow their examples, which were, in turn, patterned after the example of Christ. Amen.

DAY 71

When we suffer hardship, trials, or persecutions, we can know that Christ has already done the same. If we suffer, as He did, we no longer have a God who is absent in suffering but enters it alongside us, and, more than that, redeems suffering itself for our good. Today's meditation allows us to reflect on the solidarity we have with our Lord when we suffer.

Meditations from St. Bernard

How much I sympathize with your trouble only He knows who bore the griefs of all in His own body. How willingly would I advise you if I knew what to say, or help you if I were able, as efficaciously as I would wish that He who knows and can do all things should advise and assist me in all my necessities. If brother Drogo had consulted me about leaving your house I should by no means have agreed with him; and now that he has left, if he were to apply to enter into mine I should not receive him. All that I was able to do in those circumstances I have done for you, and have written, as you know, to the abbot who has received him. After this, reverend father, what is there more that I am able to do on your behalf? And as regards yourself, your Holiness knows well with me that men are accustomed to be perfected not only in hope, but also to glory in tribulation. The Scripture consoles them, saying: The furnace proveth the potter's vessels, and temptation the righteous man (Ecclus. xxvii. 6, Vulg.); The Lord is nigh unto them that are of a contrite heart (Ps. xxxiv. 18); and We must through much tribulation enter into the kingdom of God (Acts xiv. 21); and All who will live godly in Christ suffer persecution (2 Tim. iii. 12). Yet none the less ought we to sympathize with our friends whom we see placed in care and grief; because we do not know what will be the issue of such, and fear lest it may be for ill; since whilst, indeed, to saints and the elect tribulation worketh patience, patience experience, experience hope, and hope maketh not ashamed (Rom. v. 3–5), to the condemnable and reprobate, on the contrary, tribulation causes discouragement, and discouragement confusion, and confusion despair, which destroys them.

In order, then, that this dreadful tempest may not submerge you, nor the frightful abyss swallow you up, and the unfathomable pit shut her mouth upon you, employ all the efforts of your prudence not to be overcome of evil, but to overcome evil with good. You will overcome if you fix solidly your hope in God, and wait patiently the issue of the affair. If that monk shall return to a sense of his duty, whether for fear of you, or because of his own painful condition, well and good; but if not, it is good for you to humble yourself under the mighty hand of God, nor to wish uselessly to resist His supreme ordering; because if it is of God it cannot be undone?

St. Bernard of
Clairvaux, *Letter to the
Abbot of Satin Nicasius
at Rheims.*

Additional Biblical Reflections: Philippians 3:10; James 1:2-4; 1 Peter 5:10.

Prayer

Lord, you are the great redeemer. Even the curse we earned for our sin—the curse of death and suffering—has been redeemed in your Son. May your cross be ever before our eyes during our trials and tribulations so that we might see that, in you, the path of suffering is one that leads to glory in your resurrection. Amen.

DAY 72

There is no mathematical equation that can "balance" out the debt of love we owe God. Rather, St. Bernard suggests that we love God immeasurably as He loves us immeasurably. Our limits to love are set only by our capacity. However, in Him, we also have an eternal existence whereby we might love God each day with all that we are.

Meditations from St. Bernard

Admit that God deserves to be loved very much, yea, boundlessly, because He loved us first, He infinite and we nothing, loved us, miserable sinners, with a love so great and so free. This is why I said at the beginning that the measure of our love to God is to love immeasurably. For since our love is toward God, who is infinite and immeasurable, how can we bound or limit the love we owe Him? Besides, our love is not a gift but a debt. And since it is the Godhead who loves us, Himself boundless, eternal, supreme love, of whose greatness there is no end, yea, and His wisdom is infinite, whose peace passeth all understanding; since it is He who loves us, I say, can we think of repaying Him grudgingly? 'I will love Thee, O Lord, my strength. The Lord is my rock and my fortress and my deliverer, my God, my strength, in whom I will trust' (Ps. 18.1f). He is all that I need, all that I long for. My God and my help, I will love Thee for Thy great goodness; not so much as I might, surely, but as much as I can. I cannot love Thee as Thou deservest to be loved, for I cannot love Thee more than my own feebleness permits. I will love Thee more when Thou deemest me worthy to receive greater capacity for loving; yet never so perfectly as Thou hast deserved of me. 'Thine eyes did see my substance, yet being unperfect; and in Thy book all my members were written' (PS. 139.16). Yet Thou recordest in that book all who do what they can, even though they cannot do what they ought. Surely I have said enough to show how God should be loved and why. But who has felt, who can know, who express, how much we should love him.

St. Bernard of
Clairvaux. *On Loving
God,* Ch. 6.

Additional Biblical Reflections: Romans 8:28-29; Ephesians 2:4-5; 1 John 4:7-16.

Prayer

Lord, your love is great and eternal. While we cannot match you in the measure of our love, you have granted us a share in eternity. Therefore, our love for you may also be immeasurable as we enjoy eternal life in you. Grant us the ability to love you immeasurably every day of our eternal lives. Amen.

DAY 73

Loving God cannot be a contractual agreement whereby we receive certain benefits in exchange for our love. The love of God does not merit God's benefits, but it does receive them—not for the sake of earning spiritual profits, but as spontaneous as love is itself. For, loving God is its own reward.

Meditations from St. Bernard

And now let us consider what profit we shall have from loving God. Even though our knowledge of this is imperfect, still that is better than to ignore it altogether. I have already said (when it was a question of wherefore and in what manner God should be loved) that there was a double reason constraining us: His right and our advantage. Having written as best I can, though unworthily, of God's right to be loved. I have still to treat of the recompense which that love brings. For although God would be loved without respect of reward, yet He wills not to leave love unrewarded. True charity cannot be left destitute, even though she is unselfish and seeketh not her own (I Cor. 13.5). Love is an affection of the soul, not a contract: it cannot rise from a mere agreement, nor is it so to be gained. It is spontaneous in its origin and impulse; and true love is its own satisfaction. It has its reward; but that reward is the object beloved. For whatever you seem to love, if it is on account of something else, what you do really love is that something else, not the apparent object of desire. St. Paul did not preach the Gospel that he might earn his bread; he ate that he might be strengthened for his ministry. What he loved was not bread, but the Gospel. True love does not demand a reward, but it deserves one. Surely no one offers to pay for love; yet some recompense is due to one who loves, and if his love endures he will doubtless receive it.

St. Bernard of
Clairvaux. *On Loving
God,* Ch. 7.

Additional Biblical Reflections: Deuteronomy 7:9; 1 Corinthians 12:1-13; Colossians 3:14.

Prayer

Lord, loving you is its own reward. Let us not love you as we consume goods or services, expecting certain payments for our hearts' investments. Rather, let us love recklessly, spontaneously, without reason or rationality, and simply receive whatever benefits such love might bring upon us on account of your graciousness. Amen.

DAY 74

Once again, in today's meditation, St. Bernard bids us to consider the significance of persecutions and sufferings we must endure as the Faithful. Here, St. Bernard offers several Biblical examples of how those who have been persecuted endured and were blessed on account of their sufferings.

Meditations from St. Bernard

I have learned with much pain by your letter the persecution that you are enduring for the sake of righteousness, and although the consolation given you by Christ in the promise of His kingdom may suffice amply for you, none the less is it my duty to render you both all the consolation that is in my power, and sound and faithful advice as far as I am able. For who can see without anxiety Peter stretching his arms in the midst of the billows?— or hear without grief the dove of Christ not singing, but groaning as if she said, How shall we sing the Lord's song in a strange land? (Ps. cxxxvii. 4). Who, I say, can without tears look upon the tears of Christ Himself, who from the bottom of the abyss lifts now His eyes unto the hills to see from whence cometh His help? But we to whom in your humility you say that you are looking, are not mountains of help, but are ourselves struggling with laborious endeavours in this vale of tears against the snares of a resisting enemy, and the violence of worldly malice, and with you we cry out, Our help is from the Lord, who made Heaven and earth (Ps. cxxi. 2).

All those, indeed, who wish to live piously in Christ suffer persecution (2 Tim. iii. 12). The intention to live piously is never wanting to them, but it is not always possible to carry it perfectly out, for just as it is the mark of the wicked constantly to struggle against the pious designs of the good; so it is not a reproach to the piety [of the latter], even although they are frequently unable to perfect their just and holy desires, because they are few against many opposers. Thus Aaron yielded against his will to the impious clamours of the riotous people (Exod. xxxii.). So Samuel unwillingly anointed Saul, constrained by the too eager desires of the same people for a king (1 Sam. x.). So David, when he wished to build a Temple, yet because of the numerous wars which that valorous man had constantly to sustain against enemies who molested him, he was forbidden to do what he piously proposed (2 Sam. vii.). Similarly, venerable father, I counsel you, without prejudice to the better advice of wiser persons, so to soften, for the present only, the rigour of your purpose of reform, and that of those who share it with you, that you may not be unmindful of the salvation of the weaker brethren. Those, indeed, over whom you have consented to preside in that Order of Cluny ought to be invited to a stricter life, but they ought not to be obliged to embrace it against their will. I believe that those who do desire to live more strictly ought to be persuaded either to bear with the weaker out of charity as far as they can without sin, or permitted to preserve the customs which they desire in the monastery itself, if that may be done without scandal to either party; or at least that they should be set free from the Order to associate themselves where it may seem good with other brothers who live according to their proposal.

St. Bernard of
Clairvaux. *To Simon,
Abbot of S. Nicholas.*

Additional Biblical Reflections: Jeremiah 20:11; Luke 6:22; 2 Timothy 3:12.

Prayer

Lord, the examples of the many persecuted saints whom you have preserved are many. Grant that should we face persecution in this life, we might likewise be granted a steadfast and holy endurance to see through our sufferings to the glories of eternity with you. Amen.

DAY 75

St. Bernard calls love one of humanity's "natural" affections. God made us that way. We love, but the object of our love is, at least in our carnal condition, more often the self than others. We tend to love God insofar as He satisfies our self-love—so long as He meets our needs and expectations. Thus, our love must be perfected in the image of the Son. Our self-will must die with Christ that we might be raised with godly desires.

Meditations from St. Bernard

Love is one of the four natural affections, which it is needless to name since everyone knows them. And because love is natural, it is only right to love the Author of nature first of all. Hence comes the first and great commandment, 'Thou shalt love the Lord thy God.' But nature is so frail and weak that necessity compels her to love herself first; and this is carnal love, wherewith man loves himself first and selfishly, as it is written, 'That was not first which is spiritual but that which is natural; and afterward that which is spiritual' (I Cor. 15.46). This is not as the precept ordains but as nature directs: 'No man ever yet hated his own flesh' (Eph. 5.29). But if, as is likely, this same love should grow excessive and, refusing to be contained within the restraining banks of necessity, should overflow into the fields of voluptuousness, then a command checks the flood, as if by a dike: 'Thou shalt love thy neighbor as thyself'. And this is right: for he who shares our nature should share our love, itself the fruit of nature. Wherefore if a man find it a burden, I will not say only to relieve his brother's needs, but to minister to his brother's pleasures, let him mortify those same affections in himself, lest he become a transgressor. He may cherish himself as tenderly as he chooses, if only he remembers to show the same indulgence to his neighbor. This is the curb of temperance imposed on thee, O man, by the law of life and conscience, lest thou shouldest follow thine own lusts to destruction, or become enslaved by those passions which are the enemies of thy true welfare. Far better divide thine enjoyments with thy neighbor than with these enemies. And if, after the counsel of the son of Sirach, thou goest not after thy desires but refrainest thyself from thine appetites (Ecclus. 18.30); if according to the apostolic precept having food and raiment thou art therewith content (I Tim. 6.8), then thou wilt find it easy to abstain from fleshly lusts which war against the soul, and to divide with thy neighbors what thou hast refused to thine own desires. That is a temperate and righteous love which practices self-denial in order to minister to a brother's necessity. So our selfish love grows truly social, when it includes our neighbors in its circle… But if we are to love our neighbors as we ought, we must have regard to God also: for it is only in God that we can pay that debt of love aright. Now a man cannot love his neighbor in God, except he love God Himself; wherefore we must love God first, in order to love our neighbors in Him. This too, like all good things, is the Lord's doing, that we should love Him, for He hath endowed us with the possibility of love. He who created nature sustains it; nature is so constituted that its Maker is its protector for ever. Without Him nature could not have begun to be; without Him it could not subsist at all. That we might not be ignorant of this, or vainly attribute to ourselves the beneficence of our Creator, God has determined in the depths of His wise counsel that we should be subject to tribulations. So when man's strength fails and God comes to his aid, it is meet and right that man, rescued by God's hand, should glorify Him, as it is written, 'Call upon Me in the time of trouble; so will I hear thee, and thou shalt praise Me' (Ps. 50.15). In such wise man, animal and carnal by nature, and loving only himself, begins to love God by reason of that very self-love; since he learns that in God he can accomplish all things that are good, and that without God he can do nothing.

St. Bernard of
Clairvaux. *On Loving
God*, Ch. 8.

Additional Biblical Reflections: Matthew 26:41; Romans 8:8-13; Galatians 5:19-21.

Prayer

Lord, refine our nature. Use the capacity we have to love and direct it toward you and others. In doing so, make us more closely resemble your Son, who loved us perfectly without any thought of self. Amen.

DAY 76

Love begins selfishly. However, this is but one step toward refining our love for what St. Bernard calls the second and third degrees of love—ultimately ending up loving God on His own account solely because He is God. Thus, let us examine our self-love and, from there, learn how to progress in our love rather than continue to turn it inward toward one's own interests, passions, and desires.

Meditations from St. Bernard

So then in the beginning man loves God, not for God's sake, but for his own. It is something for him to know how little he can do by himself and how much by God's help, and in that knowledge to order himself rightly towards God, his sure support. But when tribulations, recurring again and again, constrain him to turn to God for unfailing help, would not even a heart as hard as iron, as cold as marble, be softened by the goodness of such a Savior, so that he would love God not altogether selfishly, but because He is God? Let frequent troubles drive us to frequent supplications; and surely, tasting, we must see how gracious the Lord is (Ps. 34.8). Thereupon His goodness once realized draws us to love Him unselfishly, yet more than our own needs impel us to love Him selfishly: even as the Samaritans told the woman who announced that it was Christ who was at the well: 'Now we believe, not because of thy saying: for we have heard Him ourselves, and know that this is indeed the Christ, the savior of the world' (John 4.42). We likewise bear the same witness to our own fleshly nature, saying, 'No longer do we love God because of our necessity, but because we have tasted and seen how gracious the Lord is'. Our temporal wants have a speech of their own, proclaiming the benefits they have received from God's favor. Once this is recognized it will not be hard to fulfill the commandment touching love to our neighbors; for whosoever loves God aright loves all God's creatures. Such love is pure, and finds no burden in the precept bidding us purify our souls, in obeying the truth through the Spirit unto unfeigned love of the brethren (I Peter 1.22). Loving as he ought, he counts that command only just. Such love is thankworthy, since it is spontaneous; pure, since it is shown not in word nor tongue, but in deed and truth (I John 3.18); just, since it repays what it has received. Whoso loves in this fashion, loves even as he is loved, and seeks no more his own but the things which are Christ's, even as Jesus sought not His own welfare, but ours, or rather ourselves. Such was the psalmist's love when he sang: 'O give thanks unto the Lord, for He is gracious' (Ps. 118.1). Whosoever praises God for His essential goodness, and not merely because of the benefits He has bestowed, does really love God for God's sake, and not selfishly. The psalmist was not speaking of such love when he said: 'So long as thou doest well unto thyself, men will speak good of thee'(Ps. 49.18). The third degree of love, we have now seen, is to love God on His own account, solely because He is God.

St. Bernard of
Clairvaux. *On Loving
God*, Ch. 9

Additional Biblical Reflections: Psalm 49; John 4:42; 1 Peter 1:22.

Prayer

Lord, while we begin to learn to love through the love of self, let us love ourselves not on account of ego but because you love us too. For, how can we not love ourselves if we hope to fashion our hearts after yours? Let this be a holy love, though, that persists not for our own sake but for the sake of your Son. Amen.

DAY 77

Yesterday's prayer led us toward what St. Bernard calls the fourth degree of love—"wherein one loves himself only in God." While we might be tempted to believe that the cure of self-love is self-hatred, to hate oneself is to hate one whom God Himself loves! The command to love one's neighbor as oneself cannot be fulfilled without loving ourselves properly. For if we hated ourselves, to love one's neighbor as we do ourselves would not be to love him or her at all. If we desire to have hearts that reflect God's, we must learn to love ourselves like God does.

Meditations from St. Bernard

How blessed is he who reaches the fourth degree of love, wherein one loves himself only in God! Thy righteousness standeth like the strong mountains, O God. Such love as this is God's hill, in the which it pleaseth Him to dwell. 'Who shall ascend into the hill of the Lord?' 'O that I had wings like a dove; for then would I flee away and be at rest.' 'At Salem is His tabernacle; and His dwelling in Sion.' 'Woe is me, that I am constrained to dwell with Mesech!' (Ps. 24.3; 55.6; 76.2; 120.5). When shall this flesh and blood, this earthen vessel which is my soul's tabernacle, attain thereto? When shall my soul, rapt with divine love and altogether self-forgetting, yea, become like a broken vessel, yearn wholly for God, and, joined unto the Lord, be one spirit with Him? When shall she exclaim, 'My flesh and my heart faileth; but God is the strength of my heart and my portion for ever' (Ps. 73.26). I would count him blessed and holy to whom such rapture has been vouchsafed in this mortal life, for even an instant to lose thyself, as if thou wert emptied and lost and swallowed up in God, is no human love; it is celestial. But if sometimes a poor mortal feels that heavenly joy for a rapturous moment, then this wretched life envies his happiness, the malice of daily trifles disturbs him, this body of death weighs him down, the needs of the flesh are imperative, the weakness of corruption fails him, and above all brotherly love calls him back to duty. Alas! that voice summons him to re-enter his own round of existence; and he must ever cry out lamentably, 'O Lord, I am oppressed: undertake for me' (Isa. 38.14); and again, 'O wretched man that I am! who shall deliver me from the body of this death?' (Rom. 7.24).

In this life, I think, we cannot fully and perfectly obey that precept, 'Thou shalt love the Lord thy God with all thy heart, and with all thy soul, and with all thy strength, and with all thy mind' (Luke 10.27). For here the heart must take thought for the body; and the soul must energize the flesh; and the strength must guard itself from impairment. And by God's favor, must seek to increase. It is therefore impossible to offer up all our being to God, to yearn altogether for His face, so long as we must accommodate our purposes and aspirations to these fragile, sickly bodies of ours. Wherefore the soul may hope to possess the fourth degree of love, or rather to be possessed by it, only when it has been clothed upon with that spiritual and immortal body, which will be perfect, peaceful, lovely, and in everything wholly subjected to the spirit. And to this degree no human effort can attain: it is in God's power to give it to whom He wills. Then the soul will easily reach that highest stage, because no lusts of the flesh will retard its eager entrance into the joy of its Lord, and no troubles will disturb its peace. May we not think that the holy martyrs enjoyed this grace, in some degree at least, before they laid down their victorious bodies? Surely that was immeasurable strength of love which enraptured their souls, enabling them to laugh at fleshly torments and to yield their lives gladly. But even though the frightful pain could not destroy their peace of mind, it must have impaired somewhat its perfection.

St. Bernard of
Clairvaux. *On Loving
God*, Ch. 10.

Additional Biblical Reflections: Leviticus 19:18; Matthew 22:1-46; Luke 10:27.

Prayer

Lord, you loved us when we were yet unlovable. Help us to love ourselves only through the lens of your longing gaze, which drove you not to puff us up in the ways of the flesh but love us to the point of sacrifice and death. Therefore, let us love ourselves in such a way that we are willing to crucify the flesh and see ourselves raised anew in our love of you. Amen.

DAY 78

To be apart from the body is to be with the Lord. However, as St. Bernard reminds us, our hope is not for a bodiless existence as souls floating around in God's heavenly glory. Rather, as we confess in the Creed, the resurrection of the body remains our hope. This impacts how we view our flesh—not as though it is the enemy of the soul, but as a part of the self that must be redeemed.

Meditations from St. Bernard

What of the souls already released from their bodies? We believe that they are overwhelmed in that vast sea of eternal light and of luminous eternity. But no one denies that they still hope and desire to receive their bodies again: whence it is plain that they are not yet wholly transformed, and that something of self remains yet unsurrendered. Not until death is swallowed up in victory, and perennial light overflows the uttermost bounds of darkness, not until celestial glory clothes our bodies, can our souls be freed entirely from self and give themselves up to God. For until then souls are bound to bodies, if not by a vital connection of sense, still by natural affection; so that without their bodies they cannot attain to their perfect consummation, nor would they if they could. And although there is no defect in the soul itself before the restoration of its body, since it has already attained to the highest state of which it is by itself capable, yet the spirit would not yearn for reunion with the flesh if without the flesh it could be consummated.

And finally, 'Right dear in the sight of the Lord is the death of His saints' (Ps. 116.15). But if their death is precious, what must such a life as theirs be! No wonder that the body shall seem to add fresh glory to the spirit; for though it is weak and mortal, it has availed not a little for mutual help. How truly he spake who said, 'All things work together for good to them that love God' (Rom. 8.28). The body is a help to the soul that loves God, even when it is ill, even when it is dead, and all the more when it is raised again from the dead: for illness is an aid to penitence; death is the gate of rest; and the resurrection will bring consummation. So, rightly, the soul would not be perfected without the body, since she recognizes that in every condition it has been needful to her good.

St. Bernard of
Clairvaux. *On Loving
God*, Ch. 11.

Additional Biblical Reflections: John 6:40; 2 Corinthians 4:14; Romans 6:5.

Prayer

Lord, you have made us in body and soul and declared our whole selves good. Let us not despise our bodies but despise only fleshly desire rooted in sin so that we might still hope for the redemption of our bodies along with our souls, as we await the new heaven and earth promised in your Word. Amen.

DAY 79

Many of us have laws unto ourselves that are not laws from the Lord. This may be beneficial or detrimental to our faith. Thus, we must make sure that any laws we establish for ourselves do not supplant God's law or revise how we apply God's truths to our lives. Therefore, the Scriptures declare that in the Spirit, the law ceases to be the burden so that to the flesh, it is but a delight.

Meditations from St. Bernard

Furthermore, the slave and the hireling have a law, not from the Lord, but of their own contriving; the one does not love God, the other loves something else more than God. They have a law of their own, not of God, I say; yet it is subject to the law of the Lord. For though they can make laws for themselves, they cannot supplant the changeless order of the eternal law. Each man is a law unto himself, when he sets up his will against the universal law, perversely striving to rival his Creator, to be wholly independent, making his will his only law. What a heavy and burdensome yoke upon all the sons of Adam, bowing down our necks, so that our life draweth nigh unto hell. 'O wretched man that I am! Who shall deliver me from the body of this death?' (Rom. 7.24). I am weighed down, I am almost overwhelmed, so that 'If the Lord had not helped me, it had not failed but my soul had been put to silence' (Ps. 94.17). Job was groaning under this load when he lamented: 'Why hast Thou set me as a mark against Thee, so that I am a burden to myself?' (Job 7.20). He was a burden to himself through the law which was of his own devising: yet he could not escape God's law, for he was set as a mark against God. The eternal law of righteousness ordains that he who will not submit to God's sweet rule shall suffer the bitter tyranny of self: but he who wears the easy yoke and light burden of love (Matt. 11.30) will escape the intolerable weight of his own self-will. Wondrously and justly does that eternal law retain rebels in subjection, so that they are unable to escape. They are subject to God's power, yet deprived of happiness with Him, unable to dwell with God in light and rest and glory everlasting. O Lord my God, 'why dost Thou not pardon my transgression and take away mine iniquity?' (Job 7.21). Then freed from the weight of my own will, I can breathe easily under the light burden of love. I shall not be coerced by fear, nor allured by mercenary desires; for I shall be led by the Spirit of God, that free Spirit whereby Thy sons are led, which beareth witness with my spirit that I am among the children of God (Rom. 8.16). So shall I be under that law which is Thine; and as Thou art, so shall I be in the world. Whosoever do what the apostle bids, 'Owe no man anything, but to love one another' (Rom. 13.8), are doubtless even in this life conformed to God's likeness: they are neither slaves nor hirelings but sons.

St. Bernard of
Clairvaux. *On Loving
God,* Ch. 13.

Additional Biblical Reflections: Romans 8:15-23; Galatians 3:28; Ephesians 1:5.

Prayer

Lord, let us delight in your law so that we might better know your ways. For you have made us and know what is best for our lives. Grant this, so we might enjoy the gift of life and reflect your glory in all we say and do. Amen.

DAY 80

We live in a critical age—a time when many are willing to criticize others without understanding. Often, such attacks are waged out of the attacker's own flawed heart and insecurity. Thus, the Pharisees—insecure because the law they had followed offered no such security—attacked our Lord. Men of this stripe have existed in every generation, and such was the case in St. Bernard's day. In today's meditation, he offers encouragement to several abbots who have unfairly been assaulted in such a way.

Meditations from St. Bernard

Let those depart both from me and from You who say: We do not desire to be better than our fathers; declaring themselves to be the sons of lukewarm and lax persons, whose memory is in execration, since they have eaten sour grapes, and their children's teeth are set on edge. Or if they pretend that their fathers were holy men, whose memory is blessed, let them imitate their sanctity, and not defend, as laws instituted by them, the indulgences and dispensations which they have merely endured. Although holy Elias says, I am not better than my fathers (2 Kings xix. 4), yet he has not said that he did not wish to be. Jacob saw upon the ladder Angels ascending and descending (Gen. xxviii. 12); but was any one of them either sitting, or standing still? It was not for angels to stand still on the uncertain rounds of a frail ladder; nor can anything remain fixed in the same condition during the uncertain period of this mortal life. Here have we no continuing city; nor do we yet possess, but always seek for, that which is to come. Of necessity you either ascend or descend, and if you try to stand still you cannot but fall. It may be held as certain that the man is not good at all who does not wish to be better; and where you begin not to care to make advance in goodness there also you leave off being good.

Let those depart both from me and from you who call good evil and evil good. If they call the pursuit of righteousness evil, what good thing will be good in their eyes? The Lord once spoke a single word, and the Pharisees were scandalized (S. Matt. xv. 12). But now these new Pharisees are scandalized not even at a word, but at silence. You plainly see then that they seek only the occasion to attack you. But leave them alone; they be blind leaders of the blind. Take thought for the salvation of the little ones, not of the murmurs of the evil-disposed. Why do you so much fear to give scandal to those who are not to be cured unless you become sick with them? It is not even desirable to wait to see whether your resolutions are pleasing to all of you in all respects, otherwise you will determine upon little or no good. You ought to consult not the views, but the needs of all; and faithfully to draw them towards God, even although they be unwilling, rather than abandon them to the desires of their heart. I commend myself to your holy prayers.

St. Bernard of
Clairvaux, *To the Abbots
Assembled at Soissons.*

Additional Biblical Reflections: Matthew 15:12; Romans 12:2; Philippians 3:23.

Prayer

Lord, we are easily swayed by our times. Let us not be taken captive by hollow philosophies but may our consciences be bound to your truth. Let us, nonetheless, learn to love in the way of your Incarnation in the world, as we find it not as we would have it be. In Jesus's name. Amen.

DAY 81

The law of God alone evokes reason to fear. For, when we measure ourselves up to the standard of the law, we fall short. However, when accompanying the law, love rescues us of such fear. It turns the fulfillment of love into a godly fear—a reverence for the mysteries of God—and even joy.

Meditations from St. Bernard

Now the children have their law, even though it is written, 'The law is not made for a righteous man' (I Tim. 1.9). For it must be remembered that there is one law having to do with the spirit of servitude, given to fear, and another with the spirit of liberty, given in tenderness. The children are not constrained by the first, yet they could not exist without the second: even as St. Paul writes, 'Ye have not received the spirit of bondage again to fear; but ye have received the spirit of adoption, whereby we cry, Abba, Father' (Rom. 8.15). And again to show that that same righteous man was not under the law, he says: 'To them that are under the law, I became as under the law, that I might gain them that are under the law; to them that are without law, as without law (being not without law to God, but under the law to Christ)' (I Cor. 9.20f). So it is rightly said, not that the righteous do not have a law, but, 'The law is not made for a righteous man', that is, it is not imposed on rebels but freely given to those willingly obedient, by Him whose goodness established it. Wherefore the Lord saith meekly: 'Take My yoke upon you', which may be paraphrased thus: 'I do not force it on you, if you are reluctant; but if you will you may bear it. Otherwise it will be weariness, not rest, that you shall find for your souls.'

Love is a good and pleasant law; it is not only easy to bear, but it makes the laws of slaves and hirelings tolerable; not destroying but completing them; as the Lord saith: 'I am not come to destroy the law, but to fulfill' (Matt. 5.17). It tempers the fear of the slave, it regulates the desires of the hireling, it mitigates the severity of each. Love is never without fear, but it is godly fear. Love is never without desire, but it is lawful desire. So love perfects the law of service by infusing devotion; it perfects the law of wages by restraining covetousness. Devotion mixed with fear does not destroy it, but purges it.

St. Bernard of
Clairvaux. *On Loving
God*, Ch. 14

Additional Biblical Reflections: Joshua 1:9; Isaiah 41:10; 1 John 4:18.

Prayer

Lord, perfect your love within us so that all fear might be cast out and replaced with godly reverence. For, you do not desire that we would be timid creatures consumed by terror but confident children of you, our Father, who revere your law and live according to your will. Amen.

DAY 82

The flesh, St. Bernard says, is where we begin but not where we should end. From the beginnings in the flesh, by God's grace, we must proceed through degrees so that in the spirit we come to know more than what we see merely by the flesh. In this way, we come to know true love and thereby enter God's joy and the plenteousness of His house.

Meditations from St. Bernard

Nevertheless, since we are carnal and are born of the lust of the flesh, it must be that our desire and our love shall have its beginning in the flesh. But rightly guided by the grace of God through these degrees, it will have its consummation in the spirit: for that was not first which is spiritual but that which is natural; and afterward that which is spiritual (I Cor. 15.46). And we must bear the image of the earthy first, before we can bear the image of the heavenly. At first, man loves himself for his own sake. That is the flesh, which can appreciate nothing beyond itself. Next, he perceives that he cannot exist by himself, and so begins by faith to seek after God, and to love Him as something necessary to his own welfare. That is the second degree, to love God, not for God's sake, but selfishly. But when he has learned to worship God and to seek Him aright, meditating on God, reading God's Word, praying and obeying His commandments, he comes gradually to know what God is, and finds Him altogether lovely. So, having tasted and seen how gracious the Lord is (Ps. 34.8), he advances to the third degree, when he loves God, not merely as his benefactor but as God. Surely he must remain long in this state; and I know not whether it would be possible to make further progress in this life to that fourth degree and perfect condition wherein man loves himself solely for God's sake. Let any who have attained so far bear record; I confess it seems beyond my powers. Doubtless it will be reached when the good and faithful servant shall have entered into the joy of his Lord (Matt. 25.21), and been satisfied with the plenteousness of God's house (Ps. 36.8). For then in wondrous wise he will forget himself and as if delivered from self, he will grow wholly God's. Joined unto the Lord, he will then be one spirit with Him (I Cor. 6.17). This was what the prophet meant, I think, when he said: ' I will go forth in the strength of the Lord God: and will make mention of Thy righteousness only' (Ps. 71.16). Surely he knew that when he should go forth in the spiritual strength of the Lord, he would have been freed from the infirmities of the flesh, and would have nothing carnal to think of, but would be wholly filled in his spirit with the righteousness of the Lord.

St. Bernard of
Clairvaux. *On Loving
God,* Ch. 15.

Additional Biblical Reflections: Proverbs 3:3-8; Psalm 101:1-8; 2 Corinthians 5:16-18.

Prayer

Lord, you have granted us lives in this world not that we might lament or feel pain alone but progress toward you in the way of the Spirit. Thus, you sent your Spirit into the world. We also pray that you would send your Spirit into our hearts and that our lives might follow an upward path toward your glory. Amen.

DAY 83

Our lives are not lives of wandering. Rather, they are lives fixed on a destination. The destination has been determined by God and is revealed in the Word. Namely, it is life in the Kingdom of God. Today's meditation from St. Bernard helps us focus our eyes on our ultimate hope in His Kingdom.

Meditations from St. Bernard

In that day the members of Christ can say of themselves what St. Paul testified concerning their Head: 'Yea, though we have known Christ after the flesh, yet now henceforth know we Him no more' (II Cor. 5.16). None shall thereafter know himself after the flesh; for 'flesh and blood cannot inherit the Kingdom of God' (I Cor. 15.50). Not that there will be no true substance of the flesh, but all carnal needs will be taken away, and the love of the flesh will be swallowed up in the love of the spirit, so that our weak human affections will be made divinely strong. Then the net of charity which as it is drawn through the great and wide sea doth not cease to gather every kind of fish, will be drawn to the shore; and the bad will be cast away, while only the good will be kept (Matt. 13.48). In this life the net of all-including love gathers every kind of fish into its wide folds, becoming all things to all men, sharing adversity or prosperity, rejoicing with them that do rejoice, and weeping with them that weep (Rom. 12.15). But when the net is drawn to shore, whatever causes pain will be rejected, like the bad fish, while only what is pleasant and joyous will be kept. Do you not recall how St. Paul said: 'Who is weak and I am not weak? Who is offended and I burn not?' And yet weakness and offense were far from him. So too he bewailed many which had sinned already and had not repented, though he was neither the sinner nor the penitent. But there is a city made glad by the rivers of the flood of grace (Ps. 46.4), and whose gates the Lord loveth more than all the dwellings of Jacob (Ps. 87.2). In it is no place for lamentation over those condemned to everlasting fire, prepared for the devil and his angels (Matt. 25.41). In these earthly dwellings, though men may rejoice, yet they have still other battles to fight, other mortal perils to undergo. But in the heavenly Fatherland no sorrow nor sadness can enter: as it is written, 'The habitation of all rejoicing ones is in Thee' (Ps. 87. 7, Vulg.); and again, 'Everlasting joy shall be unto them' (Isa. 61.7). Nor could they recall things piteous, for then they will make mention of God's righteousness only. Accordingly, there will be no need for the exercise of compassion, for no misery will be there to inspire pity.

St. Bernard of
Clairvaux. *On Loving
God,* Ch. 15.

Additional Biblical Reflections: 1 Corinthians 9:24-25; Hebrews 10:26; Titus 3:5.

Prayer

Lord, let us live our lives with our eyes firmly fixed on the destination that is your Kingdom. Thus, we pray that thy Kingdom is not only realized in the world but likewise in our hearts and lives. Amen.

DAY 84

In today's meditation, St. Bernard writes to an abbot who, having written to Bernard for advice, had recently seen several monks— or "religious" persons—depart his monastery and is questioning whether it might be his fault. At first, Bernard struggles to offer a response, not knowing the full context or cause by which many left. However, regardless of the cause, he begs the abbot to consider the situation as a mirror—what might he learn from the occurrence? How might the Lord be using this situation to refine His service?

Meditations from St. Bernard

You write to me from beyond the sea to ask of me advice which I should have preferred that you had sought from some other. I am held between two difficulties, for if I do not reply to you, you may take my silence for a sign of contempt; but if I do reply I cannot avoid danger, since whatever I reply I must of necessity either give scandal to some one or give to some other a security which they ought not to have, or at all events more than they ought to have. That your brethren have departed from you was not with the knowledge nor by the advice or persuasion of me or of my brethren. But I incline to believe that it was of God, since their purpose could not be shaken by all your efforts; and that the brethren themselves thought this also who so earnestly sought my advice about themselves; their conscience troubling them, as I suppose, because they quitted you.

Here is a mirror. In it let your Religious consider, not the features of their faces, but the fact of their turning back. Here let them determine and distinguish their motives, their thoughts, accusing or excusing them with that sentence which the spiritual man passes who judges all things, and is himself judged by no one. I, indeed, cannot rashly determine whether the state which they have left or that which they have embraced was the greater or less, the higher or lower, the severer or the more lax. Let them judge according to the rule of S. Gregory. But to you, Reverend Father, I declare, with as much positive assurance as plain truth, that it is not at all desirable that you should set yourself to quench the Spirit. Hinder not him, it is said, who is able to do good, but if thou canst, do good also thyself (Prov. iii. 27, Vulg.). It more befits you to be proud of the good works of your sons, since a wise son is the glory of his father (Prov. x. 1). For the rest, let no one make it a cause of complaint against me that I have not hidden in my heart the righteousness of God, unless, perhaps, I have spoken less of it than I ought, for the sake of avoiding scandal.

St. Bernard of
Clairvaux, *To the Abbot
of a Certain Monastery at
York.*

Additional Biblical Reflections: Matthew 13:11; Ephesians 3:2-6; Colossians 2:1-3.

Prayer

Lord, you work in mysterious ways. Let us find solace not in our examination of the ways by which you appear to be acting but rather in our knowledge of you and your character. For, all who love you, you are constantly working all things for our good, even redeeming our flaws for your sake. In Jesus's name. Amen.

DAY 85

In today's meditation, St. Bernard praises an abbot not for his personal piety or religious action but on account of his charity and love of the poor. Here, we see that what merits more in God's sight is not our commitment to ritual or prayer, but when such things launch us toward lives steeped in love and charity.

Meditations from St. Bernard

To the very dear father and Reverend Lord Thurstan, by the Grace of God Archbishop of York, Bernard, Abbot of Clairvaux, wishes the fullest health.

The general good report of men, as I have experienced, has said nothing in your favour which the splendour of your good works does not justify. Your actions, in fact, show that your high reputation, which fame had previously spread everywhere, was neither false nor ill-founded, but manifest and certain. Especially of late how brilliantly has your zeal for righteousness and your sacerdotal energy shone forth in the defence of the poor Religious who had no other helper. Once, indeed, the whole assembly of the saints used to venerate your works of mercy and alms deeds; but in doing so it narrated always what is common to you with very many, since whosoever possesses the goods of this world is bound to share them with the poor. But this is your episcopal task, this the noble proof of your paternal affection, this your truly divine fervour, the zeal which no doubt has inspired and aroused in you who makes His angels spirits and His ministers a flaming fire. This, I say, belongs entirely to you. It is the ornament of your dignity, the badge of your office, the adornment of your crown. It is one thing to fill the belly of the hungry, and quite another thing to have a zeal for holy poverty. The one serves nature, the other grace. Thou shalt visit thy kind, He says, and thou shalt not sin (Job v. 24, Vulg.). Therefore he who nourishes the flesh of another sins not in so doing, but he who honours the sanctity of another does good to his own soul; therefore he says again, Keep your alms in your own hand until you shall find a righteous man to whom to give it. For what advantage? Because He who receives a righteous man in the name of a righteous man shall receive a righteous man's reward (S. Matt. x. 41). Let us, then, discharge the debt that nature requires of us, that we may avoid sin; but let us be co-workers with grace, that we may merit to become sharers of it. It is this that I so admire in you, as I acknowledge that it was given to you from above. O, Father, truly reverend and to be regarded with the sincerest affection; the praise for what you have laid out of your temporal means to the relief of our necessities, will be blended with the praises of God for ever.

St. Bernard of
Clairvaux, *To Thurstan,
Archbishop of York.*

Additional Biblical Reflections: Proverbs 19:17; Luke 12:22; 1 John 3:17.

Prayer

Lord, you have given us all things, even your Son, without cause or merit. Let us also be cheerful givers so that we might be your instruments of love for the sake of the poor and all those in need. Amen.

DAY 86

In today's mediation, St. Bernard praises a monastic community for continuing to strive toward greater degrees of holiness despite how praiseworthy they already are.

Meditations from St. Bernard

How marvellous are those things which I have heard and learned, and which the two Geoffries have announced to me, that you have become newly fervent with the fire from on high, that from weakness you have become strong, that you have flourished again with new sanctity.

This is the finger of God secretly working, softly renewing, healthfully changing not, indeed, bad men into good, but making good men better. Who will grant unto me to cross over to you and see this great sight? For that progress in holiness is not less wonderful or less delightful than that conversion. It is much more easy, in fact, to find many men of the world converted to good than one Religious who is good becoming better than he is. The rarest bird in the world is the monk who ascends ever so little from the point which he has once reached in the religious life. Thus the spectacle which you present, dearest brethren, is the more rare and salutary, not only to men who desire greatly to be the helper of your sanctity, but it rightly rejoices the whole Church of God as well; since the rarer it is the more glorious it is also. For prudence made it a duty to you to pass beyond that mediocrity so dangerously near to defect, and to escape from that lukewarmness which provokes God to reject you, it was even a duty of conscience for you to do so, since you know that it is not safe for men who have embraced the holy Rule to halt before having attained the goal to which it leads. I am exceedingly grieved that I am obliged by the pressing obligations of the day and the haste of the messenger to express the fulness of my affection with a pen so briefs and to comprise the breadth of my kindness for you within the narrow limits of this billet. But if anything is wanting, brother Geoffrey will supply it by word of mouth.

St. Bernard of
Clairvaux, *To Richard,*
Abbot of Fountains, And
His Companions.

Additional Biblical Reflections: Matthew 5:48; James 1:4; 1 John 2:5.

Prayer

Lord, you are perfect, and no matter how far we progress in this life, we fall short of your glory. Therefore, let us never grow weary of spiritual progress so that we might come to know you and your glory all the more in your presence until all is finally revealed on the last day. Amen.

DAY 87

When Bernard was separated from his Monks at Clairvaux, he did not write them solely so that they might have their longing for his return pacified, but because he genuinely found that he was more enriched by his brothers than they were by him. We must never forget that God has called us into holy communities of faith so that, as members of His body, we might grow together in holiness.

Meditations from St. Bernard

To his dearly-loved brethren the Monks of Clairvaux, the converts, and the novices, their brother Bernard sends greeting, bidding them rejoice in the Lord always. Judge by yourselves what I am suffering. If my absence is painful to you, let no one doubt that it is far more painful to me. The loss is not equal, the burden is not the same, for you are deprived of but one individual, while I am bereft of all of you. It cannot but be that I am weighed down by as many anxieties as you are in number; I grieve for the absence of each one of you, and fear the dangers which may attack you. This double grief will not leave me until I am restored to my children.

And since you know these things, you must not be angry at my long absence, which is not according to my will, but is due to the necessities of the Church; rather pity me. I hope that it will not be a long absence now; do you pray that it may not be unfruitful. Let any losses which may in the meantime happen to befall you be regarded as gains, for the cause is God's. And since He is gracious and all-powerful, He will easily make any losses good, and even add greater riches. Therefore, let us be of good courage, since we have God with us, in whom I am present with you, though we may seem to be separated by a long distance.

St. Bernard of
Clairvaux, *To His Monks
of Clairvaux.*

Additional Biblical Reflections: Acts 2:43-47; Colossians 1:18; Hebrews 10:25.

Prayer

Lord, your Church is your Bride. Spare us of the notion that we might love you, the Bridegroom, while we reject your Bride. Grant us the holy consolation of our fellow believers so that we might recognize your presence in our lives through their holy company. Amen.

DAY 88

The unity of the Church is a mystery. However, when we live charitably together as believers and follow the Lord, we find that all the Church benefits. However, when dissension and pride threaten the body, we find that all of us fall far from God's presence. Today, St. Bernard reminds us of the importance of our unity as His believers.

Meditations from St. Bernard

Let no one among you who shows himself attentive to his duties, humble, reverent, devoted to reading, watchful unto prayer, anxious for brotherly love, think that I am absent from him. For can I be anything but present with him in spirit when we are of one heart and one mind? But if, which God forbid, there be among you any whisperer, or any that is double-tongued, a murmurer, or rebellious, or impatient of discipline, or restless or truant, and who is not ashamed to eat the bread of idleness, from such I should be far absent in soul even though present in body, just because he would have already set himself far from God by a distance of character and not of space.

In the meanwhile, brethren, until I come, serve the Lord in fear, that in Him being delivered from the hand of your enemies you may serve Him without fear. Serve Him in hope, for He is faithful that promised; serve Him by good works, for He is bountiful to reward. To say nothing else, He rightly claims this life of ours as His own, because He laid down His own to obtain it. Let none, therefore, live to himself, but to Him who died for him. For whom can I more justly live than for Him whose death was my life? for whom with more profit to myself than for Him who promises eternal life?

for whom under a greater necessity than for Him who threatens me with everlasting flames? But I serve Him willingly, because love gives liberty. To this I exhort my children. Serve Him in that love which casteth out fear, which feels no labours, seeks for no reward, thinks of no merit, and yet is more urgent than all. No terror is so powerful, no rewards so inviting, no righteousness so exacting. May it join me to you never to be divided, may it also bring me before you, especially at your hours of prayer, my brethren, dearly beloved and greatly longed for.

St. Bernard of
Clairvaux, *To His Monks
of Clairvaux.*

Additional Biblical Reflections: Psalm 122:1; 1 Corinthians 1:10; 1 Peter 3:8.

Prayer

Lord, even as your body cannot be divided against itself, let your Church, your body by virtue of being your Bride and one-in-flesh with you, be spared of fruitless divisions. Let us bear with one another charitably, placing the best construction on others' words and actions so that in all things, we might be built up in your image. Amen.

DAY 89

To ponder our future hope is not to dwell in the clouds, absent of the present. Rather, a future-oriented joy invades the present in such a way where even things that might cause us to despair are not devoid of joy in God's presence. With many biblical citations, St. Bernard reminds us to fix our eyes on the hope of God's promises.

Meditations from St. Bernard

But it will be well to note what class of people takes comfort in the thought of God. Surely not that perverse and crooked generation to whom it was said, 'Woe unto you that are rich; for ye have received your consolation' (Luke 6.24). Rather, those who can say with truth, 'My soul refuseth comfort' (Ps. 77.2). For it is meet that those who are not satisfied by the present should be sustained by the thought of the future, and that the contemplation of eternal happiness should solace those who scorn to drink from the river of transitory joys. That is the generation of them that seek the Lord, even of them that seek, not their own, but the face of the God of Jacob. To them that long for the presence of the living God, the thought of Him is sweetest itself: but there is no satiety, rather an ever-increasing appetite, even as the Scripture bears witness, 'they that eat me shall yet be hungry' (Ecclus. 24.21); and if the one an-hungred spake, 'When I awake up after Thy likeness, I shall be satisfied with it.' Yea, blessed even now are they which do hunger and thirst after righteousness, for they, and they only, shall be filled. Woe to you, wicked and perverse generation; woe to you, foolish and abandoned people, who hate Christ's memory, and dread His second Advent! Well may you fear, who will not now seek deliverance from the snare of the hunter; because 'they that will be rich fall into temptation and a snare, and into many foolish and hurtful lusts' (I Tim. 6.9). In that day we shall not escape the dreadful sentence of condemnation, 'Depart from Me, ye cursed, into everlasting fire' (Matt. 25.41). O dreadful sentence indeed, O hard saying! How much harder to bear than that other saying which we repeat daily in church, in memory of the Passion: 'Whoso eateth My flesh and drinketh My blood hath eternal life' (John 6.54). That signifies, whoso honors My death and after My example mortifies his members which are upon the earth (Col. 3.5) shall have eternal life, even as the apostle says, 'If we suffer, we shall also reign with Him' (II Tim. 2.12). And yet many even today recoil from these words and go away, saying by their action if not with their lips, 'This is a hard saying; who can hear it?' (John 6.60). 'A generation that set not their heart aright, and whose spirit cleaveth not steadfastly unto God' (Ps. 78.8), but chooseth rather to trust in uncertain riches, it is disturbed at the very name of the Cross, and counts the memory of the Passion intolerable. How can such sustain the burden of that fearful sentence, 'Depart from Me, ye cursed, into everlasting fire, prepared for the devil and his angels'? 'On whomsoever that stone shall fall it will grind him to powder' (Luke 20.18); but 'the generation of the faithful shall be blessed' (Ps. 112.2), since, like the apostle, they labor that whether present or absent they may be accepted of the Lord (II Cor. 5.9). At the last day they too shall hear the Judge pronounce their award, 'Come, ye blessed of My Father, inherit the kingdom prepared for you from the foundation of the world' (Matt. 25.34).

St. Bernard of Clairvaux. *On Loving God*, Ch. 4.

Additional Biblical Reflections: Jeremiah 29:11; Matthew 6:33; James 4:12-15.

Prayer

Lord, by securing our future, you have also redeemed our present and past. Let us not live with a hope that is devoid of impact on the future but let your hope change our lives here and now, so we might see today not as a time we must merely endure but as the beginning of our lives in your eternity. In Jesus's name. Amen.

DAY 90

While we have cause to lament in this world, our lament is not merely on account of our sufferings. Rather, as the Bridegroom nears, and we are His Bridegroom, we lament for those who do not know the coming joy that consumes our lives. We lament not because we suffer, for we know that our suffering is temporary, but for those whose futures know only wrath.

Meditations from St. Bernard

In that day those who set not their hearts aright will feel, too late, how easy is Christ's yoke, to which they would not bend their necks and how light His burden, in comparison with the pains they must then endure. O wretched slaves of Mammon, you cannot glory in the Cross of our Lord Jesus Christ while you trust in treasures laid up on earth: you cannot taste and see how gracious the Lord is, while you are hungering for gold. If you have not rejoiced at the thought of His coming, that day will be indeed a day of wrath to you.

But the believing soul longs and faints for God; she rests sweetly in the contemplation of Him. She glories in the reproach of the Cross, until the glory of His face shall be revealed. Like the Bride, the dove of Christ, that is covered with silver wings (Ps. 68.13), white with innocence and purity, she reposes in the thought of Thine abundant kindness, Lord Jesus; and above all she longs for that day when in the joyful splendor of Thy saints, gleaming with the radiance of the Beatific Vision, her feathers shall be like gold, resplendent with the joy of Thy countenance.

Rightly then may she exult, 'His left hand is under my head and His right hand doth embrace me.' The left hand signifies the memory of that

179

matchless love, which moved Him to lay down His life for His friends; and the right hand is the Beatific Vision which He hath promised to His own, and the delight they have in His presence. The Psalmist sings rapturously, 'At Thy right hand there is pleasure for evermore' (Ps. 16.11): so we are warranted in explaining the right hand as that divine and deifying joy of His presence.

Rightly too is that wondrous and ever-memorable love symbolized as His left hand, upon which the Bride rests her head until iniquity be done away: for He sustains the purpose of her mind, lest it should be turned aside to earthly, carnal desires. For the flesh wars against the spirit: 'The corruptible body presseth down the soul, and the earthly tabernacle weigheth down the mind that museth upon many things' (Wisdom 9.15). What could result from the contemplation of compassion so marvelous and so undeserved, favor so free and so well attested, kindness so unexpected, clemency so unconquerable, grace so amazing except that the soul should withdraw from all sinful affections, reject all that is inconsistent with God's love, and yield herself wholly to heavenly things? No wonder is it that the Bride, moved by the perfume of these unctions, runs swiftly, all on fire with love, yet reckons herself as loving all too little in return for the Bridegroom's love. And rightly, since it is no great matter that a little dust should be all consumed with love of that Majesty which loved her first and which revealed itself as wholly bent on saving her. For 'God so loved the world that He gave His only-begotten Son, that whosoever believeth in Him should not perish but have everlasting life' (John 3.16). This sets forth the Father's love. But 'He hath poured out His soul unto death,' was written of the Son (Isa. 53.12). And of the Holy Spirit it is said, 'The Comforter which is the Holy Ghost whom the Father will send in My name, He shall teach you all things, and bring all things to your remembrance, whatsoever I have said unto you' (John 14.26). It is plain, therefore, that God loves us, and loves us with all His heart; for the Holy Trinity altogether loves us, if we may venture so to speak of the infinite and incomprehensible Godhead who is essentially one.

St. Bernard of
Clairvaux. *On Loving
God*, Ch. 4.

Additional Biblical Reflections: Matthew 25:1-13; 2 Corinthians 11:2; Revelation 19:7.

Prayer

We wait for you, Lord, as a bride longing for the coming of her bridegroom. May we long for you with holy eyes, always alert and ready, so, should you reappear, we will be ready to embrace you covered by the grace merited by you on the cross. Wash us clean of our iniquities, as a bride washed for her bridegroom so that we might be pleasing to you in every way. In His name. Amen.

DAY 91

In today's meditation, St. John of the Cross reminds us how, after a time of being nurtured as a mother does a new infant, those who progress in the faith are often set upon challenges. The child must learn to walk. In the process, the child might stumble and bruise a knee or elbow. So, too, for those who progress in the faith, after a time, we are no longer nursed and nurtured but set to labor in the things of God, tested with trials and doubts, not that we might fall but that we might learn to walk and even run into God's arms more fervently.

Meditations from St. John of the Cross

It must be known, then, that the soul, after it has been definitely converted to the service of God, is, as a rule, spiritually nurtured and caressed by God, even as is the tender child by its loving mother, who warms it with the heat of her bosom and nurtures it with sweet milk and soft and pleasant food, and carries it and caresses it in her arms; but, as the child grows bigger, the mother gradually ceases caressing it, and, hiding her tender love, puts bitter aloes upon her sweet breast, sets down the child from her arms and makes it walk upon its feet, so that it may lose the habits of a child and betake itself to more important and substantial occupations. The loving mother is like the grace of God, for, as soon as the soul is regenerated by its new warmth and fervour for the service of God, He treats it in the same way; He makes it to find spiritual milk, sweet and delectable, in all the things of God, without any labour of its own, and also great pleasure in spiritual exercises, for here God is giving to it the breast of His tender love, even as to a tender.

St. John of the
Cross. *Dark Night of the
Soul*

Additional Biblical Reflections: 1 Corinthians 3:1-3; 1 Peter 2:1-25; Hebrews 5:11-14.

Prayer

Lord, now that we have been nurtured like babes on your sweet milk, we are tasked to begin taking steps through the challenges of life. Guide us through the "dark night" of the soul as we learn to rely on you, to trust your direction, and follow your voice even as we wander through the wilderness of the world. Amen.

DAY 92

One of the most common temptations that befall the young of faith is that when eager to perform acts of piety and good works, pride quickly wells up, and one begins to think they have become something godly. Here, St. John of the Cross reminds us about the trapping of the Pharisee, who believed he was greater than other men. Instead, as we grow in the faith, we must come to see ourselves evermore in contrast to the glories of God, whom we come to know more intimately. The more we know God, the more we should see, by comparison, that we are flawed and broken creatures dependent on His grace and mercy.

Meditations from St. John of the Cross

As these beginners feel themselves to be very fervent and diligent in spiritual things and devout exercises, from this prosperity (although it is true that holy things of their own nature cause humility) there often comes to them, through their imperfections, a certain kind of secret pride, whence they come to have some degree of satisfaction with their works and with themselves. And hence there comes to them likewise a certain desire, which is somewhat vain, and at times very vain, to speak of spiritual things in the presence of others, and sometimes even to teach such things rather than to learn them. They condemn others in their heart when they see that they have not the kind of devotion which they themselves desire; and sometimes they even say this in words, herein resembling the Pharisee, who boasted of himself, praising God for his own good works and despising the publican.

In these persons the devil often increases the fervour that they have and the desire to perform these and other works more frequently, so that their pride and presumption may grow greater. For the devil knows quite well that all these works and virtues which they perform are not only valueless to them, but even become vices in them. And such a degree of evil are some of these persons wont to reach that they would have none appear good save themselves; and thus, in deed and word, whenever the opportunity occurs, they condemn them and slander them, beholding the mote in their brother's eye and not considering the beam which is in their own; they strain at another's gnat and themselves swallow a camel.

St. John of the
Cross. *The Dark Night
of the Soul.*

Additional Biblical Reflections: Proverbs 16:18; Luke 18:11ff.; James 4:6

Prayer

Dearest Lord, as we draw nearer to you, let us always see that by comparison to your glory, we are but humble creatures, dependent on your every grace. Grant this: that pride might not set us on a course in the opposite direction from which we were first set when you granted us your Spirit. Amen.

DAY 93

It is easy to be distracted by all the *methods* of achieving piety and lose focus on the heart of the matter, which is, quite literally, the devotion of the *heart* itself. How quickly—although starting on the path toward piety with the right intentions—do we fail to see the results we seek and end up jumping from practice to practice as if it is the external thing that must change rather than the condition of our hearts. In today's mediation, St. John of the Cross warns of such ritualism—vain repetitions devoid of the heart's devotion.

Meditations from St. John of the Cross

Many of these beginners have also at times great spiritual avarice. They will be found to be discontented with the spirituality which God gives them; and they are very disconsolate and querulous because they find not in spiritual things the consolation that they would desire. Many can never have enough of listening to counsels and learning spiritual precepts, and of possessing and reading many books which treat of this matter, and they spend their time on all these things rather than on works of mortification and the perfecting of the inward poverty of spirit which should be theirs. Furthermore, they burden themselves with images and rosaries which are very curious; now they put down one, now take up another; now they change about, now change back again; now they want this kind of thing, now that, preferring one kind of cross to another, because it is more curious. And others you will see adorned with agnus deis and relics and tokens, like children with trinkets. Here I condemn the attachment of the heart, and the affection which they have for the nature, multitude and curiosity of these things, inasmuch as it is quite contrary to poverty of spirit which considers only the substance of devotion, makes use only of what suffices for that end and grows weary of this other kind of multiplicity and curiosity. For true devotion must issue from the heart, and consist in the truth and substances alone of what is represented by spiritual things; all the rest is affection and attachment proceeding from imperfection; and in order that one may pass to any kind of perfection it is necessary for such desires to be killed.

St. John of the
Cross. *A Life*. Chapter
19

Additional Biblical Reflections: Proverbs 14:12-15; Matthew 6:7; Mark 7:3-9.

Prayer

Lord, you have blessed us with many means and methods whereby we might draw closer to you. Let us not forget the ends of our piety for the sake of the means. Guide us ever by your presence so that we might engage in true piety with the devotion of our hearts and not satisfy our vanities. Amen.

DAY 94

It is easy to assume that amid pious acts, attending mass, saying our prayers, or even receiving the Eucharist, we are immune from spiritual weakness or diabolical assault. This is because we are vulnerable during such moments, so human flesh, the Devil and his demons, or even fear, can lead us astray. This is a part of the "dark night" of the soul that St. John of the Cross describes—a period of growth in the faith where it sometimes seems that no matter what we do, the Lord is absent, and we are left alone, wandering as spiritual beggars.

Meditations from St. John of the Cross

Many of these beginners have many other imperfections than those which I am describing with respect to each of the deadly sins, but these I set aside, in order to avoid prolixity, touching upon a few of the most important, which are, as it were, the origin and cause of the rest. And thus, with respect to this sin of luxury (leaving apart the falling of spiritual persons into this sin, since my intent is to treat of the imperfections which have to be purged by the dark night), they have many imperfections which might be described as spiritual luxury, not because they are so, but because the imperfections proceed from spiritual things. For it often comes to pass that, in their very spiritual exercises, when they are powerless to prevent it, there arise and assert themselves in the sensual part of the soul impure acts and motions, and sometimes this happens even when the spirit is deep in prayer, or engaged in the Sacrament of Penance or in the Eucharist. These things are not, as I say, in their power; they proceed from one of three causes.

The first cause from which they often proceed is the pleasure which human nature takes in spiritual things. For when the spirit and the sense are pleased, every part of a man is moved by that pleasure to delight according to its proportion and nature. For then the spirit, which is the higher part, is moved to pleasure and delight in God; and the sensual nature, which is the lower part, is moved to pleasure and delight of the senses, because it cannot possess and lay hold upon aught else, and it therefore lays hold upon that which comes nearest to itself, which is the impure and sensual…

The second cause whence these rebellions sometimes proceed is the devil, who, in order to disquiet and disturb the soul, at times when it is at prayer or is striving to pray, contrives to stir up these motions of impurity in its nature; and if the soul gives heed to any of these, they cause it great harm. For through fear of these not only do persons become lax in prayer—which is the aim of the devil when he begins to strive with them—but some give up prayer altogether, because they think that these things attack them more during that exercise than apart from it, which is true, since the devil attacks them then more than at other times, so that they may give up spiritual exercises…

The third source whence these impure motions are apt to proceed in order to make war upon the soul is often the fear which such persons have conceived for these impure representations and motions. Something that they see or say or think brings them to their mind, and this makes them afraid, so that they suffer from them through no fault of their own.

St. John of the
Cross. *Dark Night of the Soul*

Additional Biblical Reflections: Matthew 26:24; Mark 14:38; Ephesians 6:7.

Prayer

Dear Lord, guard our hearts and make us ever mindful that the flesh and the Devil, even our fear, is always working against our desire to know you more. Sustain us through your presence, especially when we are in prayer and engaged in spiritual disciplines so that through them, we might be led more closely toward you. Amen.

DAY 95

The Catechism describes the sin of wrath as the taking out of one's anger on an innocent person, or at least, unworthy of the degree of "wrath" we levy against them. According to St. John of the Cross, this is one of the temptations that beginners in spiritual paths are most vulnerable to. This often stems from the fact that early in our spiritual development, the feelings that we mistake for spiritual progress are often fleeting. When our emotions wane, we often think we have lost our contact with the divine and that our progress has been for naught. Then, out of desperation, we often fall prey to the sin of wrath.

Meditations from St. John of the Cross

By reason of the concupiscence which many beginners have for spiritual consolations, their experience of these consolations is very commonly accompanied by many imperfections proceeding from the sin of wrath; for, when their delight and pleasure in spiritual things come to an end, they naturally become embittered, and bear that lack of sweetness which they have to suffer with a bad grace, which affects all that they do; and they very easily become irritated over the smallest matter—sometimes, indeed, none can tolerate them. This frequently happens after they have been very pleasantly recollected in prayer according to sense; when their pleasure and delight therein come to an end, their nature is naturally vexed and disappointed, just as is the child when they take it from the breast of which it was enjoying the sweetness. There is no sin in this natural vexation, when it is not permitted to indulge itself, but only imperfection, which must be purged by the aridity and severity of the dark night.

There are other of these spiritual persons, again, who fall into another

190

kind of spiritual wrath: this happens when they become irritated at the sins of others, and keep watch on those others with a sort of uneasy zeal. At times the impulse comes to them to reprove them angrily, and occasionally they go so far as to indulge it and set themselves up as masters of virtue. All this is contrary to spiritual meekness.

St. John of the
Cross. *Dark Night of the
Soul*

Additional Biblical Reflections: Psalm 37:8; Proverbs 14:29; Ephesians 4:26.

Prayer

Lord, you are a God of mercy and grace. Yet we often turn easily to anger and wrath. Grant us your peace and make us ever aware of our anger so that it does not turn into wrath. Lead us, instead, to your mercies so that we might remain grateful rather than angry, even when the emotions of our faith wane. In Jesus's name. Amen.

DAY 96

To this point, most of St. John of the Cross's meditations have not been entirely encouraging. He insists the spiritual life must go through a "dark night of the soul," a period where we see all that we lack so that we might gratefully receive the gifts the Lord wishes us to have. It is during this "dark night," the time when it *feels* that God is far away, that He is actually drawing near and doing some of His most important work on our spirits through His Spirit.

Meditations from St. John of the Cross

This is the first and principal benefit caused by this arid and dark night of contemplation: the knowledge of oneself and of one's misery. For, besides the fact that all the favours which God grants to the soul are habitually granted to them enwrapped in this knowledge, these aridities and this emptiness of the faculties, compared with the abundance which the soul experienced aforetime and the difficulty which it finds in good works, make it recognize its own lowliness and misery, which in the time of its prosperity it was unable to see... In the first place, the soul learns to commune with God with more respect and more courtesy, such as a soul must ever observe in converse with the Most High. These it knew not in its prosperous times of comfort and consolation, for that comforting favour which it experienced made its craving for God somewhat bolder than was fitting, and discourteous and ill-considered... And here we must note another excellent benefit which there is in this night and aridity of the desire of sense, since we have had occasion to speak of it. It is that, in this dark night of the desire (to the end that the words of the Prophet may be fulfilled, namely: 'Thy light shall shine in the darkness'), God will enlighten the soul, giving it knowledge, not only of its lowliness and wretchedness, as we have said, but likewise of the greatness and excellence of God… Let it suffice here to have described these imperfections, among the many to be found in the lives of those that are in this first state of beginners, so that it may be seen how greatly they need God to set them in the state of proficients. This He does by bringing them into the dark night whereof we now speak; wherein He weans them from the breasts of these sweetnesses and pleasures, gives them pure aridities and inward darkness, takes from them all these irrelevances and puerilities, and by very different means causes them to win the virtues. For, however assiduously the beginner practises the mortification in himself of all these actions and passions of his, he can never completely succeed—very far from it—until God shall work it in him passively by means of the purgation of the said night. Of this I would fain speak in some way that may be profitable; may God, then, be pleased to give me His Divine light, because this is very needful in a night that is so dark and a matter that is so difficult to describe and to expound.

St. John of the
Cross, *The Dark Night
of the Soul*

Additional Biblical Reflections: Exodus 33:3; Isiah 53:10; Psalm 38:3.

Prayer

Dearest Lord, while we go through many trials, temptations, and tribulations in this world, you are always at work through it all. Lead us to see your light as it penetrates the darkness of our lives so that we might endure through the shadowy sufferings of this life and persist into life everlasting. Amen.

DAY 97

For St. John of the Cross, spiritual progress is not linear. One does not pass through the dark night, find the light, and never experience spiritual darkness again. Rather, as one progresses, it is more a cyclical pattern whereby one gains spiritual insight through darkness, enjoys God's good things, and then might be subject to darkness again in a season when the flesh again exerts itself. But every time one passes through this darkness, God uses it to bring one through to the light with new insight, greater awareness of God's ways, and growth toward better holiness.

Meditations from St. John of the Cross

This night, which, as we say, is contemplation, produces in spiritual persons two kinds of darkness or purgation, corresponding to the two parts of man's nature—namely, the sensual and the spiritual. And thus the one night or purgation will be sensual, wherein the soul is purged according to sense, which is subdued to the spirit; and the other is a night or purgation which is spiritual, wherein the soul is purged and stripped according to the spirit, and subdued and made ready for the union of love with God. The night of sense is common and comes to many: these are the beginners; and of this night we shall speak first. The night of the spirit is the portion of very few, and these are they that are already practised and proficient, of whom we shall treat hereafter. The first purgation or night is bitter and terrible to sense, as we shall now show. The second bears no comparison with it, for it is horrible and awful to the spirit, as we shall show presently. Since the night of sense is first in order and comes first, we shall first of all say something about it briefly, since more is written of it, as of a thing that is more common; and we shall pass on to treat more fully of the spiritual night, since very little has been said of this, either in speech or in writing, and very little is known of it, even by experience. Since, then, the conduct of these beginners upon the way of God is ignoble, and has much to do with their love of self and their own inclinations, as has been explained above, God desires to lead them farther. He seeks to bring them out of that ignoble kind of love to a higher degree of love for Him, to free them from the ignoble exercises of sense and meditation (wherewith, as we have said, they go seeking God so unworthily and in so many ways that are unbefitting), and to lead them to a kind of spiritual exercise wherein they can commune with Him more abundantly and are freed more completely from imperfections. For they have now had practice for some time in the way of virtue and have persevered in meditation and prayer, whereby, through the sweetness and pleasure that they have found therein, they have lost their love of the things of the world and have gained some degree of spiritual strength in God; this has enabled them to some extent to refrain from creature desires, so that for God's sake they are now able to suffer a light burden and a little aridity without turning back to a time which they found more pleasant. When they are going about these spiritual exercises with the greatest delight and pleasure, and when they believe that the sun of Divine favour is shining most brightly upon them, God turns all this light of theirs into darkness, and shuts against them the door and the source of the sweet spiritual water which they were tasting in God whensoever and for as long as they desired…For, as I have said, God now sees that they have grown a little, and are becoming strong enough to lay aside their swaddling clothes and be taken from the gentle breast; so He sets them down from His arms and teaches them to walk on their own feet; which they feel to be very strange, for everything seems to be going wrong with them.

St. John of the
Cross, *The Dark Night
of the Soul*

Additional Biblical Reflections: Romans 5:3-5; John 16:33; James 1:2-4.

Prayer

Lord, let us never imagine in this life that we have arrived at spiritual perfection. For the moment we think we have achieved it, our pride and other various sins arise from the flesh to remind us that we have not, in fact, achieved perfect godliness. Let us embrace the darkness and the light alike, knowing that you are in all and work through all to bring us closer to you. Amen.

DAY 98

Today, St. John of the Cross offers practical advice for when we are going through the dark night of the soul. At such moments, we may feel restless, with the need to do *something* to lift ourselves out of the discomfort of our condition. However, in such moments, becoming a busybody is often counterproductive. Instead, St. John of the Cross recommends that we simply find time to do *nothing*. We should find moments of peace and quiet—when we do not focus on any particular object or meditation but simply allow ourselves to exist in the knowledge that God is present, not because of the discomfort of the dark night, but, in many ways, because of it.

Meditations from St. John of the Cross

During the time, then, of the aridities of this night of sense (wherein God effects the change of which we have spoken above, drawing forth the soul from the life of sense into that of the spirit—that is, from meditation to contemplation—wherein it no longer has any power to work or to reason with its faculties concerning the things of God, as has been said), spiritual persons suffer great trials, by reason not so much of the aridities which they suffer, as of the fear which they have of being lost on the road, thinking that all spiritual blessing is over for them and that God has abandoned them since they find no help or pleasure in good things. Then they grow weary, and endeavour (as they have been accustomed to do) to concentrate their faculties with some degree of pleasure upon some object of meditation, thinking that, when they are not doing this and yet are conscious of making an effort, they are doing nothing. This effort they make not without great inward repugnance and unwillingness on the part of their soul, which was taking pleasure in being in that quietness and ease, instead of working with its faculties. So they have abandoned the one pursuit, yet draw no profit from the other; for, by seeking what is prompted by their own spirit, they lose the spirit of tranquillity and peace which they had before. And thus they are like to one who abandons what he has done in order to do it over again, or to one who leaves a city only to re-enter it, or to one who is hunting and lets his prey go in order to hunt it once more. This is useless here, for the soul will gain nothing further by conducting itself in this way, as has been said... t is well for those who find themselves in this condition to take comfort, to persevere in patience and to be in no wise afflicted. Let them trust in God, Who abandons not those that seek Him with a simple and right heart, and will not fail to give them what is needful for the road, until He bring them into the clear and pure light of love. This last He will give them by means of that other dark night, that of the spirit, if they merit His bringing them thereto.

The way in which they are to conduct themselves in this night of sense is to devote themselves not at all to reasoning and meditation, since this is not the time for it, but to allow the soul to remain in peace and quietness, although it may seem clear to them that they are doing nothing and are wasting their time, and although it may appear to them that it is because of their weakness that they have no desire in that state to think of anything. The truth is that they will be doing quite sufficient if they have patience and persevere in prayer without making any effort.

St. John of the
Cross. *The Dark Night
of the Soul*

Additional Biblical Reflections: 1 Kings 19:11-13; Psalm 46:10; 2 Corinthians 6:4-8.

Prayer

Lord, you often come to us in the stillness. During your earthly pilgrimage, you, too, took moments to depart from the business of the world to simply commune with the Father in quiet. Quell our restlessness, particularly during seasons of the dark night in the soul, so we might hear your voice, which will lead us through every condition of this life. Amen.

DAY 99

There is no shame in recognizing that we are spiritual children. Jesus, himself, exhorted His hearers—who thought themselves more advanced in spiritual matters than they truly were—to become *like* the little children (Matt. 18:1-5). It is quite dangerous when we are spiritual children to behave as if we are adults. Imagine a child attempting to drive a car or wield a weapon. To mature in the faith, we must embrace our childhood and take from this season of our growth what we ought to receive *as* children and allow the Spirit to give us growth in due course.

Meditations from St. John of the Cross

Therefore, since these proficients are still at a very low stage of progress, and follow their own nature closely in the intercourse and dealings which they have with God, because the gold of their spirit is not yet purified and refined, they still think of God as little children, and speak of God as little children, and feel and experience God as little children, even as Saint Paul says, because they have not reached perfection, which is the union of the soul with God. In the state of union, however, they will work great things in the spirit, even as grown men, and their works and faculties will then be Divine rather than human, as will afterwards be said. To this end God is pleased to strip them of this old man and clothe them with the new man, who is created according to God, as the Apostle says, in the newness of sense. He strips their faculties, affections and feelings, both spiritual and sensual, both outward and inward, leaving the understanding dark, the will dry, the memory empty and the affections in the deepest affliction, bitterness and constraint, taking from the soul the pleasure and experience of spiritual blessings which it had aforetime, in order to make of this privation one of the principles which are requisite in the spirit so that there may be introduced into it and united with it the spiritual form of the spirit, which is the union of love. All this the Lord works in the soul by means of a pure and dark contemplation.

St. John of the
Cross. *The Dark Night
of the Soul*

Additional Biblical Reflections: Matthew 18:1-5; 1 Corinthians 12:11; Ephesians 4:24.

Prayer

Dearest Lord, let us approach you as little children, eager to hear every word without any pretense that we have grown or matured more than we have, for you give us what we need in due season. Grant us such humility so that we might truly become mature disciples. Amen.

DAY 100

S t. John of the Cross does not exhort his hearers because he is more learned than other men; rather, he speaks of his own experience enduring a "dark night." Likewise, from his experience, he knows the blessings and happiness that follow. In today's meditation, we might take comfort from his example.

Meditations from St. John of the Cross

This was a great happiness and a good chance for me; for, when the faculties had been perfectly annihilated and calmed, together with the passions, desires and affections of my soul, wherewith I had experienced and tasted God after a lowly manner, I went forth from my own human dealings and operations to the operations and dealings of God. That is to say, my understanding went forth from itself, turning from the human and natural to the Divine; for, when it is united with God by means of this purgation, its understanding no longer comes through its natural light and vigour, but through the Divine Wisdom wherewith it has become united. And my will went forth from itself, becoming Divine; for, being united with Divine love, it no longer loves with its natural strength after a lowly manner, but with strength and purity from the Holy Spirit; and thus the will, which is now near to God, acts not after a human manner, and similarly the memory has become transformed into eternal apprehensions of glory. And finally, by means of this night and purgation of the old man, all the energies and affections of the soul are wholly renewed into a Divine temper and Divine delight.

St. John of the
Cross, *The Dark Night
of the Soul*

Additional Biblical Reflections: Proverbs 3:12-18; Job 5:17-27; Philippians 4:7.

Prayer

Lord, you do not grant us a period of trial so that we might be miserable; rather, you press us through the "dark night," so we might come to know true happiness as creatures made in your image. Let us take comfort from the example of those who have gone before us, and, together with your word, trust that the path you've set us on is not one destined for misery, but one that, while suffering might befall us in the end, will result in genuine contentment. Amen.

DAY 101

According to St. John of the Cross, there are multiple nights of the soul through which one might progress in his way to spiritual perfection. In today's meditation, he bids us to consider the example of Tobias, as contained in the Book of Tobit, as he endured hardship and trial in the pursuit of his would-be wife. We hear not only the unique character of each of these three nights of the soul but the way the Lord worked through each of them to prepare Tobias for the life He had intended for him.

Meditations from St. John of the Cross

We may say that there are three reasons for which this journey made by the soul to union with God is called night. The first has to do with the point from which the soul goes forth, for it has gradually to deprive itself of desire for all the worldly things which it possessed, by denying them to itself... The second reason has to do with the mean, or the road along which the soul must travel to this union — that is, faith, which is likewise as dark as night to the understanding. The third has to do with the point to which it travels — namely, God, Who, equally, is dark night to the soul in this life. These three nights must pass through the soul — or, rather, the soul must pass through them — in order that it may come to Divine union with God.

In the book of the holy Tobias these three kinds of night were shadowed forth by the three nights which, as the angel commanded, were to pass ere the youth Tobias should be united with his bride. In the first he commanded him to burn the heart of the fish in the fire, which signifies the heart that is affectioned to, and set upon, the things of the world; which, in order that one may begin to journey toward God, must be burned and purified from all that is creature, in the fire of the love of God. And in this purgation the devil flees away, for he has power over the soul only when it is attached to things corporeal and temporal.

On the second night the angel told him that he would be admitted into the company of the holy patriarchs, who are the fathers of the faith. For, passing through the first night, which is self-privation of all objects of sense, the soul at once enters into the second night, and abides alone in faith to the exclusion, not of charity, but of other knowledge acquired by the understanding, as we shall say hereafter, which is a thing that pertains not to sense.

On the third night the angel told him that he would obtain a blessing, which is God; Who, by means of the second night, which is faith, continually communicates Himself to the soul in such a secret and intimate manner that He becomes another night to the soul, inasmuch as this said communication is far darker than those others, as we shall say presently. And, when this third night is past, which is the complete accomplishment of the communication of God in the spirit, which is ordinarily wrought in great darkness of the soul, there then follows its union with the Bride, which is the Wisdom of God. Even so the angel said likewise to Tobias that, when the third night was past, he should be united with his bride in the fear of the Lord; for, when this fear of God is perfect, love is perfect, and this comes to pass when the transformation of the soul is wrought through its love.

These three parts of the night are all one night; but, after the manner of night, it has three parts. For the first part, which is that of sense, is comparable to the beginning of night, the point at which things begin to fade from sight. And the second part, which is faith, is comparable to midnight, which is total darkness. And the third part is like the close of night, which is God, the which part is now near to the light of day. And, that we may understand this the better, we shall treat of each of these reasons separately as we proceed.

St. John of the
Cross, *Ascent of Mount
Carmel*

Additional Biblical Reflections: Deuteronomy 31:5; Psalm 88:1; Tobit 8-14.

Prayer

Lord, all good things come from you, even our various dark nights, through which we might pass as we make spiritual progress. Guide us through each of these, as you did for your servant Tobias, so we might enjoy the blessings you have chosen to bestow upon us. Amen.

DAY 102

In today's meditation, St. John of the Cross speaks of various kinds of fasting—fasting of all the various senses (not just abstaining from food)—and the ways that we might grow through such a spiritual practice. Through various kinds of fasts, we are told, the soul comes to realize its true condition and finds instead its delights in the things of God. According to St. John of the Cross, this is necessary if we are to attain union with God.

Meditations from St. John of the Cross

Let us take an example from each of the faculties. When the soul deprives its desire of the pleasure of all that can delight the sense of hearing, the soul remains unoccupied and in darkness with respect to this faculty. And, when it deprives itself of the pleasure of all that can please the sense of sight, it remains unoccupied and in darkness with respect to this faculty also. And, when it deprives itself of the pleasure of all the sweetness of perfumes which can give it pleasure through the sense of smell, it remains equally unoccupied and in darkness according to this faculty. And, if it also denies itself the pleasure of all food that can satisfy the palate, the soul likewise remains unoccupied and in darkness. And finally, when the soul mortifies itself with respect to all the delights and pleasures that it can receive from the sense of touch, it remains, in the same way, unoccupied and in darkness with respect to this faculty. So that the soul that has denied and thrust away from itself the pleasures which come from all these things, and has mortified its desire with respect to them, may be said to be, as it were, in the darkness of night, which is naught else than an emptiness within itself of all things.

The reason for this is that, as the philosophers say, the soul, as soon as

God infuses it into the body, is like a smooth, blank board upon which nothing is painted; and, save for that which it experiences through the senses, nothing is communicated to it, in the course of nature, from any other source. And thus, for as long as it is in the body, it is like one who is in a dark prison and who knows nothing, save what he is able to see through the windows of the said prison; and, if he saw nothing through them, he would see nothing in any other way. And thus the soul, save for that which is communicated to it through the senses, which are the windows of its prison, could acquire nothing, in the course of nature, in any other way.

Wherefore, if the soul rejects and denies that which it can receive through the senses, we can quite well say that it remains, as it were, in darkness and empty; since, as appears from what has been said, no light can enter it, in the course of nature, by any other means of illumination than those aforementioned.

St. John of the
Cross, *Ascent of Mount
Carmel*

Additional Biblical Reflections: Isaiah 58:3-7; Ezra 8:21-23; Matthew 6:16-18.

Prayer

Dear Lord, you have given us all of our senses. These things are good. Yet, in the flesh, we often find ourselves blinded from spiritual matters on account of sensual delights. Grant that we might learn, through proper fasting, our true condition, and the true satisfaction that comes only through communion with you. Amen.

DAY 103

When we set our affection and attention on earthly things, are spiritual estate is limited to that upon which our hearts and minds dwell. For those whose lives are consumed by the pursuit of riches, they might become very wealthy in this life, but all they have perishes with them. St. John of the Cross evokes the example of the Israelites, who grumbled that they were hungry. The Lord provided bread from Heaven. But what if they had obsessed instead over the need to know the Lord, who'd brought them out of Egypt? Then, they might have been ready to receive the promised land, a place flowing with milk and honey, and could feast more sumptuously than they did on manna.

Meditations from St. John of the Cross

From what has been said it may be seen in some measure how great a distance there is between all that the creatures are in themselves and that which God is in Himself, and how souls that set their affections upon any of these creatures are at as great a distance as they from God; for, as we have said, love produces equality and likeness. This distance was clearly realized by Saint Augustine, who said in the Sololoquies, speaking with God: 'Miserable man that I am, when will my littleness and imperfection be able to have fellowship with Thy uprightness? Thou indeed art good, and I am evil; Thou art merciful, and I am impious; Thou art holy, I am miserable; Thou art just, I am unjust; Thou art light, I am blind; Thou, life, I, death; Thou, medicine, I, sick; Thou, supreme truth, I, utter vanity.' All this is said by this Saint.

Wherefore, it is supreme ignorance for the soul to think that it will be able to pass to this high estate of union with God if first it void not the desire of all things, natural and supernatural, which may hinder it, according as we shall explain hereafter; for there is the greatest possible distance between these things and that which comes to pass in this estate, which is naught else than transformation in God. For this reason Our Lord, when showing us this path, said through Saint Luke: Qui non renuntiat omnibus quae possidet, non potest meus esse discipulus. This signifies: He that renounces not all things that he possesses with his will cannot be My disciple. And this is evident; for the doctrine that the Son of God came to teach was contempt for all things, whereby a man might receive as a reward the Spirit of God in himself. For, as long as the soul rejects not all things, it has no capacity to receive the Spirit of God in pure transformation… Oh, did spiritual persons but know how much good and what great abundance of spirit they lose through not seeking to raise up their desires above childish things, and how in this simple spiritual food they would find the sweetness of all things, if they desired not to taste those things! But such food gives them no pleasure, for the reason why the children of Israel received not the sweetness of all foods that was contained in the manna was that they would not reserve their desire for it alone.

St. John of the
Cross, *Ascent of Mount
Carmel*

Additional Biblical Reflections: Exodus 34:2-3; Wisdom 16:20; Luke 14:33.

Prayer

Dear Lord, we are so easily distracted by our bodily needs, cares, concerns, and even the pleasures of this life. But you are the great giver of all good things. Let us set our hearts not on the things we seek, but on you, the great giver, so we might receive all you would give us in your abundant mercies and love. In Jesus's name. Amen.

DAY 104

In yesterday's meditation, we heard how the things that consume our passions could distract us from God's good things. Today, we hear how otherworldly matters, namely the kinds of torments and afflictions we experience in this world, can do the same. Citing several scriptures, St. John of the Cross does not minimize or dismiss such sufferings but urges us, instead, to consider God's presence and His promise as our comforter and sustainer. In such times, when the turmoil we are experiencing has become our focus, we should rather be directed to focus on the Lord.

Meditations from St. John of the Cross

The second kind of positive evil which the desires cause the soul is in their tormenting and afflicting of it, after the manner of one who is in torment through being bound with cords from which he has no relief until he be freed. And of these David says: The cords of my sins, which are my desires, have constrained me round about. And, even as one that lies naked upon thorns and briars is tormented and afflicted, even so is the soul tormented and afflicted when it rests upon its desires. For they take hold upon it and distress it and cause it pain, even as do thorns. Of these David says likewise: They compassed me about like bees, wounding me with their stings, and they were enkindled against me, like fire among thorns; for in the desires, which are the thorns, increases the fire of anguish and torment… he more intense is the desire, the greater is the torment which it causes the soul. So that the torment increases with the desire; and the greater are the desires which possess the soul, the greater are its torments; for in such a soul is fulfilled, even in this life, that which is said in the Apocalypse concerning

Babylon, in these words: As much as she has wished to exalt and fulfil her desires, so much give ye to her torment and anguish. And even as one that falls into the hands of his enemies is tormented and afflicted, even so is the soul tormented and afflicted that is led away by its desires… This attaining to fatness is a going forth from all pleasures of the creatures; for the creatures torment, but the Spirit of God refreshes. And thus He calls us through Saint Matthew, saying: All ye that go about tormented, afflicted and burdened with the burden of your cares and desires, go forth from them, come to Me, and I will refresh you and ye shall find for your souls the rest which your desires take from you, wherefore they are a heavy burden.

St. John of the
Cross. *Ascent of Mount Carmel*

Additional Biblical Reflections: Psalm 118:61; Matthew 11:28-29; Revelation 18:7.

Prayer

Your Spirit, Lord, is greater than any affliction. Let not the troubles of this world blind us from your presence. Rather, amid the most difficult seasons of life, let us fix our eyes all the more firmly upon you so that you might raise us from our misery through your promises and blessings. Amen.

DAY 105

In today's meditation, St. John of the Cross bids us to consider our desires, which have a way of blinding us from spiritual matters. He insists that the major problem many face in their hollow pursuits of piety is they focus immediately upon trying to attain spiritual things without mortifying the flesh. This, the saint reminds us, is akin to growing a garden in a field already populated by weeds. While "weeding" the garden of our souls can be a painful and arduous process, it is necessary to experience the growth we seek.

Meditations from St. John of the Cross

The third evil that the desires cause in the soul is that they blind and darken it. Even as vapours darken the air and allow not the bright sun to shine; or as a mirror that is clouded over cannot receive within itself a clear image; or as water defiled by mud reflects not the visage of one that looks therein; even so the soul that is clouded by the desires is darkened in the understanding and allows neither the sun of natural reason nor that of the supernatural Wisdom of God to shine upon it and illumine it clearly. And thus David, speaking to this purpose, says: Mine iniquities have taken hold upon me, and I could have no power to see…Desire blinds and darkens the soul; for desire, as such, is blind, since of itself it has no understanding in itself, the reason being to it always, as it were, a child leading a blind man. And hence it comes to pass that, whensoever the soul is guided by its desire, it becomes blind; for this is as if one that sees were guided by one that sees not, which is, as it were, for both to be blind. And that which follows from this is that which Our Lord says through Saint Matthew: 'If the blind lead the blind, both fall into the pit.'… For this reason one must greatly lament the ignorance of certain men, who burden themselves with extraordinary penances and with many other voluntary practices, and think that this practice or that will suffice to bring them to the union of Divine Wisdom; but such will not be the case if they endeavour not diligently to mortify their desires. If they were careful to bestow half of that labour on this, they would profit more in a month than they profit by all the other practices in many years. For, just as it is necessary to till the earth if it is to bear fruit, and unless it be tilled it bears naught but weeds, just so is mortification of the desires necessary if the soul is to profit. Without this mortification, I make bold to say, the soul no more achieves progress on the road to perfection and to the knowledge of God of itself, however many efforts it may make, than the seed grows when it is cast upon untilled ground. Wherefore the darkness and rudeness of the soul will not be taken from it until the desires be quenched. For these desires are like cataracts, or like motes in the eye, which obstruct the sight until they be taken away.

St. John of the
Cross. *The Interior
Castle.* First Mansions,
Ch. 2

Additional Biblical Reflections: Psalm 6:4, 49:13-20; Isiah 59:10; Matthew 15:14.

Prayer

Lord, we pray that you would do the painful work of weeding our lives of our sins and thereby mortify the garden of our flesh, so the garden of our souls might spring up to the bountiful life you created us to have from the beginning. Grant us the endurance to see through the arduous process of mortification so that we might see the benefits of your bounty. Amen.

DAY 106

We are often like dogs who return to their vomit. Yes, we might make great progress, but how easily do we defile ourselves by returning to old sins that we previously confessed and had purged from our souls. Thus, the saint urges us to take great care about the things we subject our souls to in this world, for all progress can easily be lost when we allow the things that stain and defile our souls to take root.

Meditations from St. John of the Cross

The fourth evil which the desires cause in the soul is that they stain and defile it, as is taught in Ecclesiasticus, in these words: He that toucheth pitch shall be defiled with it. And a man touches pitch when he allows the desire of his will to be satisfied by any creature. Here it is to be noted that the Wise Man compares the creatures to pitch; for there is more difference between excellence of soul and the best of the creatures than there is between pure diamond, or fine gold, and pitch. And just as gold or diamond, if it were heated and placed upon pitch, would become foul and be stained by it, inasmuch as the heat would have cajoled and allured the pitch, even so the soul that is hot with desire for any creature draws forth foulness from it through the heat of its desire and is stained by it. And there is more difference between the soul and other corporeal creatures than between a liquid that is highly clarified and mud that is most foul. Wherefore, even as such a liquid would be defiled if it were mingled with mud, so is the soul defiled that clings to creatures, since by doing this it becomes like to the said creatures. And in the same way that traces of soot would defile a face that is very lovely and perfect, even in this way do disordered desires befoul and defile the soul that has them, the which soul is in itself a most lovely and perfect image of God... It is impossible to explain in words, or to cause to be understood by the understanding, what variety of impurity is caused in the soul by a variety of desires. For, if it could be expressed and understood, it would be a wondrous thing, and one also which would fill us with pity, to see how each desire, in accordance with its quality and degree, be it greater or smaller, leaves in the soul its mark and deposit of impurity and vileness, and how one single disorder of the reason can be the source of innumerable different impurities, some greater, some less, each one after its kind. For, even as the soul of the righteous man has in one single perfection, which is uprightness of soul, innumerable gifts of the greatest richness, and many virtues of the greatest loveliness, each one different and full of grace after its kind according to the multitude and the diversity of the affections of love which it has had in God, even so the unruly soul, according to the variety of the desires which it has for the creatures, has in itself a miserable variety of impurities and meannesses, wherewith it is endowed by the said desires.

St. John of the
Cross, *Ascent of Mount Carmel*

Additional Biblical Reflections: Ecclesiasticus 13:1; Lamentations 4:7-8; Proverbs 26:11.

Prayer

Dear Lord, there are many ways that we might, by our inattentiveness or passions, defile our souls and find ourselves far from you. Give us the wisdom to see the difference between good things and sinful ones and grant us the resilience to stand up against temptation, so we might rather cherish the intimacy our souls share with you. Amen.

DAY 107

Today, St. John of the Cross reminds us about the danger of a half-hearted or lukewarm faith. This is one of the many ways in which our desires can plague the soul. With a lukewarm faith, we lack the resolve to stick to any good practice or virtue but are quickly and easily distracted and dissuaded from spiritual pursuits.

Meditations from St. John of the Cross

The fifth way in which the desires harm the soul is by making it lukewarm and weak, so that it has no strength to follow after virtue and to persevere therein. For as the strength of the desire, when it is set upon various aims, is less than if it were set wholly on one thing alone, and as, the more are the aims whereon it is set, the less of it there is for each of them, for this cause philosophers say that virtue in union is stronger than if it be dispersed. Wherefore it is clear that, if the desire of the will be dispersed among other things than virtue, it must be weaker as regards virtue. And thus the soul whose will is set upon various trifles is like water, which, having a place below wherein to empty itself, never rises; and such a soul has no profit. For this cause the patriarch Jacob compared his son Ruben to water poured out, because in a certain sin he had given rein to his desires. And he said: 'Thou art poured out like water; grow thou not.' As though he had said: Since thou art poured out like water as to the desires, thou shalt not grow in virtue. And thus, as hot water, when uncovered, readily loses heat, and as aromatic spices, when they are unwrapped, gradually lose the fragrance and strength of their perfume, even so the soul that is not recollected in one single desire for God loses heat and vigour in its virtue. This was well understood by

David, when he said, speaking with God: I will keep my strength for Thee That is, concentrating the strength of my desires upon Thee alone.

St. John of the
Cross, *Ascent of Mount
Carmel*

Additional Biblical Reflections: Genesis 49:4; Psalm 58:10; Luke 12:35-40.

Prayer

Dear Lord, stoke a fire in our souls and a passion for you so that we might be tepid or lukewarm in spiritual matters. Continue to tinder our flames, so we might always grow spiritually and not be easily doused by the storms of life. In Jesus's name. Amen.

DAY 108

In the preceding meditations, St. John of the Cross went after the notion of human desire so poignantly that one might get the idea that it is inappropriate to desire anything at all. In today's meditation, the saint offers helpful clarification about the sorts of desires that are both appropriate and unavoidable as natural creatures and distinguishes these from those that can harm the soul. It is not unholy, for instance, to desire food, clothing, or shelter. However, such desires must be coupled with a pursuit of God. It is not unholy that we should desire our children's safety or other such natural things. These are holy desires, and we must take care not to forsake holy desires as we seek to suppress unholy ones.

Meditations from St. John of the Cross

I expect that for a long time the reader has been wishing to ask whether it be necessary, in order to attain to this high estate of perfection, to undergo first of all total mortification in all the desires, great and small, or if it will suffice to mortify some of them and to leave others, those at least which seem of little moment. For it appears to be a severe and most difficult thing for the soul to be able to attain to such purity and detachment that it has no will and affection for anything.

To this I reply: first, that it is true that all the desires are not equally hurtful, nor do they all equally embarrass the soul. I am speaking of those that are voluntary, for the natural desires hinder the soul little, if at all, from attaining to union, when they are not consented to nor pass beyond the first movements (I mean, all those wherein the rational will has had no part, whether at first or afterward); and to take away these — that is, to mortify them wholly in this life — is impossible. And these hinder not the soul in such a way as to prevent its attainment to Divine union, even though they be not, as I say, wholly mortified; for the natural man may well have them, and yet the soul may be quite free from them according to the rational spirit. For it will sometimes come to pass that the soul will be in the full union of the prayer of quiet in the will at the very time when these desires are dwelling in the sensual part of the soul, and yet the higher part, which is in prayer, will have nothing to do with them. But all the other voluntary desires, whether they be of mortal sin, which are the gravest, or of venial sin, which are less grave, or whether they be only of imperfections, which are the least grave of all, must be driven away every one, and the soul must be free from them all, howsoever slight they be, if it is to come to this complete union; and the reason is that the state of this Divine union consists in the soul's total transformation, according to the will, in the will of God, so that, there may be naught in the soul that is contrary to the will of God, but that, in all and through all, its movement may be that of the will of God alone.

St. John of the
Cross, *Ascent of Mount
Carmel*

Additional Biblical Reflections: Psalm 37:4, 145:19; Luke 6:21; Colossians 3:1-25.

Prayer

Lord, refine our desires so that we might seek only good things in this world, for you created us as creatures in communion with the earth and one another. Thus, let us still seek the good things of this life that you have intended for us, but let us never attach our passions to such things in a way that the creation—rather than you, our creator— becomes God. In Jesus's name. Amen.

DAY 109

We have all prayed, many times, "Thy will be done." Today, St. John of the Cross reminds us about the difference between "thine" and "mine." While we see our will to be conformed to God's, often we find what we desire and what God wills are two different things. However, through spiritual progress, we come to see that our will gradually begins to mirror God's. Yet we can still, even in a state of relative piety, believe that it is thereby safe to pursue our will, for the flesh is always eager to pervert our will. Thus, it is in God's heart that we should always seek His will and check our will accordingly.

Meditations from St. John of the Cross

It is for this reason that we say of this state that it is the making of two wills into one — namely, into the will of God, which will of God is likewise the will of the soul. For if this soul desired any imperfection that God wills not, there would not be made one will of God, since the soul would have a will for that which God has not. It is clear, then, that for the soul to come to unite itself perfectly with God through love and will, it must first be free from all desire of the will, howsoever slight. That is, that it must not intentionally and knowingly consent with the will to imperfections, and it must have power and liberty to be able not so to consent intentionally. I say knowingly, because, unintentionally and unknowingly, or without having the power to do otherwise, it may well fall into imperfections and venial sins, and into the natural desires whereof we have spoken; for of such sins as these which are not voluntary and surreptitious it is written that the just man shall fall seven times in the day and shall rise up again. But of the voluntary desires, which, though they be for very small things, are, as

I have said, intentional venial sins, any one that is not conquered suffices to impede union.[4] I mean, if this habit be not mortified; for sometimes certain acts of different desires have not as much power when the habits are mortified. Still, the soul will attain to the stage of not having even these, for they likewise proceed from a habit of imperfection. But some habits of voluntary imperfections, which are never completely conquered, prevent not only the attainment of Divine union, but also progress in perfection.

St. John of the
Cross, *Ascent of Mount
Carmel*

Additional Biblical Reflections: Matthew 6:9-13; Ephesians 1:11; 1 John 2:17.

Prayer

Dearest Lord, might your will be done on Earth as it is in Heaven, not only in our lives but throughout the world. Let our will always be subjected to yours, even as our will comes to reflect yours more consistently. Grant this so that we might progress toward righteousness rather than carnality and constantly grow to be a better reflection of your love and mercy in the world. In Jesus's name. Amen.

DAY 110

It is interesting that St. John of the Cross speaks of faith as the second part of the "dark night" of the soul, which is striving toward God. Nonetheless, faith is truly tested in darkness. When there is light, and all is seen and clear, having faith is easy. When we must traverse through the darkness, unsure about what is in front of us, we must trust the guiding voice of God, who promises to navigate us through this dark night.

Meditations from St. John of the Cross

We now go on to treat of the second part of this night, which is faith; this is the wondrous means which, as we said, leads to the goal, which is God, Who, as we said,] is also to the soul, naturally, the third cause or part of this night. For faith, which is the means, is compared with midnight. And thus we may say that it is darker for the soul either than the first part or, in a way, than the third; for the first part, which is that of sense, is compared to the beginning of night, or the time when sensible objects can no longer be seen, and thus it is not so far removed from light as is midnight. The third part, which is the period preceding the dawn, is quite close to the light of day, and it, too, therefore, is not so dark as midnight; for it is now close to the enlightenment and illumination of the light of day, which is compared with God. For, although it is true, if we speak after a natural manner, that God is as dark a night to the soul as is faith, still, when these three parts of the night are over, which are naturally night to the soul, God begins to illumine the soul by supernatural means with the ray of His Divine light; which is the beginning of the perfect union that follows, when the third night is past, and it can thus be said to be less dark.

It is likewise darker than the first night, for this belongs to the lower part of man, which is the sensual part, and, consequently, the more exterior; and this second part, which is of faith, belongs to the higher part of man, which is the rational part, and, in consequence, more interior and more obscure, since it deprives it of the light of reason, or, to speak more clearly, blinds it; and thus it is aptly compared to midnight, which is the depth of night and the darkest part thereof.

We have now to prove how this second part, which is faith, is night to the spirit, even as the first part is night to sense. And we shall then also describe the things that are contrary to it, and how the soul must prepare itself actively to enter it. For, concerning the passive part, which is that which God works in it, when He brings it into that night, we shall speak in its place, which I intend shall be the third book.

St. John of the
Cross, *Ascent of Mount
Carmel*

Additional Biblical Reflections: Proverbs 3:5-6; Matthew 21:21-22; Hebrews 11:6.

Prayer

Lord, faith is a great gift that you have given us, whereby we must trust your call and heed your voice while navigating periods of darkness. When we need help through our unbelief so that we might persist, see us through the darkness into your light. Amen.

DAY 111

Faith is how we encounter the mysteries of God. When confronted with such mysteries, the rational mind seeks to comprehend God's transcendence, but faith simply accepts it and adores the mysteries, for the goodness of God's mysteries is not contingent on our understanding but His generosity. When we pass through this dark period of the soul, St. John of the Cross reminds us to find ourselves content to adore rather than investigate God's mysteries.

Meditations from St. John of the Cross

Faith, say the theologians, is a habit of the soul, certain and obscure. And the reason for its being an obscure habit is that it makes us believe truths revealed by God Himself, which transcend all natural light, and exceed all human understanding, beyond all proportion. Hence it follows that, for the soul, this excessive light of faith which is given to it is thick darkness, for it overwhelms greater things and does away with small things, even as the light of the sun overwhelms all other lights whatsoever, so that when it shines and disables our visual faculty they appear not to be lights at all. So that it blinds it and deprives it of the sight that has been given to it, inasmuch as its light is great beyond all proportion and transcends the faculty of vision. Even so the light of faith, by its excessive greatness, oppresses and disables that of the understanding; for the latter, of its own power, extends only to natural knowledge, although it has a faculty for the supernatural, whenever Our Lord is pleased to give it supernatural activity.

Even so is faith with respect to the soul; it tells us of things which we have never seen or understood, nor have we seen or understood aught that resembles them, since there is naught that resembles them at all. And thus, we have no light of natural knowledge concerning them, since that which we are told of them bears no relation to any sense of ours; we know it by the ear alone, believing that which we are taught, bringing our natural light into subjection and treating it as if it were not. For, as Saint Paul says, Fides ex auditu. As though he were to say: Faith is not knowledge which enters by any of the senses but is only the consent given by the soul to that which enters through the ear.

St. John of the
Cross, *Ascent of Mount
Carmel*

Additional Biblical Reflections: Matthew 17:20; Luke 17:5; Romans 10:17.

Prayer

Lord, your majesty is far beyond our comprehension. Yet, we are so bold as to presume that we can master our spirituality and, likewise, your Divinity. Grant us humility so that, through faith, we might come to adore your mysteries rather than attempt to subject them to our haughty intellects. Amen.

DAY 112

The irony and wonder of faith is that while it does not grant us complete comprehension of the things of God, it does grant us *understanding*. In today's meditation, we learn that there is a difference between these different sorts of knowledge, for our pursuit of information and knowledge often leads us only deeper into darkness but, with faith, is accompanied by God's revelation, and we find we are illuminated in His truth.

Meditations from St. John of the Cross

And faith far transcends even that which is indicated by the examples given above. For not only does it give no information and knowledge, but, as we have said, it deprives us of all other information and knowledge, and blinds us to them, so that they cannot judge it well. For other knowledge can be acquired by the light of the understanding; but the knowledge that is of faith is acquired without the illumination of the understanding, which is rejected for faith; and in its own light, if that light be not darkened, it is lost. Wherefore Isaias said: If ye believe not, ye shall not understand. It is clear, then, that faith is dark night for the soul, and it is in this way that it gives it light; and the more the soul is darkened, the greater is the light that comes to it. For it is by blinding that it gives light, according to this saying of Isaias. For if ye believe not, ye shall not (he says) have light. And thus faith was foreshadowed by that cloud which divided the children of Israel and the Egyptians when the former were about to enter the Red Sea, whereof Scripture says: that cloud was full of darkness and gave light to the night.

A wondrous thing it is that, though it was dark, it should give light to the night. This was said to show that faith, which is a black and dark cloud to the soul (and likewise is night, since in the presence of faith the soul is deprived of its natural light and is blinded), can with its darkness give light and illumination to the darkness of the soul, for it was fitting that the disciples should thus be like the master. For man, who is in darkness, could not fittingly be enlightened save by other darkness, even as David teaches us, saying: Day unto day uttereth and aboundeth in speech, and night unto night showeth knowledge. Which, to speak more clearly, signifies: The day, which is God in bliss, where it is day to the blessed angels and souls who are now day, communicates and reveals to them the Word, which is His Son, that they may know Him and enjoy Him. And the night, which is faith in the Church Militant, where it is still night, shows knowledge is night to the Church, and consequently to every soul, which knowledge is night to it, since it is without clear beatific wisdom; and, in the presence of faith, it is blind as to its natural light.

So that which is to be inferred from this that faith, because it is dark night, gives light to the soul, which is in darkness, that there may come to be fulfilled that which David likewise says to this purpose, in these works: the night will be illumination in my delights. Which is as much as to say: In the delights of my pure contemplation and union with God, the night of faith shall be my guide. Wherein he gives it clearly to be understood that the soul must be in darkness in order to have light for this road.

St. John of the
Cross, *Ascent of Mount
Carmel*

Additional Biblical Reflections: Exodus 14:20; Isaiah 7:9; Psalm 18:3.

Prayer

Lord, only in faith and trust do we find true understanding. Let us be content with whatever knowledge we might have, not that we might become conceited in our study of your word, but that through it, you might illuminate us in your Spirit. Amen.

DAY 113

Working through St. John of the Cross and his meditations can be a dark night in its own right. As you have undoubtedly experienced, he spends much effort expounding on the darkness or the night of the soul. But this he does for a reason—for even the slightest light shines more brightly in a dark room than one merely dim or already lit. Today, we get a bit of that light to draw us out of the darkness as he explores the benefits we receive when passing through the dark night in faith.

Meditations from St. John of the Cross

Wherefore, passing beyond all that can be known and understood, both spiritually and naturally, the soul will desire with all desire to come to that which in this life cannot be known, neither can enter into its heart. And, leaving behind all that it experiences and feels, both temporally and spiritually, and all that it is able to experience and feel in this life, it will desire with all desire to come to that which surpasses all feeling and experience. And, in order to be free and void to that end, it must in no wise lay hold upon that which it receives, either spiritually or sensually, within itself (as we shall explain presently, when we treat this in detail), considering it all to be of much less account. For the more emphasis the soul lays upon what it understands, experiences and imagines, and the more it esteems this, whether it be spiritual or no, the more it loses of the supreme good, and the more it is hindered from attaining thereto. And the less it thinks of what it may have, however much this be, in comparison with the highest good, the more it dwells upon that good and esteems it, and, consequently, the more nearly it approaches it. And in this wise the soul approaches a

228

great way towards union, in darkness, by means of faith, which is likewise dark, and in this wise faith wondrously illumines it. It is certain that, if the soul should desire to see, it would be in darkness much more quickly, with respect to God, than would one who opens his eyes to look upon the great brightness of the sun.

Wherefore, by blinding itself in its faculties upon this road, the soul will see the light, even as the Saviour says in the Gospel, in this wise: I am come into this world for judgment; that they which see not may see, and that they which see may become blind. This, as it will be supposed, is to be understood of this spiritual road, where the soul that is in darkness, and is blinded as regards all its natural and proper lights, will see supernaturally; and the soul that would depend upon any light of its own will become the blinder and will halt upon the road to union.

St. John of the
Cross. *Ascent of Mount
Carmel*

Additional Biblical Reflections: Proverbs 2:2-5; John 9:39; 2 Timothy 2:7.

Prayer

Lord, too often, we fail to see your light because we have attempted to illuminate our lives artificially. However, your true light can shine more brightly than ever when we pass through the dark nights in faith. Grant us such perseverance. Amen.

DAY 114

Today, St. John of the Cross gives us another metaphor to understand God's work in our souls as He leads us from darkness into light. He compares the process to light striking a window—if the light illumines a room to its greatest capacity, the window must be clean, not stained, fogged, or covered in dust. Today's meditation will help us appreciate the work that God is doing in us as we undergo the process of spiritual refinement.

Meditations from St. John of the Cross

In order that both these things may be the better understood, let us make a comparison. A ray of sunlight is striking a window. If the window is in any way stained or misty, the sun's ray will be unable to illumine it and transform it into its own light, totally, as it would if it were clean of all these things, and pure; but it will illumine it to a lesser degree, in proportion as it is less free from those mists and stains; and will do so to a greater degree, in proportion as it is cleaner from them, and this will not be because of the sun's ray, but because of itself; so much so that, if it be wholly pure and clean, the ray of sunlight will transform it and illumine it in such wise that it will itself seem to be a ray and will give the same light as the ray. Although in reality the window has a nature distinct from that of the ray itself, however much it may resemble it, yet we may say that that window is a ray of the sun or is light by participation. And the soul is like this window, whereupon is ever beating (or, to express it better, wherein is ever dwelling) this Divine light of the Being of God according to nature, which we have described.

In thus allowing God to work in it, the soul (having rid itself of every mist and stain of the creatures, which consists in having its will perfectly united with that of God, for to love is to labour to detach and strip itself for God's sake of all that is not God) is at once illumined and transformed in God, and God communicates to it His supernatural Being, in such wise that it appears to be God Himself, and has all that God Himself has. And this union comes to pass when God grants the soul this supernatural favour, that all the things of God and the soul are one in participant transformation; and the soul seems to be God rather than a soul, and is indeed God by participation; although it is true that its natural being, though thus transformed, is as distinct from the Being of God as it was before, even as the window has likewise a nature distinct from that of the ray, though the ray gives it brightness.

This makes it clearer that the preparation of the soul for this union, as we said, is not that it should understand or perceive or feel or imagine anything, concerning either God or aught else, but that it should have purity and love — that is, perfect resignation and detachment from everything for God's sake alone; and, as there can be no perfect transformation if there be not perfect purity, and as the enlightenment, illumination and union of the soul with God will be according to the proportion of its purity, in greater or in less degree; yet the soul will not be perfect, as I say, if it be not wholly and perfectly bright and clean.

St. John of the
Cross, *Ascent of Mount
Carmel*

Additional Biblical Reflections: Matthew 13:13-16; John 1:13; 1 John 2:11.

Prayer

Lord, cleanse our sin-stained hearts so that your light might illumine our souls more perfectly. We pray that you would help us endure your refinement for the sake of knowing you more intimately, for spiritual progress does not happen when we allow our lives to be clouded by distractions, the things of this world, and sin. In Jesus's name. Amen.

DAY 115

The second "faculty" of the soul which St. John of the Cross says must be refined, after faith, is memory. Memory is a powerful thing. The Israelites were told, for instance, to place a letter on their brows to call the Lord's works to mind. Throughout the Old Testament, how often do we hear God's people reminded about what God did when He rescued Israel from Egypt? So, too, the Passover and other rituals were meant to codify God's actions, in memory, in the hearts and minds of God's people. However, selectively, we often remember only the things that justify our resentments, or we use them to explain our past sins. The memory must be refined like the rest of us so that we aim to increase our recollection of God's good things.

Meditations from St. John of the Cross

The first faculty of the soul, which is the understanding, has now been instructed, through all its apprehensions, in the first theological virtue, which is faith, to the end that, according to this faculty, the soul may be united with God by means of the purity of faith. It now remains to do likewise with respect to the other two faculties of the soul, which are memory and will, and to purify them likewise with respect to their apprehensions, to the end that, according to these two faculties also, the soul may come to union with God in perfect hope and charity... Beginning, then, with natural knowledge, I say that natural knowledge in the memory consists of all the kinds of knowledge that the memory can form concerning the objects of the five bodily senses — namely: hearing, sight, smell, taste and touch — and all kinds of knowledge of this type which it is possible to form and fashion. Of all these forms and kinds of knowledge the soul must strip and void itself, and it must strive to lose the imaginary apprehension of them, so that there may be left in it no kind of impression of knowledge, nor trace of aught soever, but rather the soul must remain barren and bare, as if these forms had never passed through it, and in total oblivion and suspension. And this cannot happen unless the memory be annihilated as to all its forms, if it is to be united with God. For it cannot happen save by total separation from all forms which are not God; for God comes beneath no definite form or kind of knowledge whatsoever, as we have said in treating of the night of the understanding. And since, as Christ says, no man can serve two masters,[1] the memory cannot be united both with God and with forms and distinct kinds of knowledge and, as God has no form or image that can be comprehended by the memory, it follows that, when the memory is united with God (as is seen, too, every day by experience), it remains without form and without figure, its imagination being lost and itself being absorbed in a supreme good, and in a great oblivion, remembering nothing. For that Divine union voids its fancy and sweeps it clean of all forms and kinds of knowledge and raises it to the supernatural.

St. John of the
Cross, *Ascent of Mount
Carmel*

Additional Biblical Reflections: Exodus 12:14; Luke 22:19-20; John 14:26.

Prayer

Lord, recall to our minds the good deeds you have done so that we might ever remember your love and faithfulness through these recollections. Let the memories of our failings serve not as self-justifications but as causes to rebuff the temptations of the flesh, and may the memories of your grace, most especially the sacrifice of your Son, be front and center in our minds. Amen.

DAY 116

After considering the refinement of both faith and memory, St. John of the Cross speaks of the will's conversion. Without the refinement of the will, all of our faculties will be bent awry. To pursue godliness, we must first desire it. This is another purpose of the dark night of the soul—for having gone through such a time, our desire and craving for God's light should grow all the more.

Meditations from St. John of the Cross

We should have accomplished nothing by the purgation of the understanding in order to ground it in the virtue of faith, and by the purgation of the memory in order to ground it in hope, if we purged not the will also according to the third virtue, which is charity, whereby the works that are done in faith live and have great merit, and without it are of no worth. For, as Saint James says: 'Without works of charity, faith is dead.' And, now that we have to treat of the active detachment and night of this faculty, in order to form it and make it perfect in this virtue of the charity of God, I find no more fitting authority than that which is written in the sixth chapter of Deuteronomy, where Moses says: 'Thou shalt love the Lord thy God with thy whole heart and with thy whole soul and with thy whole strength.' Herein is contained all that the spiritual man ought to do, and all that I have here to teach him, so that he may truly attain to God, through union of the will, by means of charity. For herein man is commanded to employ all the faculties and desires and operations and affections of his soul in God, so that all the ability and strength of his soul may serve for no more than this… The strength of the soul consists in its faculties, passions and desires, all of which are governed by the will. Now when these faculties, passions and desires are directed by the will toward God, and turned away from all that is not God, then the strength of the soul is kept for God, and thus the soul is able to love God with all its strength. And, to the end that the soul may do this, we shall here treat of the purgation from the will of all its unruly affections, whence arise unruly operations, affections and desires, and whence also arises its failure to keep all its strength for God. These affections and passions are four, namely: Joy, hope, grief and fear. These passions, when they are controlled by reason according to the way of God, so that the soul rejoices only in that which is purely the honour and glory of God, and hopes for naught else, neither grieves save for things that concern this, neither fears aught save God alone, it is clear that the strength and ability of the soul are being directed toward God and kept for Him. For, the more the soul rejoices in any other thing than God, the less completely will it centre its rejoicing in God; and the more it hopes in aught else, the less will it hope in God; and so with the other passions.

St. John of the
Cross, *Ascent of Mount
Carmel*

Additional Biblical Reflections: Deuteronomy 6:5; Psalm 58:10; James 2:20.

Prayer

Lord, while we desire to know you more, our will is often weak, vacillating between our desires of this world and our desire to embrace your path. Grant us not only access to your holiness but a fervent desire for it. In Jesus's name. Amen.

DAY 117

Our meditations from St. John of the Cross now turn to his *Spiritual Canticle*, consisting largely of songs sung between the bride (the Church) and the bridegroom (Christ). Here we learn more of the intimacy that God intends for those who have passed through the dark night of the soul and what enjoyment there might be for those who come to experience His illumination.

Meditations from St. John of the Cross

The chief object of the soul in these words is not to ask only for that affective and sensible devotion, wherein there is no certainty or evidence of the possession of the Bridegroom in this life; but principally for that clear presence and vision of His Essence, of which it longs to be assured and satisfied in the next. This, too, was the object of the bride who, in the divine song desiring to be united to the Divinity of the Bridegroom Word, prayed to the Father, saying, "Show me where You feed, where You lie in the midday." For to ask to be shown the place where He fed was to ask to be shown the Essence of the Divine Word, the Son; because the Father feeds nowhere else but in His only begotten Son, Who is the glory of the Father. In asking to be shown the place where He lies in the midday, was to ask for the same thing, because the Son is the sole delight of the Father, Who lies in no other place, and is comprehended by no other thing, but in and by His beloved Son, in Whom He reposes wholly, communicating to Him His whole Essence, in the "midday," which is eternity, where the Father is ever begetting and the Son ever begotten.

St. John of the

Cross, *The Spiritual Canticle*

Additional Biblical Reflections: Song of Solomon 1:6; John 14:3; Revelation 22:17.

Prayer

Dear Lord, to know you is to be members of your Bride united one-in-flesh to the Bridegroom, who is Christ. Let us always keep your Son at the center of our hearts so that we might be conformed to His image in suffering as we pass through the dark night and in resurrection as we embrace the light of His life. Amen.

DAY 118

Today, we reflect on all the progress we have made in the first twenty-seven days, wherein we considered St. John of the Cross's program toward spiritual progress. We are reminded about the things that distress the soul, the theological virtues, and the aspects of the human soul upon which the Lord works to draw us unto Him. All these things work for our good—for the Lord knows better what we require than we know for ourselves.

Meditations from St. John of the Cross

Here the soul speaks of three things that distress it: namely, languor, suffering, and death; for the soul that truly loves God with a love in some degree perfect, suffers in three ways in His absence, in its three powers ordinarily — the understanding, the will, and the memory. In the understanding it languishes because it does not see God, Who is the salvation of it, as the Psalmist says: "I am your salvation."

These three things which distress the soul are grounded on the three theological virtues — faith, charity, and hope, which relate, in the order here assigned them, to the three faculties of the soul — understanding, will, and memory. Observe here that the soul does no more than represent its miseries and pain to the Beloved: for he who loves wisely does not care to ask for that which he wants and desires, being satisfied with hinting at his necessities, so that the beloved one may do what shall to him seem good. Thus the Blessed Virgin at the marriage feast of Cana asked not directly for wine, but only said to her Beloved Son, "They have no wine." The sisters of Lazarus sent to Him, not to ask Him to heal their brother, but only to say that he whom He loved was sick: "Lord, behold, he whom You love is sick."

There are three reasons for this. Our Lord knows what is expedient for us better than we do ourselves. Secondly, the Beloved is more compassionate towards us when He sees our necessities and our resignation. Thirdly, we are more secured against self-love and self-seeking when we represent our necessity, than when we ask for that which we think we need. It is in this way that the soul represents its three necessities; as if it said: "Tell my Beloved, that as I languish, and as He only is my salvation, to save me; that as I am suffering, and as He only is my joy, to give me joy; that as I am dying, and as He only is my life, to give me life."

St. John of the
Cross, *The Spiritual
Canticle*

Additional Biblical Reflections: Psalm 34:3; John 2:3; John 11:3.

Prayer

Lord, the path of spiritual progress has been laid out in our word and expounded upon by the faithful saint. Grant us the desire to see it through and the perseverance to endure the promises that await us who seek you. Amen.

DAY 119

Spiritual progress is chiefly the work of the Spirit in our hearts. However, if we take such a truth and imagine that we can remain idle and expect God to work on us in our sloth, we are mistaken. Today, St. John of the Cross reminds us that God has made us creatures capable of working, pursuing His word, and striving toward His promised illuminations of the soul.

Meditations from St. John of the Cross

Here the soul makes it known that to find God it is not enough to pray with the heart and the tongue, or to have recourse to the help of others; we must also work ourselves, according to our power. God values one effort of our own more than many of others on our behalf; the soul, therefore, remembering the saying of the Beloved, "Seek and you shall find," is resolved on going forth, as I said just now, to seek Him actively, and not rest till it finds Him, as many do who will not that God should cost them anything but words, and even those carelessly uttered, and for His sake will do nothing that will cost them anything. Some, too, will not leave for His sake a place which is to their taste and liking, expecting to receive all the sweetness of God in their mouth and in their heart without moving a step, without mortifying themselves by the abandonment of a single pleasure or useless comfort.

But until they go forth out of themselves to seek Him, however loudly they may cry they will not find Him; for the bride in the Canticle sought Him in this way, but she found Him not until she went out to seek Him: "In my little bed in the nights I have sought Him Whom my soul loves: I have sought Him and have not found Him. I will rise and will go about the city: by the streets and highways I will seek Him Whom my soul loves." She afterwards adds that when she had endured certain trials she "found Him."

He, therefore, who seeks God, consulting his own ease and comfort, seeks Him by night, and therefore finds Him not. But he who seeks Him in the practice of virtue and of good works, casting aside the comforts of his own bed, seeks Him by day; such a one shall find Him, for that which is not seen by night is visible by day. The Bridegroom Himself teaches us this, saying, "Wisdom is clear and never fades away, and is easily seen of them that love her, and is found of them that seek her. She prevents them that covet her, that she first may show herself to them. He that awakes early to seek her shall not labor; for he shall find her sitting at his doors." [62] The soul that will go out of the house of its own will, and abandon the bed of its own satisfaction, will find the divine Wisdom, the Son of God, the Bridegroom waiting at the door without, and so the soul says: "I will go over mountains and strands."

St. John of the
Cross, *The Spiritual
Canticle*

Additional Biblical Reflections: Song of Solomon 2:1-4; Wisdom 6:13; Luke 11:9.

Prayer

Lord, we too often ask for your spiritual blessings from a posture of idleness, unwilling to do all that is in us to strive toward your graces. Certainly, grace comes by your merits, but we pray you would vivify our efforts so that you might use every step we take to draw us closer to you. In Jesus's name. Amen.

DAY 120

Everything we have learned during our thirty days of prayer with St. John of the Cross—if it were to be comprehended in a single truth—has been focused on the person of Jesus Christ, the Son of God. For He passed through a dark night so that we who follow Him, taking up our crosses in pursuit of Him, might also go with Him through the darkness and be restored alongside Him in the glory of His resurrected life.

Meditations from St. John of the Cross

The son of God is, in the words of St. Paul, "the brightness of His glory and the figure of His substance." God saw all things only in the face of His Son. This was to give them their natural being, bestowing upon them many graces and natural gifts, making them perfect, as it is written in the book of Genesis: "God saw all the things that He had made: and they were very good." To see all things very good was to make them very good in the Word, His Son. He not only gave them their being and their natural graces when He beheld them, but He also clothed them with beauty in the face of His Son, communicating to them a supernatural being when He made man, and exalted him to the beauty of God, and, by consequence, all creatures in him, because He united Himself to the nature of them all in man. For this cause the Son of God Himself said, "And I, if I be lifted up from the earth will draw all things to Myself." And thus in this exaltation of the incarnation of His Son, and the glory of His resurrection according to the flesh, the Father not only made all things beautiful in part, but also, we may well say, clothed them wholly with beauty and dignity.

But beyond all this — speaking now of contemplation as it affects the soul and makes an impression on it — in the vivid contemplation and knowledge of created things the soul beholds such a multiplicity of graces, powers, and beauty with which God has endowed them, that they seem to it to be clothed with admirable beauty and supernatural virtue derived from the infinite supernatural beauty of the face of God, whose beholding of them clothed the heavens and the earth with beauty and joy; as it is written: "You open Your hand and fill with blessing every living creature." Hence the soul wounded with love of that beauty of the Beloved which it traces in created things, and anxious to behold that beauty which is the source of this visible beauty.

St. John of the
Cross, *The Spiritual
Canticle*

Additional Biblical Reflections: Genesis 1:31; Psalm 144:16; John 12:32.

Prayer

Dear Lord, we have access to you only on account of the merits and person of your Son, Jesus Christ. May our lives every be a reflection of His, bearing our crosses so that we might find Him there and endure alongside Him into resurrected life and the illumination of your Spirit. In His name. Amen

DAY 121

St. Francis placed a great deal of emphasis on the Eucharist in his discussions of the Christian life. How can one draw near to the Lord without receiving with awe and gratitude the very means, ordained by Christ, that He has instituted as His way of drawing near to us? Thus, St. Francis goes to great lengths in his writings to reinforce the proper posture and awe a Christian should have when taking the Eucharistic host. While many people seek God in many and various places, in the Eucharist, God seeks us, He comes to us on His terms, and therefore, it is the one place where we can be certain that we are genuinely encountering the Lord.

Meditations from St. Francis

The Lord Jesus said to His disciples: "I am the Way, and the Truth, and the Life. No man cometh to the Father, but by Me. If you had known Me you would, without doubt, have known My Father also: and from henceforth you shall know Him, and you have seen Him. Philip saith to Him: Lord, show us the Father, and it is enough for us. Jesus saith to him: Have I been so long a time with you and have you not known Me? Philip, he that seeth Me seeth [My] Father also. How sayest thou, Shew us the Father?" The Father "inhabiteth light inaccessible," and "God is a spirit," and "no man hath seen God at any time." Because God is a spirit, therefore it is only by the spirit He can be seen, for "it is the spirit that quickeneth; the flesh profiteth nothing." For neither is the Son, inasmuch as He is equal to the Father, seen by any one other than by the Father, other than by the Holy Ghost. Wherefore, all those who saw the Lord Jesus Christ according to humanity and did not see and believe according to the Spirit and the

Divinity, that He was the Son of God, were condemned. In like manner, all those who behold the Sacrament of the Body of Christ which is sanctified by the word of the Lord upon the altar by the hands of the priest in the form of bread and wine, and who do not see and believe according to the Spirit and Divinity that It is really the most holy Body and Blood of our Lord Jesus Christ, are condemned, He the Most High having declared it when He said, "This is My Body, and the Blood of the New Testament," and "he that eateth My Flesh and drinkety My Blood hath everlasting life."

Wherefore [he who has] the Spirit of the Lord which dwells in His faithful, he it is who receives the most holy Body and Blood of the Lord: all others who do not have this same Spirit and who presume to receive Him, eat and drink judgment to themselves. Wherefore, "O ye sons of men, how long will you be dull of heart?" Why will you not know the truth and "believe in the Son of God?" Behold daily He humbles Himself as when from His "royal throne" He came into the womb of the Virgin; daily He Himself comes to us with like humility; daily He descends from the bosom of His Father upon the altar in the hands of the priest. And as He appeared in true flesh to the Holy Apostles, so now He shows Himself to us in the sacred Bread; and as they by means of their fleshly eyes saw only His flesh, yet contemplating Him with their spiritual eyes, believed Him to be God, so we, seeing bread and wine with bodily eyes, see and firmly believe it to be His most holy Body and true and living Blood. And in this way our Lord is ever with His faithful, as He Himself says: "Behold I am with you all days, even to the consummation of the world."

St. Francis of Assisi.
Of the Lord's Body.

Additional Biblical Reflections: Matthew 28:29–20; John 14:6; 1 Corinthians 11:29.

Prayer

Lord, while we see the accidents of bread and wine, you nonetheless have chosen these crude vessels to become your body and blood, your presence. Let us receive the sacrament worthily and regularly, with proper contrition, so that by discerning your body, we might receive this gift to our glory and yours. Amen.

DAY 122

Today's meditation addresses two of Jesus's most difficult teachings. First, St. Francis speaks of renouncing the material world and possessions since such things can easily become false gods. Second, he urges that one love even those who might persecute them on account of their faithful obedience. This is why he argues that one should not abandon their superiors or people who are in authority, even if situations demand, for the sake of their soul, necessary disobedience. It is better to disobey and accept the consequences—if such disobedience is rooted in higher fidelity to God—than to disobey and flee.

Meditations from St. Francis

The Lord says in the Gospel: he "that doth not renounce all that he possesseth cannot be" a "disciple" and "he that will save his life, shall lose it." That man leaves all he possesses and loses his body and his soul who abandons himself wholly to obedience in the hands of his superior, and whatever he does and says—provided he himself knows that what he does is good and not contrary to his [the superior's] will—is true obedience. And if at times a subject sees things which would be better or more useful to his soul than those which the superior commands him, let him sacrifice his will to God, let him strive to fulfil the work enjoined by the superior. This is true and charitable obedience which is pleasing to God and to one's neighbor.

If, however, a superior command anything to a subject that is against his soul it is permissible for him to disobey, but he must not leave him [the superior], and if in consequence he suffer persecution from some, he should love them the more for God's sake. For he who would rather suffer persecution than wish to be separated from his brethren, truly abides in perfect obedience because he lays down his life for his brothers. For there are many religious who, under pretext of seeing better things than those which their superiors command, look back and return to the vomit of their own will. These are homicides and by their bad example cause the loss of many souls.

St. Francis of Assisi.
*Of Perfect and Imperfect
Obedience.*

Additional Biblical Reflections: Matthew 6:19–21; Acts 5:29; Romans 13:1–14; 1 Timothy 6:17–19.

Prayer

Lord, perfect obedience often requires we walk a tightrope between both requiring material goods to survive and worshipping them, between obeying authorities and remaining faithful to what is required of the soul. Grant us the wisdom to walk this narrow path so that we might always move constantly according to your will. Amen.

DAY 123

Today's reflection is sobering. While humankind was granted more by God from the beginning than any creature, no creature has turned against God more violently and persistently. Even the demons, St. Francis points out, were never so bold as to crucify the Lord. But the answer to this devilish side of man is not in the will but the cross. Thus, if we are to take glory or refuge in anything, it must and can only be the cross.

Meditations from St. Francis

Consider, O man, how great the excellence in which the Lord has placed you because He has created and formed you to the image of His beloved Son according to the body and to His own likeness according to the spirit. And all the creatures that are under heaven serve and know and obey their Creator in their own way better than you. And even the demons did not crucify Him, but you together with them crucified Him and still crucify Him by taking delight in vices and sins. Wherefore then can you glory For if you were so clever and wise that you possessed all science, and if you knew how to interpret every form of language and to investigate heavenly things minutely, you could not glory in all this, because one demon has known more of heavenly things and still knows more of earthly things than all men, although there may be some man who has received from the Lord a special knowledge of sovereign wisdom. In like manner, if you were handsomer and richer than all others, and even if you could work wonders and put the demons to flight, all these things are hurtful to you and in nowise belong to you, and in them you cannot glory; that, however, in which we may glory is in our infirmities, and in bearing daily the holy cross of our Lord Jesus Christ.

St. Francis of Assisi.
*That No One Should
Glory Save in the Cross of
the Lord.*

Additional Biblical Reflections: Jeremiah 17:9; Romans 7:18; Ephesians 2:1–3.

Prayer

Lord, we have so often been faithless, but you have been faithful. While we do not deserve your favor, in your grace, you've come to us through the very violence we did to you and used your cross as an instrument of our redemption. Let the cross be the object of our glory so that we might not return to the ways of the flesh but would evermore be molded after the image of your Son. Amen.

DAY 124

Nothing thwarts vice better than virtue. However, as St. Francis reminds us today, not a single virtue can be apprehended by humankind lest one first dies to the flesh. That is to say; he pursues the way of the cross. Virtue is not a habit we inculcate through self-will and discipline, but we receive virtues as gifts from God, who uses both will and discipline as a farmer who waters his crops. In such an instance, it is water that undoubtedly produces a harvest but only water as the farmer gives it. Likewise, discipline alone does not produce virtue, but when proportioned according to God's goodness, a harvest of virtue results.

Meditations from St. Francis

Hail, queen wisdom! May the Lord save thee with thy sister holy pure simplicity! O Lady, holy poverty, may the Lord save thee with thy sister holy humility! O Lady, holy charity, may the Lord save thee with thy sister holy obedience! O all ye most holy virtues, may the Lord, from whom you proceed and come, save you! There is absolutely no man in the whole world who can possess one among you unless he first die. He who possesses one and does not offend the others, possesses all; and he who offends one, possesses none and offends all; and every one [of them] confounds vices and sins. Holy wisdom confounds Satan and all his wickednesses. Pure holy simplicity confounds all the wisdom of this world and the wisdom of the flesh. Holy poverty confounds cupidity and avarice and the cares of this world. Holy humility confounds pride and all the men of this world and all things that are in the world. Holy charity confounds all diabolical and fleshly temptations and all fleshly fears. Holy obedience confounds all bodily and fleshly desires and keeps the body mortified to the obedience of the spirit and to the obedience of one's brother and makes a man subject to all the men of this world and not to men alone, but also to all beasts and wild animals, so that they may do with him whatsoever they will, in so far as it may be granted to them from above by the Lord.

St. Francis of Assisi.
Salutation of the Virtues.

Additional Biblical Reflections: 1 Corinthians 3:6–9; Philippians 4:8; 2 Peter 1:5–8.

Prayer

Lord, you are the fountain of virtue. Let us seek virtue not by our own accord but by receiving our virtues from your gracious hand. For virtue is a projection of you and your will, not us and our will. Couple the gift of virtue with gratitude so that they are not spoiled by pride and boasting but always testify to your grace and mercy. Amen.

DAY 125

The Lord's Prayer is arguably the most repeated prayer in Christendom. We pray it so regularly that the depth of its meaning might often be lost on our tongues. In today's meditation, St. Francis expands upon the Lord's Prayer by plumbing the depths of the prayer our Lord taught us.

Meditations from St. Francis

Our Father, most holy, our Creator, Redeemer, and Comforter.

Who art in heaven, in the angels and in the saints illuminating them unto knowledge, for Thou, O Lord, art light; inflaming them unto love, for Thou, O Lord, art Love; dwelling in them and filling them with blessedness, for Thou, O Lord, art the highest Good, the eternal Good from whom is all good and without whom is no good.

Hallowed be Thy Name: may Thy knowledge shine in us that we may know the breadth of Thy benefits, the length of Thy promises, the height of Thy majesty, and the depth of Thy judgments.

Thy Kingdom come, that Thou mayest reign in us by grace and mayest make us come to Thy Kingdom, where there is the clear vision of Thee, the perfect love of Thee, the blessed company of Thee, the eternal enjoyment of Thee.

Thy will be done on earth as it is in heaven, that we may love Thee with the whole heart by always thinking of Thee; with the whole soul by always desiring Thee; with the whole mind by directing all our intentions to Thee and seeking Thy honor in all things and with all our strength, by spending all the powers and senses of body and soul in the service of Thy love and not in anything else; and that we may love our neighbors even as ourselves, drawing to the best of our power all to Thy love; rejoicing in the good of others as in our own and compassionating [them] in troubles and giving offence to no one.

Give us this day, through memory and understanding and reverence for the love which He had for us and for those things which He said, did, and suffered, for us,—our daily bread, Thy Beloved Son, our Lord Jesus Christ.

And forgive us our trespasses, by Thy ineffable mercy in virtue of the Passion of Thy Beloved Son, our Lord Jesus Christ, and through the merits and intercession of the most Blessed Virgin Mary and of all Thy elect.

As we forgive their that trespass against us, and what we do not fully forgive, do Thou, O Lord, make us fully forgive, that for Thy sake we may truly love our enemies and devoutly intercede for them with Thee; that we may render no evil for evil, but in Thee may strive to do good to all.

And lead us not into temptation, hidden or visible, sudden or continuous. But deliver us from evil, past, present, and to come. Amen.

St. Francis of Assisi.
The Praises.

Additional Biblical Reflections: Matthew 6:9–13; Luke 11:1–13; Philippians 4:6.

Prayer

Lord, you have given us a wealth of wisdom in the pattern by which you taught us to pray. Let us meditate on these words so that they are not hollow but genuine pleas that fulfill the request that thy will is done in our lives. Amen.

DAY 126

Creation itself testifies to God's glory. In today's meditation, St. Francis offers a canticle that praises the earth's elements for the ways they reflect God's goodness. One can appreciate the artist by beholding his art, the architect by wondering at his structures. Likewise, when we behold the elements of this world properly, they do not become false deities but evidences and glories of our Creator God.

Meditations from St. Francis

> *Most high, omnipotent, good Lord,*
> *Praise, glory and honor and benediction all, are Thine.*
> *To Thee alone do they belong, most High,*
> *And there is no man fit to mention Thee.*
> *Praise be to Thee, my Lord, with all Thy creatures,*
> *Especially to my worshipful brother sun,*
> *The which lights up the day, and through him dost Thou brightness give;*
> *And beautiful is he and radiant with splendor great;*
> *Of Thee, most High, signification gives.*
> *Praised be my Lord, for sister moon and for the stars,*
> *In heaven Thou hast formed them clear and precious and fair.*
> *Praised be my Lord for brother wind*
> *And for the air and clouds and fair and every kind of weather,*
> *By the which Thou givest to Thy creatures nourishment.*
> *Praised be my Lord for sister water,*
> *The which is greatly helpful and humble and precious and pure.*
> *Praised be my Lord for brother fire,*
> *By the which Thou lightest up the dark.*

And fair is he and gay and mighty and strong.
Praised be my Lord for our sister, mother earth,
The which sustains and keeps us
And brings forth diverse fruits with grass and flowers bright.
Praised be my Lord for those who for Thy love forgive
And weakness bear and tribulation.
Blessed those who shall in peace endure,
For by Thee, most High, shall they be crowned.
Praised be my Lord for our sister, the bodily death,
From the which no living man can flee.
Woe to them who die in mortal sin;
Blessed those who shall find themselves in Thy most holy will,
For the second death shall do them no ill.
Praise ye and bless ye my Lord, and give Him thanks,
And be subject unto Him with great humility.

St. Francis of Assisi.
The Canticle of the Sun.

Additional Biblical Reflections: Job 12:7; Romans 1:20; 2 Peter 3:10.

Prayer

Lord, throughout your Word, you reveal yourself to us through the elements of your creation. You guided Israel by a pillar of wind and fire. You brought your people through the water, even as you have brought us all through baptism. And your Spirit descended as tongues of fire. Even the wind and the sea obeyed your Word. Let us see, in all things, your mighty hand at work so that we might always revere your glory. Amen.

DAY 127

Even God's law, which is good and holy, kills when we esteem those words unto ourselves and use our obedience to those words as a cause to become puffed up in pride. While the letter does, indeed, kill, when taken alone—for us, whom the spirit has already quickened—the letter takes a new meaning, not a deadly burden but a joyful path of obedience and holiness.

Meditations from St. Francis

The Apostle says, "the letter killeth, but the spirit quickeneth." They are killed by the letter who seek only to know the words that they may be esteemed more learned among others and that they may acquire great riches to leave to their relations and friends. And those religious are killed by the letter who will not follow the spirit of the Holy Scriptures, but who seek rather to know the words only and to interpret them to others. And they are quickened by the spirit of the Holy Scriptures who do not interpret materially every text they know or wish to know, but who by word and example give them back to God from whom is all good.

St. Francis of Assisi.
That Good Works Should
Accompany Knowledge.

Additional Biblical Reflections: Psalm 19:7; John 6:63; 2 Corinthians 3:4–6.

Prayer

Lord, while the letter kills in your spirit, we have new life after the image of your son who died and rose. Grant, Lord, that we might always approach the letter not according to the flesh but the spirit so that we might learn from you all that is right and good. Amen.

DAY 128

Community has always been an important component of Christian living. As members of one body, if one member wanders, another might pull them back in line. Since we are all prone to wander and are easily tempted, the Lord has created holy communities of brothers and sisters who might hold us accountable. Here, we see that St. Francis did not believe that brothers should be admonished for the sake of some kind of purity or to protect the community, but out of love for the sake of the one who errs.

Meditations from St. Francis

Therefore take care of your souls and of those of your brothers, for "it is a fearful thing to fall into the hands of the living God." If however one of the ministers should command some one of the brothers anything contrary to our life or against his soul, the brother is not bound to obey him, because that is not obedience in which a fault or sin is committed. Nevertheless, let all the brothers who are subject to the ministers and servants consider reasonably and carefully the deeds of the ministers and servants. And if they should see any one of them walking according to the flesh and not according to the spirit, according to the right way of our life, after the third admonition, if he will not amend, let him be reported to the minister and servant of the whole fraternity in the Whitsun Chapter, in spite of any obstacle that may stand in the way. If however among the brothers, wherever they may be, there should be some brother who desires to live according to the flesh, and not according to the spirit, let the brothers with whom he is admonish, instruct, and correct him humbly and diligently. And if after the third admonition he will not amend, let them as soon as possible send him, or make the matter known to his minister and servant, and let the minister and servant do with him what may seem to him most expedient before God.

And let all the brothers, the ministers and servants as well as the others, take care not to be troubled or angered because of the fault or bad example of another, for the devil desires to corrupt many through the sin of one; but let them spiritually help him who has sinned, as best they can; for he that is whole needs not a physician, but he that is sick.

St. Francis of Assisi.
*First Rule of the Friars
Minor.*

Additional Biblical Reflections: Proverbs 27:6; Luke 17:3; Colossians 3:16.

Prayer

Lord, thank you for calling us into your Church. These holy communities are meant not to force conformity but to ensure that all of us remain on the right path toward you. Let us hear our fellows' admonitions in such a way, and rather than taking offense, be grateful for the correction. Amen.

DAY 129

Much has been written in recent years on the topic of servant leadership. This idea, now peddled regularly in business schools, is actually ancient wisdom. Here, St. Francis picks up on this idea concerning the friars. But even St. Francis did not invent this idea—he rightly points out that this way of leading "from below" was typified by Jesus, who humbled himself so that he might become the Lord of all by being the servant of all.

Meditations from St. Francis

In like manner let not all the brothers have power and authority, especially among themselves, for as the Lord says in the Gospel: "The princes of the Gentiles lord it over them: and they that are the greater exercise power upon them." It shall not be thus among the brothers, but whosoever will be the greater among them, let him be their minister and servant, and he that is the greater among them let him be as the younger, and he who is the first, let him be as the last. Let not any brother do evil or speak evil to another; let them rather in the spirit of charity willingly serve and obey each other: and this is the true and holy obedience of our Lord Jesus Christ. And let all the brothers as often soever as they may have declined from the commandments of God, and wandered from obedience, know that, as the prophet says, they are cursed out of obedience as long as they continue consciously in such a sin. And when they persevere in the commandments of the Lord, which they have promised by the holy Gospel and their life, let them know that they abide in true obedience, and are blessed by God.

St. Francis of Assisi.
First Rule of the Friars Minor.

Additional Biblical Reflections: Matthew 20:20-28; John 13:1–17; Philippians 2:3.

Prayer

Lord, though you were Lord of all, you made yourself our servant so we might be elevated to your place of glory. Grant us, Lord, servant hearts so that through our obedience, others might also see your glory. In Jesus's name. Amen.

DAY 130

Franciscans have been known, after St. Francis, for their renunciation of material things and vows of poverty. While not all people are given such a righteous name, it is not poverty alone that engenders holiness in these monastic communities. Rather, it's a removal of other things represented by material wealth that we readily turn into "gods" in our lives.

Meditations from St. Francis

The Lord commands in the Gospel: "Take heed, beware of all malice and avarice and guard yourselves from the solicitudes of this world, and the cares of this life." Therefore, let none of the brothers, wherever he may be or whithersoever he may go, carry or receive money or coin in any manner, or cause it to be received, either for clothing, or for books, or as the price of any labor, or indeed for any reason, except on account of the manifest necessity of the sick brothers. For we ought not to have more use and esteem of money and coin than of stones. And the devil seeks to blind those who desire or value it more than stones. Let us therefore take care lest after having left all things we lose the kingdom of heaven for such a trifle. And if we should chance to find money in any place, let us no more regard it than the dust we tread under our feet, for it is "vanity of vanities, and all is vanity." And if perchance, which God forbid, it should happen that any brother should collect or have money or coin, except only because of the aforesaid necessity of the sick, let all the brothers hold him for a false brother, a thief, a robber, and one having a purse, unless he should become truly penitent. And let the brothers in nowise receive money for alms or cause it to be received, seek it or cause it to be sought, or money for other houses or places; nor let them go with any person seeking money or coin for such places. But the brothers may perform all other services which are not contrary to our life, with the blessing of God. The brothers may however for the manifest necessity of the lepers ask alms for them But let them be very wary of money. But let all the brothers likewise take great heed not to search the world for any filthy lucre.

St. Francis of Assisi,
First Rule of the Friars Minor.

Additional Biblical Reflections: Ecclesiastes 5:10; 1 Timothy 6:10; Hebrews 13:5.

Prayer

Lord, while money is not evil unto itself, the love of money can lead us down many perilous paths. Spare us from the love of material wealth so that our hearts might be fully devoted to you. In Jesus's name. Amen.

DAY 131

Community is there for more than to admonish. Our fellow believers are called to support one another in all affairs. If one is suffering, we suffer together. If one is hurting, we all hurt. If one is in need, the need is one we share and must work together to meet. In today's meditation, St. Francis encourages the friars to be aware of all the brothers' needs so that the community might meet whatever is required.

Meditations from St. Francis

If any of the brothers fall into sickness, wherever he may be, let the others not leave him, unless one of the brothers, or more if it be necessary, be appointed to serve him as they would wish to be served themselves; but in urgent necessity they may commit him to some person who will take care of him in his infirmity. And I ask the sick brother that he give thanks to the Creator for all things, and that he desire to be as God wills him to be, whether sick or well; for all whom the Lord has predestined to eternal life 1 are disciplined by the rod of afflictions and infirmities, and the spirit of compunction; as the Lord says: "Such as I love I rebuke and chastise." If, however, he be disquieted and angry, either against God or against the brothers, or perhaps ask eagerly for remedies, desiring too much to deliver his body which is soon to die, which is an enemy to the soul, this comes to him from evil and he is fleshly, and seems not to be of the brothers, because he loves his body more than his soul.

St. Francis of Assisi,
*First Rule of the Friars
Minor.*

Additional Biblical Reflections: Ecclesiastes 4:9–12; Hebrews 10:24–25; Romans 12:3–33.

Prayer

Lord, give us open eyes and ears to see the needs of our fellow believers, for we are your hands and mouthpiece, the touch that heals and the voice that restores. In this way, might all your Church be built up so that we might persist through this life until life everlasting. Amen.

DAY 132

Debate and dispute can be addictive. Lovers of controversy often seek it. They might even get a thrill from it. But it can also be damaging and destructive, particularly in the church. Rather, as God's people, St. Francis reminds us that we are to love one another and love peace rather than discord.

Meditations from St. Francis

And let all the brothers take care not to calumniate anyone, nor to contend in words; let them indeed study to maintain silence as far as God gives them grace. Let them also not dispute among themselves or with others, but let them be ready to answer with humility, saying: "we are unprofitable servants." And let them not be angry, for "whosoever is angry with his brother shall be in danger of the judgment. And whosoever shall say to his brother, Raca, shall be in danger of the council. And whosoever shall say, Thou fool, shall be in danger of hell fire." And let them love one another, as the Lord says: "This is My commandment, that you love one another, as I have loved you." And let them show their love by the works they do for each other, according as the Apostle says: "let us not love in word or in tongue, but in deed and in truth." Let them "speak evil of no man," nor murmur, nor detract others, for it is written: "Whisperers and detractors are hateful to God." And let them be "gentle, showing all mildness toward all men." Let them not judge and not condemn, and, as the Lord says, let them not pay attention to the least sins of others, but rather let them recount their own in the bitterness of their soul. And let them "strive to enter by the narrow gate," for the Lord says: "How narrow is the gate, and strait is the way that leadeth to life, and few there are that find it!"

St. Francis of Assisi,
First Rule of the Friars Minor.

Additional Biblical Reflections: Proverbs 18:17–18; 2 Timothy 3:9–11; Titus 3:9–11.

Prayer

Lord, there can be no division in your body. You have called us to pursue your truth in harmony and peace, to love you as one body, and to love one another in kind. Grant us spirits of peace and understanding so that we might always strive to grow closer to you as one people, one body. Amen.

DAY 133

Sin usually creeps in through seemingly innocent actions. Appreciation for beauty can turn into lust. Appreciation for a brother's accomplishment can turn into envy. Associating with the ungodly, out of a desire to share God's truth with them, can also impact us to follow them instead if we are not careful. In today's meditation, St. Francis takes seriously the impressions we give and the dangers we carelessly expose ourselves to so that we might act wisely.

Meditations from St. Francis

Let all the brothers, wherever they are or may go, carefully avoid unbecoming looks, and company of women, and let no one converse with them alone. Let the priests speak to them honestly, giving them penance or some spiritual counsel. And let no woman whatsoever be received to obedience by any brother, but spiritual counsel being given to her let her do penance where she wills. Let us all carefully watch over ourselves, and hold all our members in subjection, for the Lord says: "Whosoever shall look on a woman to lust after her, hath already committed adultery with her in his heart."

St. Francis of Assisi,
*First Rule of the Friars
Minor.*

Additional Biblical Reflections: Malachi 2:7; Romans 14:13–23; 1 Corinthians 8:9.

Prayer

Lord, you have called us to be a light unto the world. We are meant to demonstrate your love to others. Therefore, ensure that we embrace your ways in all we do and say so that we not become a scandal but might always be your vessels in service to your glory. Amen.

DAY 134

As St. Francis exhorted his friars to travel from place to place, his words are reminiscent of the time that Jesus sent out 72 disciples to proclaim His message and prepare His way. In every instance, what rings true is an eternal kingdom perspective. They were to go forth in faith—depending on others' generosity—and willingly take any manner of persecution without retaliation. All of this was meant to show that the cares of this world mean little compared to the eternal message they were spreading.

Meditations from St. Francis

When the brothers travel through the world, let them carry nothing by the way, neither bag, nor purse, nor bread, nor money, nor a staff. And whatsoever house they shall enter, let them first say, "Peace be to this house," and remaining in the same house, let them eat and drink what things they have. Let them not resist evil, but if anyone should strike them on the cheek, let them turn to him the other; and if anyone take away their garment, let them not forbid him the tunic also. Let them give to everyone that asketh them, and if anyone take away their goods, let them not ask them again.

St. Francis of Assisi,
*First Rule of the Friars
Minor.*

Additional Biblical Reflections: Matthew 5:28–40; Luke 10:1–23; 1 Peter 4:12–14.

Prayer

Lord, you have sent us into the world not to be consumed by the cares of this world but with a message of your kingdom. Let all we do, and the way we carry ourselves, manifest this eternal perspective so that the truth of your message might shine through the darkness of the world. Amen.

DAY 135

Today's meditation picks up on yesterday's theme. When God sends us out, He does not do so in the ways that the world would expect. He does not send His Church into the world with power and might, but with humility and charity. While it is counterintuitive, when viewed from the perspective of faith, it makes sense. For even if the wolves devour the sheep, in faith, we know that God can and will raise up His sheep again.

Meditations from St. Francis

The Lord says: "Behold, I send you as sheep in the midst of wolves. Be ye therefore wise as serpents and simple as doves." Wherefore, whoever of the brothers may wish, by divine inspiration, to go among the Saracens and other infidels, let them go with the permission of their minister and servant. But let the minister give them leave and not refuse them, if he sees they are fit to be sent; he will be held to render an account to the Lord if in this or in other things he acts indiscreetly. The brothers, however, who go may conduct themselves in two ways spiritually among them. One way is not to make disputes or contentions; but let them be "subject to every human creature for God's sake," yet confessing themselves to be Christians. The other way is that when they see it is pleasing to God, they announce the Word of God, that they may believe in Almighty God,—Father, and Son, and Holy Ghost, the Creator of all, our Lord the Redeemer and Saviour the Son, and that they should be baptized and be made Christians, because, "unless a man be born again of water and the Holy Ghost, he cannot enter into the kingdom of God." These and other things which please God they may say to them, for the Lord says in the Gospel: "Everyone that shall confess Me before men, I will also confess him before My Father who is in heaven;" and "he that shall be ashamed of Me and My words, of him the Son of Man shall be ashamed, when He shall come in His majesty and that of His Father, and of the holy angels."

St. Francis of Assisi,
*First Rule of the Friars
Minor.*

Additional Biblical Reflections: Isaiah 53:7–9; Matthew 10:16–33; Revelation 5:6.

Prayer

Lord, while you send us out as sheep amongst wolves, you were the lamb who was sent to take away the sin of the world. Let us go forth in confidence, for the lamb that was slain has arisen again. In Jesus's name. Amen.

DAY 136

According to St. Francis, citing the Bible in several places, even our bodies are not our own. For this reason, to offer our bodies in service to the Kingdom of God is not only reasonable but expected. Once again, we are reminded that an eternal perspective, rather than a temporal one, alters how we live our lives. What might we do differently, today, if we set aside temporary concerns and were focused on our heavenly goal?

Meditations from St. Francis

And let all the brothers, wherever they may be, remember that they have given themselves, and have relinquished their bodies to our Lord Jesus Christ; and for love of Him they ought to expose themselves to enemies both visible and invisible, for the Lord says: "Whosoever shall lose his life for My sake, shall save it" in eternal life. "Blessed are they that suffer persecution for justice' sake, for theirs is the kingdom of heaven." "If they have persecuted Me, they will also persecute you." If however they should persecute you in one city, flee to another. "Blessed are ye when they shall revile you, and persecute you, and speak all that is evil against you, untruly, for My sake." "Be glad in that day and rejoice, for your reward is great in heaven." "I say to you, my friends, be not afraid of them who kill the body, and after that have no more that they can do." "See that ye are not troubled." "In your patience you shall possess your souls." "But he that shall persevere unto the end, he shall be saved."

St. Francis of Assisi,
First Rule of the Friars
Minor.

Additional Biblical Reflections: Matthew 16:25; Mark 8:35; Luke 12:4.

Prayer

Dear Lord, you have given us our bodies, eyes, and ears—all our senses. However, our bodies, given from you, still belong to you. Thus, allow us to learn to live sacrificially, dedicating our bodily lives to your service and glory so that your name might be glorified, and we might achieve our heavenly goal. In Jesus's name. Amen.

DAY 137

The Lord has called us to confess our sins to one another. When we bring what is in the darkness into the light, it loses its power. Thus, confessing our sins is not only advised so that we might be forgiven and receive grace but so the sin itself would not fester in our souls and lead to further transgressions.

Meditations from St. Francis

Let my blessed brothers, both clerics and laics, confess their sins to priests of our religion. And if they cannot do this, let them confess to other discreet and Catholic priests, knowing firmly and hoping that from whatever Catholic priests they may receive penance and absolution, they will undoubtedly be absolved from these sins if they take care to observe humbly and faithfully the penance enjoined them. If however they cannot then have a priest, let them confess to their brother, as the Apostle James says: "Confess your sins to one another;" 1 but let them not on this account fail to have recourse to priests, for to priests alone the power of binding and loosing has been given. And thus contrite and having confessed, let them receive the Body and Blood of our Lord Jesus Christ with great humility and veneration, calling to mind what the Lord Himself says: "He that eateth

My Flesh and drinketh My Blood hath everlasting life," and "Do this for a commemoration of Me."

St. Francis of Assisi,
*First Rule of the Friars
Minor.*

Additional Biblical Reflections: John 6:54–56; James 5:16; 1 John 1:9–14.

Prayer

Lord, grant us the courage to confess our sins to one another. By doing so, may our hearts be purified, and our souls redeemed from transgression. Bring what festers in the darkness into the light so that we might be drawn to you. Amen.

DAY 138

We are often told to follow our hearts. However, we hear, as St. Francis reminds us, in the scriptures that out of the hearts of men proceed wickedness and all kinds of vice. Rather than following our hearts, we must submit our hearts to Jesus Christ. For what is evil comes from the heart of men. What is good and salutary comes from the heart of our Lord.

Meditations from St. Francis

Let us all, brothers, give heed to what the Lord says: "Love your enemies, and do good to them that hate you." For our Lord Jesus, whose footsteps we ought to follow, called His betrayer friend, and offered Himself willingly to His crucifiers. Therefore all those who unjustly inflict upon us tribulations and anguishes, shames and injuries, sorrows and torments, martyrdom and death, are our friends whom we ought to love much, because we gain eternal life by that which they make us suffer. And let us hate our body with its vices and sins, because by living carnally it wishes to deprive us of the love of our Lord Jesus Christ and eternal life, and to lose itself with all else in hell; for we by our own fault are corrupt, miserable, and averse to good, but prompt and willing to evil; because, as the Lord says in the Gospel: from the heart of men proceed and come evil thoughts, adulteries, fornications, murders, thefts, covetousness, wickedness, deceit, lasciviousness, an evil eye, false testimonies, blasphemy, foolishness. All these evils come from within, from the heart of man, and these are what defile a man.

St. Francis of Assisi,
*First Rule of the Friars
Minor.*

Additional Biblical Reflections: Ezekiel 28:17; Matthew 15:18–20; Mark 7:20–23.

Prayer

Lord, you made our hearts good. But now, consumed by sin, our hearts produce all kinds of vice. Create in us clean hearts so that we might be redeemed and exemplars of your love and mercy. In Jesus's name. Amen.

DAY 139

According to St. Francis, the reason for renouncing the world is not so much because they world itself is evil—God created the world and declared it good—but because this world is corrupt, and a new heaven and earth is on the way. Thus, renouncing the world, we are prepared to follow God's will and act in ways that please Him.

Meditations from St. Francis

But now, after having renounced the world, we have nothing else to do but to be solicitous, to follow the will of God, and to please Him. Let us take much care that we be not the wayside, or the stony or thorny ground, according to what the Lord says in the Gospel: The seed is the word of God. And that which fell by the wayside and was trampled under foot are they that hear the word and do not understand, then the devil cometh, and snatcheth that which has been sown in their hearts and taketh the word out of their hearts, lest believing they should be saved. But that which fell upon the rock are they who, when they hear the word, at once receive it with joy; but when tribulation and persecution arise on account of the word, they are immediately scandalized, and these have no roots in themselves, but are for a while, for they believe for a while, and in time of temptation fall away But that which fell among thorns are they who hear the word of God, and the solicitude and cares of this world, the fallacies of riches, and the desire of other things entering in choke the word, and it becomes unfruitful. But that sown on good ground are they who, in a good and best heart, hearing the word understand and keep it, and bring forth fruit in patience. And for this reason, brothers, let us, as the Lord says, "let the dead bury their dead." And let us be much on our guard against the malice and cunning of Satan, who desires that man should not give his heart and mind to the Lord

God, and who going about seeks to seduce the heart of man under pretext of some reward or benefit, to smother the words and precepts of the Lord from memory, and who wishes to blind the heart of man by worldly business and cares, and to dwell there, as the Lord says: "When an unclean spirit is gone out of a man, he walketh through dry places seeking rest and findeth none; then he saith: 'I will return into my house whence I came out.' And coming he findeth it empty, swept, and garnished. Then he goeth and taketh with him seven other spirits more wicked than himself, and they enter in, and dwell there; and the last state of that man is made worse than the first." 1 Wherefore let us all, brothers, watch much, lest under pretext of some reward or labor or aid we lose or separate our mind and heart from the Lord. But I beseech all the brothers, both the ministers and others, in the charity which God is, 2 that, overcoming all obstacles and putting aside all care and solicitude, they strive in the best manner they are able, to serve, love, and honor the Lord God with a clean heart and a pure mind, which He seeks above all.

St. Francis of Assisi,
*First Rule of the Friars
Minor.*

Additional Biblical Reflections: Luke 16:33; 1 Peter 4:7; Revelation 13:1–18.

Prayer

Lord, this world is full of many things that can sway our hearts. Grant us a holy focus and resolve to follow your will and keep material things in perspective. For, while you grant us everything in the world, these things are not ends unto themselves but tokens of your love. In Jesus's name. Amen.

DAY 140

Doctrine is more than dogma. It is life. Unlike the Pharisees, who missed the forest for the trees, the teaching of the Scriptures is meant to manifest His name and reveal His glory. As we face the cares of this world, the teaching of Christ is like a tether that ties us to our eternal destination. St. Francis urges us to retain this perspective as we seek His truth in His word.

Meditations from St. Francis

Let us therefore hold fast the words, the life and doctrine and holy Gospel of Him who deigned for us to ask His Father to manifest to us His Name, saying: Father, I have manifested Thy Name to the men whom Thou hast given Me because the words which Thou gavest Me I have given to them, and they have received them, and have known in very deed that I came forth out of Thee, and they have believed that Thou didst send Me. I pray for them, I pray not for the world, but for them whom Thou hast given Me, because they are Thine and all My things are Thine. Holy Father, keep them in Thy Name whom Thou hast given Me, that they may be one, as We also are. These things I speak in the world that they may have joy filled in themselves. I have given them Thy word, and the world hath hated them, because they are not of the world, as I also am not of the world. I pray not that Thou shouldst take them out of the world, but that Thou shouldst keep them from evil. Sanctify them in truth. Thy word is truth As Thou hast sent Me into the world, I have sent them into the world. And for them I do sanctify Myself, that they may be sanctified in truth. Not for them only do I pray, but for them also who through their word shall believe in Me, that they may be consummated in one, and that the world may know that

Thou hast sent Me, and hast loved them, as Thou hast also loved Me. And I have made known Thy Name to them, that the love wherewith Thou hast loved Me may be in them, and I in them. Father, I will that where I am, they also whom Thou hast given Me may be with Me, that they may see Thy glory in Thy kingdom.

St. Francis of Assisi,
First Rule of the Friars Minor.

Additional Biblical Reflections: Ephesians 4:14; Titus 1:9–2:1; Hebrews 13:9.

Prayer

Lord, your word is more than pure thinking; it is a light that illuminates our path. Guide us through your Spirit so that we might glean your will from your word and always pursue your truth in ways that illuminate your kingdom. Amen.

DAY 141

St. Francis did not view his role and authority as a position of power but one whereby he could serve others. By that, he urges others to follow the example of Christ, who likewise viewed himself not according to the majesty and reverence he was owed but as a servant who offered himself to others out of love.

Meditations from St. Francis

To all Christians, religious, clerics, and laics, men and women, to all who dwell in the whole world, Brother Francis, their servant and subject, presents reverent homage, wishing true peace from heaven and sincere charity in the Lord. Being the servant of all, I am bound to serve all and to administer the balm-bearing words of my Lord. Wherefore, considering in my mind that, because of the infirmity and weakness of my body, I cannot visit each one personally, I propose by this present letter and message to offer you the words of our Lord Jesus Christ who is the Word of the Father and the words of the Holy Ghost which are "spirit and life" This Word of the Father, so worthy, so holy and glorious, whose coming the most High Father announced from heaven by His holy archangel Gabriel to the holy and glorious Virgin Mary in whose womb He received the true flesh of our humanity and frailty, He, being rich above all, willed, nevertheless, with His most Blessed Mother, to choose poverty.

St. Francis of Assisi,
Letter to All the Faithful.

Additional Biblical Reflections: Mark 10:45; Galatians 5:13; 1 Peter 4:9–19.

Prayer

Lord, you are worthy of all honor and praise. But when you came to our world, you came in the form of a servant, so we, who follow you, might likewise become servants to others. Let us have servant hearts so that your life might flow through us in the care for others. Amen.

DAY 142

St. Francis frequently wrote about the Eucharist—particularly because the sacrament illuminates what he believed to be the heart of the faith, that is, the cross of Christ. It is easy to be distracted by discipline, piety, even church activities and functions. However, we must never forget that the cross is at the intersection between this life and life everlasting. More than that, the cross redefines what this very life means. Freed from sin, we can live differently.

Meditations from St. Francis

And when His Passion was nigh, He celebrated the Pasch with His disciples and, taking bread, He gave thanks and blessed and broke saying: Take ye and eat: this is My Body. And, taking the chalice, He said: This is My Blood of the New Testament, which shall be shed for you and for many unto remission of sins. After that He prayed to the Father, saying: "Father, if it be possible, let this chalice pass from Me." "And His sweat became as drops of blood, trickling down upon the ground." But withal, He gave up His will to the will of the Father, saying: Father, Thy will be done: not as I will, but as Thou wilt. Such was the will of the Father that His Son, Blessed and Glorious, whom He gave to us, and who was born for us, should by His own Blood, sacrifice, and oblation, offer Himself on the altar of the Cross, not for Himself, by whom "all things were made," but for our sins, leaving us an example that we should follow His steps. And He wishes that we should all be saved by Him and that we should receive Him with a pure heart and a chaste body. But there are few who wish to receive Him and to be saved by Him, although His yoke is sweet and His burden light.

St. Francis of Assisi,
Letter to All the Faithful.

Additional Biblical Reflections: Galatians 2:20; 1 Corinthians 1:18–24; Philippians 2:8.

Prayer

Lord, while the cross is the last thing anyone expected might manifest your glory, for us, who are baptized into your name, it is no longer a cursed tree but one that bears life-giving fruit. Grant that we would all live cruciform lives as living sacrifices, who rest in your grace and forgiveness, and with gratitude, live differently as we await the consummation of what you achieved for us at Calvary. Amen.

DAY 143

For St. Francis, the Mass was not only central to Christian piety and worship but at the heart of a Christian's life. That is because, in the mass, one finds the forgiveness of sins, a pattern for life, and the strength to live in abstention from sin and vice. This is why, according to St. Francis, the "religious" are not merely those who fast for fasting's sake but do all such things in order so that they might do "more and greater things."

Meditations from St. Francis

We ought also to fast and to abstain from vices and sins and from superfluity of food and drink, and to be Catholics. We ought also to visit Churches frequently and to reverence clerics not only for themselves, if they are sinners, but on account of their office and administration of the most holy Body and Blood of our Lord Jesus Christ, which they sacrifice on the altar and receive and administer to others. And let us all know for certain that no one can be saved except by the Blood of our Lord Jesus Christ and by the holy words of the Lord which clerics say and announce and distribute and they alone administer and not others. But religious especially, who have renounced the world, are bound to do more and greater things, but "not to leave the other undone."

St. Francis of Assisi,
Letter to All the Faithful.

Additional Biblical Reflections: John 1:29; 2 Corinthians 12:9; Hebrews 7:27.

Prayer

Lord, you have not given us rites, rituals, or laws merely so that we might prove ourselves obedient. Rather, you've given us such things so we might come into contact with you, on account of the cross of Christ. May your body and blood nourish us, grant us your grace, and sustain us until the final feast might be enjoyed in your heavenly kingdom. Amen.

DAY 144

Once again, in today's meditation, St. Francis reminds us to be wary of our bodies and urges. Many people in the world will tell us to follow our emotions and whatever we desire. Ancient philosophies rooted in the pursuit of pleasure continue to reemerge in pop philosophy and culture. But what we are called to is a life that is not controlled by the body but *in* the body that is brought into obedience under the cross's image.

Meditations from St. Francis

We ought to hate our bodies with [their] vices and sins, because the Lord says in the Gospel that all vices and sins come forth from the heart. We ought to love our enemies and do good to them that hate us. We ought to observe the precepts and counsels of our Lord Jesus Christ. We ought also to deny ourselves and to put our bodies beneath the yoke of servitude and holy obedience as each one has promised to the Lord. And let no man be bound by obedience to obey any one in that where sin or offence is committed. But let him to whom obedience has been entrusted and who is considered greater become as the lesser and the servant of the other brothers, and let him show and have the mercy toward each of his brothers that he would wish to be shown to himself if he were in the like situation. And let him not be angry with a brother on account of his offence, but let him advise him kindly and encourage him with all patience and humility.

St. Francis of Assisi,
Letter to All the Faithful.

Additional Biblical Reflections: Romans 8:5; Galatians 5:19–21; Colossians 3:1–25.

Prayer

Lord, all things that come from you are good. The same is true of our bodies. Nonetheless, sin is often the result of the misuse of good things—our bodies, desires, thoughts, and the like. Discipline us in the flesh, Lord, so that our bodies might be slaves of righteousness and we might remain free in your Spirit. Amen.

DAY 145

Today's meditation continues to reflect on the relationship between our bodies and the spiritual life. However, St. Francis's advice has more to do with individual piety, but it also impacts how we view ourselves concerning others. For we are not isolated "temples" of the Holy Spirit, but a unified temple, a Church, whom Christ has declared His singular bride.

Meditations from St. Francis

We ought not to be "wise according to the flesh" and prudent, but we ought rather to be simple, humble, and pure. And let us hold our bodies in dishonor and contempt because through our fault we are all wretched and corrupt, foul and worms, as the Lord says by the prophet: "I am a worm and no man, the reproach of men and the outcast of the people." We should never desire to be above others, but ought rather to be servants and subject "to every human creature for God's sake." And the spirit of the Lord shall rest upon all those who do these things and who shall persevere to the end, and He shall make His abode and dwelling in them, and they shall be children of the heavenly Father whose works they do, and they are the spouses, brothers and mothers of our Lord Jesus Christ. We are spouses when by the Holy Ghost the faithful soul is united to Jesus Christ. We are His brothers when we do the will of His Father who is in heaven. We are His mothers when we bear Him in our heart and in our body through pure love and a clean conscience and we bring Him forth by holy work which ought to shine as an example to others.

St. Francis of Assisi,
Letter to All the Faithful.

Additional Biblical Reflections: Isaiah 61:10; Mark 2:19–20; Revelation 19:9.

Prayer

Lord, you are the source of all wisdom. When we seek wisdom in the flesh, we pile folly upon folly. But in you, we find in the apparent foolishness of the cross great insights that defy human reason but offer eternal life and a path of righteousness. Grant us, Lord, full trust in your ways so that we might seek wisdom only in you. Amen.

DAY 146

In today's meditation, we hear how Jesus intercedes on our behalf so that His might is also ours. For what was once ours—our sin—He accepted in His flesh when He went to the cross. We do well to ponder St. Francis's exuberance for these things. So often, when we hear of these things, we forget how profound and astounding they truly are. We would do well, with St. Francis, to recapture our marvel and wonder at what our Lord did for us.

Meditations from St. Francis

O how glorious and holy and great to have a Father in heaven! O how holy, fair, and lovable to have a spouse in heaven! O how holy and how beloved, well pleasing and humble, peaceful and sweet and desirable above all to have such a brother who has laid down His life for His sheep, and who has prayed for us to the Father, saying: Father, keep them in Thy Name whom Thou hast given Me. Father, all those whom Thou hast given Me in the world were Thine, and Thou hast given them to Me. And the words which Thou gavest Me I have given to them; and they have received them, and have known in very deed that I came forth from Thee, and they have believed that Thou didst send Me. I pray for them: not for the world: bless and sanctify them. And for them I sanctify Myself that they may be sanctified in one as We also are. And I will, Father, that where I am, they also may be with Me, that they may see My glory in My kingdom. And since He has suffered so many things for us and has done and will do so much good to us, let every creature which is in heaven and on earth and in the sea and in the abysses render praise to God and glory and honor and benediction; for He is our strength and power who alone is good, alone most high, alone almighty and admirable, glorious and alone holy, praiseworthy and blessed without end forever and ever. Amen.

St. Francis of Assisi,
Letter to All the Faithful.

Additional Biblical Reflections: Hosea 11:1; John 17:1–26; Ephesians 1:13–14.

Prayer

Dearest Lord, while we were still sinners, you took our place so that we might also take your place in Heaven—even as we go to our death, in you, so, too, do we go to life everlasting with you at the right hand of God. Grant us consolation in knowing these things, so we might live lives worthy of the calling we have received and be sanctified in your image. Amen.

DAY 147

St. Francis says the whole world should tremble at God Almighty, who comes to an altar in the hands of a priest. Yet, St. Francis also cites this as a reason to praise. How different God's presence is for those who do not know Him—who do not take hold of the benefits of Christ—compared to those who do. For God Almighty is still God Almighty. To many, His presence is at error. But for those of us whom He calls His children, it is the greatest possible comfort.

Meditations from St. Francis

Consider your dignity, brothers, priests, and be holy because He Himself is holy. And as the Lord God has honored you above all through this mystery, even so do you also love and reverence and honor Him above all. It is a great misery and a deplorable weakness when you have Him thus present to care for anything else in the whole world. Let the entire man be seized with fear; let the whole world tremble; let heaven exult when Christ, the Son of the Living God, is on the altar in the hands of the priest. O admirable height and stupendous condescension! O humble sublimity! O sublime humility! that the Lord of the universe, God and the Son of God, so humbles Himself that for our salvation He hides Himself under a morsel of bread. Consider, brothers, the humility of God and "pour out your hearts before Him," and be ye humbled that ye may be exalted by

Him. Do not therefore keep back anything for yourselves that He may receive you entirely who gives Himself up entirely to you.

Francis of Assisi, *To All the Friars.*

Additional Biblical Reflections: Psalm 111:10; Proverbs 8:13; Matthew 10:28.

Prayer

Lord, no one has descended further or from greater heights to such low lows than you from the throne of Heaven to a human birth and a death reserved for criminals. However, you have comprehended all things, and your redemption covers us no matter our status in life. Grant that we might always have a healthy fear of your majesty and constant solace on account of your grace. Amen.

DAY 148

How easy is it to fall into complacency for holy things. We have attended many masses, received the Sacrament more times than we can count, and find ourselves with wandering minds, going through the motions, without the sense of awe these things demand. St. Francis reminds us of the wonder of these things, so they do not become mundane but that we always hold them in their proper reference.

Meditations from St. Francis

Consider your dignity, brothers, priests, and be holy because He Himself is holy. And as the Lord God has honored you above all through this mystery, even so do you also love and reverence and honor Him above all. It is a great misery and a deplorable weakness when you have Him thus present to care for anything else in the whole world. Let the entire man be seized with fear; let the whole world tremble; let heaven exult when Christ, the Son of the Living God, is on the altar in the hands of the priest. O admirable height and stupendous condescension! O humble sublimity! O sublime humility! that the Lord of the universe, God and the Son of God, so humbles Himself that for our salvation He hides Himself under a morsel of bread.

Francis of Assisi, *To All the Friars.*

Additional Biblical Reflections: Amos 6:1; John 1:1–3; 1 Timothy 3:16.

Prayer

Lord, you exhibit not only the greatest majesty but the most profound humility. Yet, you are without arrogance or pride. Let us, likewise, find glory in your gifts without being prideful or boastful. In these things, let your glory leave us in constant awe so that we might not become complacent in our piety. In Jesus's name. Amen.

DAY 149

Our faith is not dependent on others. While we should love even the noblest and most pious of our spiritual mentors, as we are called to love all men, they should never eclipse our love of God. For if we hinge our faith on human beings, when they fail, as humans are prone to do, our faith will fail with them. However, when we love others through the heart of Christ, our faith will never falter.

Meditations from St. Francis

I speak to thee as best I can on the subject of thy soul; that those things which impede thee in loving the Lord God and whosoever may be a hindrance to thee, whether brothers or others, even though they were to strike thee—all these things thou oughtest to reckon as a favor And so thou shouldst desire and not otherwise. And let this be to thee for true obedience from the Lord God and from me, for this I know surely to be true obedience. And love those that do such things to thee and wish not other from them, save in so far as the Lord may grant to thee; and in this thing love them—by wishing that they may be better Christians. And let this be to thee more than a hermitage. And by this I wish to know if thou lovest God and me His servant and thine, to wit: that there be no brother in the world who has sinned, how great soever his sin may be, who after he has seen thy face shall ever go away without thy mercy, if he seek mercy, and, if he seek not mercy, ask thou him if he desires mercy. And if he afterwards appears before thy face a thousand times, love him more than me, to the end that thou mayest draw him to the Lord, and on such ones always have mercy And this thou shouldst declare to the guardians, when thou canst, that thou art determined of thyself to do thus.

St. Francis of Assisi.
To a Certain Minister.

Additional Biblical Reflections: Luke 14:26; Colossians 3:1–2; Romans 12:2.

Prayer

Lord, you are the highest object of our hearts. May our love of others always be an extension of our love of you and your love for us and all people. In this way, Lord, strengthen our faith so that we might endure no matter what others might do and remain faithful to you in all things. Amen.

DAY 150

It may be tempting to ask whether some of the practices and traditions we exercise in our reverence of God, and the Eucharist, are necessary. Indeed, not all traditions that demonstrate such reverence have persisted throughout history. Nonetheless, we must maintain reverence and awe for what meets the eye—bread and wine, and even the priest are common in every respect. However, according to God's Word, what is truly occurring is the greatest and most profound mystery: An encounter with the Divine.

Meditations from St. Francis

I entreat you more than if it were a question of myself that, when it is becoming and it may seem to be expedient, you humbly beseech the clerics to venerate above all the most holy Body and Blood of our Lord Jesus Christ and His Holy Name and written words which sanctify the body. They ought to hold as precious the chalices, corporals, ornaments of the altar, and all that pertain to the Sacrifice And if the most holy Body of the Lord be lodged very poorly in any place, let It according to the command of the Church be placed by them and left in a precious place, and let It be carried with great veneration and administered to others with discretion. The Names also and written words of the Lord, wheresoever they may be found in unclean places, let them be collected, and they ought to be put in a proper place. And in all the preaching you do, admonish the people concerning penance and that no one can be saved except he that receives the most sacred Body and Blood of the Lord. And while It is being sacrificed by the priest on the altar and It is being carried to any place, let all the people on bended knees render praise, honor, and glory to the Lord God Living and True. And you shall so announce and preach His praise to all peoples that at every hour and when the bells are rung praise and thanks shall always be given to the Almighty God by all the people through the whole earth.

St. Francis of Assisi.
To All the Custodes.

Additional Biblical Reflections: Leviticus 26:2; Luke 12:5; Hebrews 12:18–29.

Prayer

Lord, not all your mysteries can be investigated, but all of them should be revered. Let us guard our practice and actions so that all we do maintains a posture of reverence that recognizes your presence and majesty. May all these things constantly arrest our hearts so we might ever be mindful of you and your will. Amen.

DAY 151

Meditations from St. Catherine

I Catherine, thy poor unworthy mother, want thee to attain that perfection for which God has chosen thee. It seems to me that one wishing so to attain should walk with and not without moderation. And yet every work of ours ought to be done both without and with moderation: it befits us to love God without moderation, putting to that love neither limit nor measure nor rule, but loving Him immeasurably. And if thou wish to reach the perfection of love, it befits thee to set thy life in order. Let thy first rule be to flee the conversation of every human being, in so far as it is simply conversation, except as deeds of charity may demand; but to love people very much, and talk with few of them. And know how to talk in moderation even with those whom thou lovest with spiritual love; reflect that if thou didst not do this, thou wouldst place a limit before perceiving it to that limitless love which thou oughtest to bear to God, by placing the finite creature between you: for the love which thou shouldst place in God thou wouldst place in the creature, loving it without moderation; and this would hinder thy perfection. Therefore thou shouldst love it spiritually, in a disciplined way.

Letter to Monna
Alessa Dei Saracinia

Additional Biblical Reflections: Ecclesiastes 3:1-8; 1 Corinthians 6:22; Philippians 4:8.

Prayer

Dearest Lord, you have called us to love you with all our heart, soul, and strength. Yet, in the very next breath, you've bid us to love our neighbors as ourselves. Give us love in its proper proportions: wholly devoted to you and likewise to our neighbor. Amen.

DAY 152

In today's meditation, St. Catherine reminds us that our spiritual growth comes in its proper order. One does not become a saint without first exercising the foundational virtues of love and piety. One does not love one's neighbor and, thereafter, discover the truth, but one sees God's truth when living a life bathed in divine love.

Meditations from St. Catherine

The soul, who is lifted by a very great and yearning desire for the honor of God and the salvation of souls, begins by exercising herself, for a certain space of time, in the ordinary virtues, remaining in the cell of self-knowledge, in order to know better the goodness of God towards her. This she does because knowledge must precede love, and only when she has attained love, can she strive to follow and to clothe herself with the truth. But, in no way, does the creature receive such a taste of the truth, or so brilliant a light therefrom, as by means of humble and continuous prayer, founded on knowledge of herself and of God; because prayer, exercising her in the above way, unites with God the soul that follows the footprints of Christ Crucified, and thus, by desire and affection, and union of love, makes her another Himself. Christ would seem to have meant this, when He said: To him who will love Me and will observe My commandment, will I manifest Myself; and he shall be one thing with Me and I with him. In several places we find similar words, by which we can see that it is, indeed, through the effect of love, that the soul becomes another Himself.

A Treatise of Divine
Providence

Additional Biblical Reflections: Psalm 119:97; Romans 13:8-10; John 14:21.

Prayer

Lord, you have set forth a path toward you that follows from love and virtue. Lead us in the basic virtues that through the practice of such piety, we might grow, as a babe on milk before moving onto solid food, and reach full maturity in our devotion to you. Amen.

DAY 153

The life of a disciple is not one of comfort and ease. Christianity is not a feel-good religion. We have a God whose heart aches for the lost, for sinners, and suffering. A love reflecting God's heart will likewise ache. However, these pains are not without their use. In pain, we learn patience, and through patience, we come to know the truth and peace that comes through God's presence.

Meditations from St. Catherine

Very pleasing to Me, dearest daughter, is the willing desire to bear every pain and fatigue, even unto death, for the salvation of souls, for the more the soul endures, the more she shows that she loves Me; loving Me she comes to know more of My truth, and the more she knows, the more pain and intolerable grief she feels at the offenses committed against Me. You asked Me to sustain you, and to punish the faults of others in you, and you did not remark that you were really asking for love, light, and knowledge of the truth, since I have already told you that, by the increase of love, grows grief and pain, wherefore he that grows in love grows in grief. Therefore, I say to you all, that you should ask, and it will be given you, for I deny nothing to him who asks of Me in truth. Consider that the love of divine charity is so closely joined in the soul with perfect patience, that neither can leave the soul without the other. For this reason (if the soul elect to love Me) she should elect to endure pains for Me in whatever mode or circumstance I may send them to her. Patience cannot be proved in any other way than by suffering, and patience is united with love as has been said. Therefore bear yourselves with manly courage, for, unless you do so, you will not prove yourselves to be spouses of My Truth, and faithful children, nor of the company of those who relish the taste of My honor, and the salvation of souls.

A Treatise of Divine
Providence

Additional Biblical Reflections: Psalm 37:7-9; Luke 8:15; Romans 12:12; 2 Peter 3:9.

Prayer

Lord, in great patience, you endure our faithlessness so that we might be preserved until life in your name. Grant us patience as we endure sorrow in the world. Let us ever be mindful that through patient suffering, we learn to rely on you more. Amen.

DAY 154

When we speak of serving God, we often imagine that whatever we direct toward God must be in some mystical sense through prayer or meditation. However, in the Bible, we are told that God is loved and hated when we love and hate our neighbor in turn. To serve our neighbor is to serve God. But the opposite is also true. If we despise our neighbor, it is as if we despise God himself.

Meditations from St. Catherine

I wish also that you should know that every virtue is obtained by means of your neighbor, and likewise, every defect; he, therefore, who stands in hatred of Me, does an injury to his neighbor, and to himself, who is his own chief neighbor, and this injury is both general and particular. It is general because you are obliged to love your neighbor as yourself, and loving him, you ought to help him spiritually, with prayer, counseling him with words, and assisting him both spiritually and temporally, according to the need in which he may be, at least with your goodwill if you have nothing else. A man therefore, who does not love, does not help him, and thereby does himself an injury; for he cuts off from himself grace, and injures his neighbor, by depriving him of the benefit of the prayers and of the sweet desires that he is bound to offer for him to Me. Thus, every act of help that he performs should proceed from the charity which he has through love of Me. And every evil also, is done by means of his neighbor, for, if he do not love Me, he cannot be in charity with his neighbor; and thus, all evils derive from the soul's deprivation of love of Me and her neighbor; whence, inasmuch as such a man does no good, it follows that he must do evil. To whom does he evil? First of all to himself, and then to his neighbor, not against Me, for no evil can touch Me, except in so far as I count done to Me that which he does to himself. To himself he does the injury of sin, which deprives him of grace, and worse than this he cannot do to his neighbor. Him he injures in not paying him the debt, which he owes him, of love, with which he ought to help him by means of prayer and holy desire offered to Me for him.

A Treatise of Divine
Providence

Additional Biblical Reflections: Leviticus 19:18; Matthew 25:31-46; Mark 12:31-31.

Prayer

Lord, you have said that you will be with us forever. So, too, did you declare that the poor would always be with us. Let us love you through our love of the needy. Let us refrain from doing evil against our fellows lest we do evil to you. In all these things, let us serve you as we serve one another. Amen.

DAY 155

S t. Catherine teaches us, following Jesus's own words, that suffering produces patience and refines our faith. She also teaches that our present suffering serves to magnify the fruit and reward of supernatural glory, the promise of Christ that a better future is in store. Thus, we can bear our sufferings patiently, knowing they are temporary. God has a better future planned for us.

Meditations from St. Catherine

Dearest brother in Christ Jesus: I Catherine, a useless servant, comfort and bless thee and invite thee to a sweet and most holy patience, for without patience we could not please God. So I beg you, in order that you may receive the fruit of your tribulations, that you assume the armor of patience. And should it seem very hard to you to endure your many troubles, bear in memory three things, that you may endure more patiently. First, I want you to think of the shortness of your time, for on one day you are not certain of the morrow. We may truly say that we do not feel past trouble, nor that which is to come, but only the moment of time at which we are. Surely, then, we ought to endure patiently, since the time is so short. The second thing is, for you to consider the fruit which follows our troubles. For St. Paul says there is no comparison between our troubles and the fruit and reward of supernal glory. The third is, for you to consider the loss which results to those who endure in wrath and impatience; for loss follows this here, and eternal punishment to the soul.

*To Benincasa Her
Brother When He Was in
Florence*

Additional Biblical Reflections: Romans 8:18-31; 2 Corinthians 4:16; 1 Peter 5:10.

Prayer

Lord, you have planned an incredible and glorious future for your children. Grant us patience amidst this world's tribulations, knowing that these things are temporary, and the glory you have promised is eternal. In Jesus's name. Amen.

DAY 156

It is easy to remain in our faith when life is going well. However, when bad things befall us, we are forced upon a crossroads—to turn away from God and follow our own path with resentment harbored against Him, or turn to God all the more and trust Him despite the unclear path ahead. In today's meditation, St. Catherine urges us to follow the Lord's path at all times.

Meditations from St. Catherine

Once our sweet Saviour said to a very dear daughter of His, "Dost thou know how those people act who want to fulfil My will in consolation and in sweetness and joy? When they are deprived of these things, they wish to depart from My will, thinking to do well and to avoid offence; but false sensuality lurks in them, and to escape pains it falls into offence without perceiving it. But if the soul were wise and had the light of My will within, it would look to the fruit and not to the sweetness. What is the fruit of the soul? Hatred of itself and love of Me. This hate and love are the issue of self-knowledge; then the soul knows its faulty self to be nothing, and it sees in itself My goodness, which keeps its will good; and it sees what a person I have made it, in order that it may serve Me in greater perfection, and judges that I have made it for the best, and for its own greatest good. Such a man as this, dearest daughter, does not wish for time to suit himself, because he has learned humility; knowing his infirmity, he does not trust in his own wish, but is faithful to Me. He clothes him in My highest and eternal will, because he sees that I neither give nor take away, save for your sanctification; and he sees that love alone impels Me to give you sweetness and to take it from you. For this cause he cannot grieve over any consolation that might be taken from him within or without, by demon or fellow-creature— because he sees that, were this not for his good, I should not permit it. Therefore this man rejoices because he has light within and without, and is so illumined that when the devil approaches his mind with shadows to confuse him, saying, 'This is for thy sins,' he replies like a person who shrinks not from suffering, saying, 'Thanks be to my Creator, who has remembered me in the time of shadows, punishing me by pain in finite time. Great is this love, which will not punish me in the infinite future.' Oh, what tranquility of mind has this soul, because it has freed itself from the self-will which brings storm! But not thus does he whose self-will is lively within, seeking things after his own way!"

To The Venerable Religious, Brother Antonio of Nizza, of The Order of The Hermit Brothers of Saint Augustine at the Wood of The Lake

Additional Biblical Reflections: Luke 22:42; John 8:11; 2 Peter 2:22.

Prayer

Lord, your promises are always sure. Let us always remember the future you have set before us in your word so that when life's trials befall us and the Devil deceives us to believe that all things are helpless, we will nonetheless remain steadfast in pursuit of you. Amen.

DAY 157

Today, St. Catherine encourages us to guard against hollow penance or corporal exercises that are done without the affection of the soul. In other words, she cautions against "going through the motions" without a heart that fervently seeks God alongside such action. Prayer, piety, and ritual are fine and good—but if performed merely for the sake of the action without the worshipper's devotion, they merit little.

Meditations from St. Catherine

I wish therefore that the works of penance, and of other corporal exercises, should be observed merely as means, and not as the fundamental affection of the soul. For, if the principal affection of the soul were placed in penance, I should receive a finite thing like a word, which, when it has issued from the mouth, is no more, unless it has issued with affection of the soul, which conceives and brings forth virtue in truth; that is, unless the finite operation, which I have called a word, should be joined with the affection or love, in which case it would be grateful and pleasant to Me. And this is because such a work would not be alone, but accompanied by true discretion, using corporal works as means, and not as the principal foundation; for it would not be becoming that that principal foundation should be placed in penance only, or in any exterior corporal act, such works being finite, since they are done in finite time, and also because it is often profitable that the creature omit them, and even that she be made to do so.

A Treatise of Discretion

Additional Biblical Reflections: Matthew 15:2-6; 2 Thessalonians 3:6; 1 Timothy 1:4.

Prayer

Lord, you have given us a wealth of tradition and practice that can draw us closer to you if accompanied by affection and devotion. However, ensure, Lord, that we do not misuse these gifts in exercises of vanity but that they might be rightly cherished and revered, with you always at the heart of our prayers and devotions. Amen.

DAY 158

Often, spiritual seekers imagine themselves as merely lost looking for a single path—and there might be many—whereby one might escape their darkness and see some light. However, what St. Catherine reminds us is that sin has done more than left us wandering lost. It has come upon us like a deluge and would drown us if the Lord had not offered His Bridge to rescue us. When in peril, who would reject a single hand that reaches out because it is not the hand one chose for oneself, or it isn't the sort of rescuer one had imagined? Such a person we would rightly deem a fool. Thus, it is not unloving that God should demand that if we hope to be saved, we should take home of Christ alone. It is the height of love, in fact, that He would bid us cling to Him and no other.

Meditations from St. Catherine

"Wherefore I have told you that I have made a Bridge of My Word, of My only-begotten Son, and this is the truth. I wish that you, My children, should know that the road was broken by the sin and disobedience of Adam, in such a way, that no one could arrive at Eternal Life. Wherefore men did not render Me glory in the way in which they ought to have, as they did not participate in that Good for which I had created them, and My truth was not fulfilled. This truth is that I have created man to My own image and similitude, in order that he might have Eternal Life, and might partake of Me, and taste My supreme and eternal sweetness and goodness. But, after sin had closed Heaven and bolted the doors of mercy, the soul of man produced thorns and prickly brambles, and My creature found in himself rebellion against himself.

"And the flesh immediately began to war against the Spirit, and, losing the state of innocence, became a foul animal, and all created things rebelled against man, whereas they would have been obedient to him, had he remained in the state in which I had placed him. He, not remaining therein, transgressed My obedience, and merited eternal death in soul and body. And, as soon as he had sinned, a tempestuous flood arose, which ever buffets him with its waves, bringing him weariness and trouble from himself, the devil, and the world. Every one was drowned in the flood, because no one, with his own justice alone, could arrive at Eternal Life. And so, wishing to remedy your great evils, I have given you the Bridge of My Son, in order that, passing across the flood, you may not be drowned, which flood is the tempestuous sea of this dark life. See, therefore, under what obligations the creature is to Me, and how ignorant he is, not to take the remedy which I have offered, but to be willing to drown."

A Treatise of Discretion

Additional Biblical Reflections: Deuteronomy 6:4; John 14:6; 1 Timothy 2:5.

Prayer

Lord, in our desperation, you sent your Son to rescue us from our perilous estate. Thank you, Lord, for your salvation. Let us not be foolishly deceived by false saviors or paths of our own making, but let us always hold fast to your salvation so that we might be drawn from the water and live forever in your image. Amen.

DAY 159

In today's meditation, St. Catherine continues speaking from a revelation from God, according to the metaphor of God's Bridge, Jesus, who is our salvation. Here the full scope of His redemptive plan is in view. He came not merely to save some, but to save all the earth, those who would cling to His bridge and be lifted from the flood of sin.

Meditations from St. Catherine

"*Open, my daughter, the eye of your intellect, and you will see the accepted and the ignorant, the imperfect, and also the perfect who follow Me in truth, so that you may grieve over the damnation of the ignorant, and rejoice over the perfection of My beloved servants.*

"*You will see further how those bear themselves who walk in the light, and those who walk in the darkness. I also wish you to look at the Bridge of My only-begotten Son, and see the greatness thereof, for it reaches from Heaven to earth, that is, that the earth of your humanity is joined to the greatness of the Deity thereby. I say then that this Bridge reaches from Heaven to earth, and constitutes the union which I have made with man.*

"*This was necessary, in order to reform the road which was broken, as I said to you, in order that man should pass through the bitterness of the world, and arrive at life; but the Bridge could not be made of earth sufficiently large to span the flood and give you Eternal Life, because the earth of human nature was not sufficient to satisfy for guilt, to remove the stain of Adam's sin. Which stain corrupted the whole human race and gave out a stench, as I have said to you above. It was, therefore, necessary to join human nature with the height of My nature, the Eternal Deity, so that it might be sufficient to satisfy for the whole human race, so that human nature should sustain the punishment, and that the Divine nature, united with the human, should make acceptable the sacrifice of My only Son, offered to Me to take death from you and to give you life.*

"So the height of the Divinity, humbled to the earth, and joined with your humanity, made the Bridge and reformed the road. Why was this done? In order that man might come to his true happiness with the angels. And observe, that it is not enough, in order that you should have life, that My Son should have made you this Bridge, unless you walk thereon."

A Treatise of Discretion

Additional Biblical Reflections: Genesis 12:1-9; Luke 19:10; John 3:16-17.

Prayer

Lord, you have a heart that beats for the whole world, all the creatures you have made. As such, let us readily take hold of your redemption – the great Bridge that your Son has forged – and be saved so that all the world might come to know you. Amen.

DAY 160

The Holy Spirit was sent by the Father and the Son following Christ's ascension, in which He might guide us in the truth and be an ever-present consoler even as our Lord began His reign at the right hand of the Father. Furthermore, should we hope to find Christ, we must pursue Him through the Spirit, the Word through which the Spirit speaks, and through the Sacrament of Christ's Body and Blood.

Meditations from St. Catherine

"When My only-begotten Son returned to Me, forty days after the resurrection, this Bridge, namely Himself, arose from the earth, that is, from among the conversation of men, and ascended into Heaven by virtue of the Divine Nature and sat at the right hand of Me, the Eternal Father, as the angels said, on the day of the Ascension, to the disciples, standing like dead men, their hearts lifted on high, and ascended into Heaven with the wisdom of My Son – 'Do not stand here any longer, for He is seated at the right hand of the Father!' When He, then, had thus ascended on high, and returned to Me the Father, I sent the Master, that is the Holy Spirit, who came to you with My power and the wisdom of My Son, and with His own clemency, which is the essence of the Holy Spirit. He is one thing with Me, the Father, and with My Son. And He built up the road of the doctrine which My Truth had left in the world. Thus, though the bodily presence of My Son left you, His doctrine remained, and the virtue of the stones founded upon this doctrine, which is the way made for you by this Bridge. For first, He practiced this doctrine and made the road by His actions, giving you His doctrine by example rather than by words; for He

practiced, first Himself, what He afterwards taught you, then the clemency of the Holy Spirit made you certain of the doctrine, fortifying the minds of the disciples to confess the truth, and to announce this road, that is, the doctrine of Christ crucified, reproving, by this means, the world of its injustice and false judgment, of which injustice and false judgment, I will in time discourse to you at greater length."

A Treatise of Discretion

Additional Biblical Reflections: Genesis 1:1-2; John 14:26; 16:27; Acts 2.

Prayer

Lord, you did not abandon us when you ascended into Heaven but sent your Spirit that you might be with us, no matter from whence we hail, and guide us in your truth until your final return. Preserve us through your Spirit so that we might not waiver from your doctrine until all truth is revealed in the coming of your Son. Amen.

DAY 161

In today's meditation, St. Catherine discerns between three different kinds of prayer: perpetual, verbal, and mental. Perpetually, we maintain a sort of connection with God on a spiritual level, like an open channel between ourselves and God, constantly open to His voice and guidance. Then, we learn to pray verbally—but this is not about merely verbalizing words. Verbal prayer is meant to arrest the mind with holy desire. Thus, it is not sufficient to simply speak words while the mind wanders. Rather, the mind must take hold of the words of prayer so that the whole person is united to God.

Meditations from St. Catherine

Prayer is of three sorts. The one is perpetual: it is the holy perpetual desire, which prays in the sight of God, whatever thou art doing; for this desire directs all thy works, spiritual and corporal, to His honour, and therefore it is called perpetual. Of this it seems that Saint Paul the glorious was talking when he said: Pray without ceasing.

The other kind is vocal prayer, when the offices or other prayers are said aloud. This is ordained to reach the third— that is, mental prayer: your soul reaches this when it uses vocal prayer in prudence and humility, so that while the tongue speaks the heart is not far from God. But one must exert one's self to hold and establish one's heart in the force of divine charity. And whenever one felt one's mind to be visited by God, so that it was drawn to think of its Creator in any wise, it ought to abandon vocal prayer, and to fix its mind with the force of love upon that wherein it sees God visit it; then, if it has time, when this has ceased, it ought to take up the vocal prayer again, in order that the mind may always stay full and not empty. And although many conflicts of diverse kinds should abound in prayer, and darkness of mind with much confusion, the devil making the soul feel that her prayer was not pleasing to God— nevertheless, she ought not to give up on account of those conflicts and shadows, but to abide firm in fortitude and long perseverance, considering that the devil so does to draw her away from prayer the mother, and God permits it to test the fortitude and constancy of that soul. Also, in order that by those conflicts and shadows she may know herself not to be, and in the goodwill which she feels preserved within her may know the goodness of God, Who is Giver and Preserver of good and holy wills: such wills as are not vouchsafed to all who want them.

By this means she attains to the third and last— mental prayer, in which she receives the reward for the labours she underwent in her imperfect vocal prayer. Then she tastes the milk of faithful prayer. She rises above herself— that is, above the gross impulses of the senses— and with angelic mind unites herself with God by force of love, and sees and knows with the light of thought, and clothes herself with truth. She is made the sister of angels; she abides with her Bridegroom on the table of crucified desire, rejoicing to seek the honour of God and the salvation of souls; since well she sees that for this the Eternal Bridegroom ran to the shameful death of the Cross, and thus fulfilled obedience to the Father, and our salvation.

To Sister Eugenia,
Her Niece at the Convent
of Saint Agnes

Additional Biblical Reflections: Psalm 102; Matthew 6:16-18; 1 Thessalonians 5:17.

Prayer

Lord, envelop our lives in prayer. Let us maintain perpetual prayer, constantly aligned with your word and will. Grant that the words we pray not be said in vain, but that by arresting our hearts and minds, our prayers might rise to you like sweet incense. Grant these requests, Lord, so that we might live according to your will.

DAY 162

Writing at a time when it was common amongst monastics to engage in self-flagellation, follow extreme fasts, and other methods meant to mortify the flesh, St. Catherine warns that the body is not itself the seat of sin, but the self-will that operates through the flesh. Whatever spiritual discipline we engage, we must not lose the forest for the trees. Sin is not a flaw in the body—God created the body and declared it good. The sinful "flesh," rather, is as such because of the inward focus of the will.

Meditations from St. Catherine

The soul must not stay content because it has arrived at gaining the general light; nay, it ought to go on with all zeal to the perfect light. For since men are at first imperfect rather than perfect, they should advance in light to perfection. Two kinds of perfect people walk in this perfect light. There are some who give themselves to castigating their body perfectly, doing very great harsh penance; and that the flesh may not rebel against the reason, they have placed all their desire rather on mortifying their body than on slaying their self-will. These people feed at the table of penitence and are good and perfect; but unless they have a great humility and conform themselves not wholly to judge according to the will of God and not according to that of men, they often wrong their perfection, making themselves judges of those who do not walk in the same way in which they do. This happens to them because they have put more thought and desire on mortifying their body than on slaying their self-will.

> *To Brother William*
> *of England of the Hermit*
> *Brothers of St. Augustine*

Additional Biblical Reflections: Luke 12:22-23; Romans 7:12-25; 1 Corinthians 6:13-20; 9:25-27.

Prayer

Lord, you created us in the body and declared our bodies good. Let us not abuse our bodies, neither let us be overindulgent in the pleasures of the flesh. Rather, let our disciplines and pieties conform our will to you so that we will not desire what pleases ourselves but only and always what pleases you. Amen.

DAY 163

It is easy to miss the forest for the trees. Often in our efforts toward piety, we lose the heart of it—the pursuit of God—for the sake of self-serving disciplines. Furthermore, in our effort to enjoy the life God has given us, we are prone to self-indulgence. Today's meditation picks up on the theme of moderation—to discipline the flesh, but not abuse it. To enjoy God's gifts but not link one's passions to worldly things, Christ must remain at the center of all we do.

Meditations from St. Catherine

Be a dispenser to the poor of your temporal substance. Submit you to the yoke of holy and true obedience. Kill, kill your own will, that it may not be so tied to your relatives, and mortify your body, and do not so pamper it in delicate ways. Despise yourself, and have in regard neither rank nor riches, for virtue is the only thing that makes us gentlefolk, and the riches of this life are the worst of poverty when possessed with inordinate love apart from God. Recall to memory what the glorious Jerome said about this, which one can never repeat often enough, forbidding that widows should abound in daintiness, or keep their face anointed, or their garments choice or delicate. Nor should their conversation be with vain or dissolute young women, but in the cell: they should do like the turtle- dove, who, when her companion has died, mourns forever, and keeps to herself, and wants no other company. Limit your intercourse, dearest and most beloved Sister, to Christ crucified; set your affection and desire on following Him by the way of shame and true humility, in gentleness, binding you to the Lamb with the bands of charity. This my soul desires, that you may be a true daughter, and a bride consecrated to Christ, and a fruitful field, not sterile, but full of the sweet fruits of true virtues. Hasten, hasten, for time is short and the road is long. And if you gave all you have in the world, time would not pause for you from running its course. I say no more. Remain in the holy and sweet grace of God.

To Monna Colomba
in Lucca

Additional Biblical Reflections: Deuteronomy 14:12; Romans 8:30-39; 1 Corinthians 10:31.

Prayer

Lord, it is easy to be distracted by the things of this world. So, too, can we be distracted from you by blindly pursuing the very practices that ought to drive us toward you more fervently. May your Son always be at the heart of our faith and His light always in our eyes so that we might see clearly and not be blinded by the passions of this flesh and world. Amen.

DAY 164

It has been said that while the Devil is a lion, he is a lion on a leash, the length of which is determined by God. Today, St. Catherine reminds us that even the Devil—like how God once used ungodly Babylon as his instrument to discipline Israel—is His instrument of justice, and when he attacks, we might prove ourselves virtuous and faithful.

Meditations from St. Catherine

The Devil, dearest daughter, is the instrument of My Justice to torment the souls who have miserably offended Me. And I have set him in this life to tempt and molest My creatures, not for My creatures to be conquered, but that they may conquer, proving their virtue, and receive from Me the glory of victory. And no one should fear any battle or temptation of the Devil that may come to him, because I have made My creatures strong, and have given them strength of will, fortified in the Blood of my Son, which will, neither Devil nor creature can move, because it is yours, given by Me. You therefore, with free arbitration, can hold it or leave it, according as you please. It is an arm, which, if you place it in the hands of the Devil, straightway becomes a knife, with which he strikes you and slays you. But if man do not give this knife of his will into the hands of the Devil, that is, if he do not consent to his temptations and molestations, he will never be injured by the guilt of sin in any temptation, but will even be fortified by it, when the eye of his intellect is opened to see My love which allowed him to be tempted, so as to arrive at virtue, by being proved. For one does not arrive at virtue except through knowledge of self, and knowledge of Me, which knowledge is more perfectly acquired in the time of temptation, because then man knows himself to be nothing, being unable to lift off himself the pains and vexations which he would flee; and he knows Me in his will, which is fortified by My goodness, so that it does not yield to these thoughts.

A Treatise of
Discretion

Additional Biblical Reflections: Jeremiah 51:20-25; Job 1:6-12; 1 Peter 4:12-13.

Prayer

Lord, we need not fear the Devil for he is but an instrument in your hand whose threats can extend no further than you permit. Grant us steadfastness when afflicted by the foe so that we will not be destroyed but refined in the faith and endure unto life everlasting. Amen.

DAY 165

Amid temptation—be it from the Devil or the flesh—St. Catherine reminds us that Christ is still present. His presence, His truth, abides with us, giving us the strength to extinguish the fiery darts of the foe. Of course, we do not always *feel* His presence beside us. Here, St. Catherine simply bids us consider the will. If we desire that the Lord be with us, we can be certain He is, regardless of whether we feel His presence, for He has promised to be amongst those who desire Him in faith.

Meditations from St. Catherine

I remember that I heard this said once to a servant of God, and it was said to her by the Sweet Primal Truth, when she was abiding in very great pain and temptation, and among other things, felt the greatest confusion, in so much that the devil said: "What wilt thou do? for all the time of thy life thou shalt abide in these pains, and then thou shalt have hell." She then answered with manly heart, and without any fear, and with holy hatred of herself, saying: "I do not avoid pains, for I have chosen pains for my refreshment. And if at the end He should give me hell, I will not therefore abandon serving my Creator. For I am she who am worthy of abiding in hell, because I wronged the Sweet Primal Truth; so, did He give me hell, He would do me no wrong, since I am His." Then our Saviour, in this sweet and true humility, scattered the shadows and torments of the devil, as it happens when the cloud passes that the sun remains; and suddenly came the Presence of Our Saviour. Thence she melted into a river of tears, and said in a sweet glow of love: "O sweet and good Jesus, where wast thou when my soul was in such affliction?" Sweet Jesus, the Spotless Lamb, replied: "I was beside thee. For I move not, and never leave My creature, unless the creature leave Me through mortal sin." And that woman abode in sweet converse with Him, and said: "If Thou wast with me, how did I not feel Thee? How can it be that being by the fire, I should not feel the heat? And I felt nothing but freezing cold, sadness, and bitterness, and seemed to myself full of mortal sins." He replied sweetly, and said: "Dost thou wish Me to show thee, daughter mine, how in those conflicts thou didst not fall into mortal sin, and how I was beside thee? Tell me, what is it that makes sin mortal? Only the will. For sin and virtue consist in the consent of the will; there is no sin nor virtue, unless voluntarily wrought. This will was not in thee; for had it been, thou wouldst have taken joy and delight in the suggestions of the devil; but since the will was not there, thou didst grieve over them, and suffer for fear of doing wrong. So thou seest that sin and virtue consist in choice— wherefore I tell thee that thou shouldst not, on account of these conflicts, fall into disordered confusion.

To Sister Bartolomea
Della Seta Nun in the
Convent of Santo Stefano
At Pisa

Additional Biblical Reflections: Exodus 33:14; Psalm 140:13; Matthew 28:18-20.

Prayer

Lord, your presence is not contingent on a feeling or our circumstances. You promised that you would be with us and, therefore, we can be sure that so long as we desire it, you will be with us come what may. Let this truth be ever before us and that we might not lose hope amid hardship. Amen.

DAY 166

Fear can be one of the most controlling and paralyzing forces in life. Some fears are rational, and others do not make much sense, but they can be paralyzing no less. Regardless, we all know fear. However, fear can be dangerous. It can lead to sin. It also stems from doubt rather than faith. Today, St. Catherine reminds us that we have nothing to fear in Christ and that we can put on the armor of God and face all of our fears.

Meditations from St. Catherine

And I tell you on behalf of Christ crucified, most sweet and holy father, not to fear for any reason whatsoever. Come in security: trust you in Christ sweet Jesus: for, doing what you ought, God will be above you, and there will be no one who shall be against you. Up, father, like a man! For I tell you that you have no need to fear. You ought to come; come, then. Come gently, without any fear. And if any at home wish to hinder you, say to them bravely, as Christ said when St. Peter, through tenderness, wished to draw Him back from going to His passion; Christ turned to him, saying, "Get thee behind Me, Satan; thou art an offence to Me, seeking the things which are of men, and not those which are of God. Wilt thou not that I fulfil the will of My Father?" Do you likewise, sweetest father, following Him as His vicar, deliberating and deciding by yourself, and saying to those who would hinder you, "If my life should be spent a thousand times, I wish to fulfil the will of my Father." Although bodily life be laid down for it, yet seize on the life of grace and the means of winning it forever. Now comfort you and fear not, for you have no need. Put on the armour of the most holy

Cross, which is the safety and the life of Christians. Let talk who will, and hold you firm in your holy resolution.

To Gregory XI

Additional Biblical Reflections: Isaiah 41:10; 2 Timothy 1:7; 1 John 4:18.

Prayer

Lord, you are the source of our courage. When faced with the burden of the world's sin and the curse of the cross, you had no fear but stepped forward toward Golgotha with unwavering resolve. Let us follow your example and know that there is nothing to fear, for you have conquered all threats and emerged again in victory. Amen.

DAY 167

It is easy to grow weary in this life, particularly when our efforts do not seem to bear fruit. This can also be our experience with faith. No matter how many times we attend mass, how many sermons we hear, how many prayers we pray, we often find ourselves stagnant without any real spiritual growth. Today, St. Catherine reminds us to persevere in virtue—for perseverance is what stands between fortitude and patience and prevents us from falling into sin.

Meditations from St. Catherine

Dearest brother in Christ sweet Jesus: I Catherine, servant and slave of the servants of Jesus Christ, write to you in His precious Blood, with desire to see you constant and persevering in virtue; for it is not he who begins who is crowned, but only he who perseveres. For Perseverance is the Queen who is crowned; she stands between Fortitude and true Patience, but she alone receives a crown of glory. So I want you, dearest brother, to be constant and persevering in virtue, that you may receive the reward of your every labour. I hope in the great goodness of God that He will fortify you in such wise that neither demon nor fellow-creature can make you look back to your vomit.

*To Messer Ristoro
Canigiani*

Additional Biblical Reflections: Matthew 24:13; James 1:2-12; Hebrews 12:1-15.

Prayer

Lord, give us a spirit of perseverance to face all hardship, all temptation, and all doubt without wavering from the course of faith that you have set before us. Grant us an unwavering commitment to your path so that we might not fall into sin but endure and receive your crown of glory. Amen.

DAY 168

It is easy to pray for those whom we love. We can even manage to pray for acquaintances, magistrates, and presidents we do not know personally. Praying for our enemies, for those who conspire against us, is another thing altogether. Yet, as Jesus tells us, and St. Catherine reminds us, if we wish our hearts to beat after our Lord's, we must also love and pray for our enemies as well as our friends.

Meditations from St. Catherine

You seem, according to what you write me, to have made a good beginning, in which I rejoice greatly for your salvation, seeing your holy desire. First, you say that you have forgiven every man who had wronged you or wished to wrong you. This is a thing which is very necessary, if you wish to have God in your soul through grace, and to be at rest even according to the world. For he who abides in hate is deprived of God and is in a state of condemnation, and has in this life the foretaste of hell; for he is always gnawing at himself, and hungers for vengeance, and abides in fear. Believing to slay his enemy, he has first killed himself, for he has slain his soul with the knife of hate. Such men as these, who think to slay their enemy, slay themselves. He who truly forgives through the love of Christ crucified, has peace and quiet, and suffers no perturbation; for the wrath that perturbs is slain in his soul, and God the Rewarder of every good gives him His grace and at the last eternal life. What joy the soul, then, receives, and gladness and rest in its conscience, the tongue could never tell. And even according to the world, very great honour is given to the man who through love of virtue and magnanimity does not greedily desire to wreak vengeance on his enemy. So I summon you and comfort you, to persevere in this holy resolution.

To Messer Ristoro
Canigiani

Additional Biblical Reflections: Leviticus 19:18; Proverbs 25:21-22; Matthew 5:43-48.

Prayer

Lord, despite how the world rejected you, you came to embrace the world and redeem it. Let us exhibit this in our lives and love even those who despise us or who would do us harm so that we might draw nearer to you and follow the past of your cross. Amen.

DAY 169

The Lord works through men and women in various ways. Whether through the call of prophets, apostles, or simple worshippers, He nonetheless desires that all come to manifest His will, truth, and presence in the world by embracing holy virtue and resting in grace. Thus, we are all called to seek the Lord. May he manifest himself through us however He wills.

Meditations from St. Catherine

Do you know how I manifest Myself to the soul who loves Me in truth, and follows the doctrine of My sweet and amorous Word? In many is My virtue manifested in the soul in proportion to her desire, but I make three special manifestations. The first manifestation of My virtue, that is to say, of My love and charity in the soul, is made through the Word of My Son, and shown in the Blood, which He spilled with such fire of love. Now this charity is manifested in two ways; first, in general, to ordinary people, that is to those who live in the ordinary grace of God. It is manifested to them by the many and diverse benefits which they receive from Me. The second mode of manifestation, which is developed from the first, is peculiar to those who have become My friends in the way mentioned above, and is known through a sentiment of the soul, by which they taste, know, prove, and feel it. This second manifestation, however, is in men themselves; they manifesting Me, through the affection of their love. For though I am no Acceptor of creatures, I am an Acceptor of holy desires, and Myself in the soul in that precise degree of perfection which she seeks in Me. Sometimes I manifest Myself (and this is also a part of the second manifestation) by endowing men with the spirit of prophecy, showing them the things of the future. This I do in many and diverse ways, according as I see need in the soul herself and in other creatures. At other times the third manifestation takes place. I then form in the mind the presence of the Truth, My only-begotten Son, in many ways, according to the will and the desire of the soul. Sometimes she seeks Me in prayer, wishing to know My power, and I satisfy her by causing her to taste and see My virtue. Sometimes she seeks Me in the wisdom of My Son, and I satisfy her by placing His wisdom before the eye of her intellect, sometimes in the clemency of the Holy Spirit and then My Goodness causes her to taste the fire of Divine charity, and to conceive the true and royal virtues, which are founded on the pure love of her neighbor.

*A Treatise of
Discretion*

Additional Biblical Reflections: Isaiah 46:9-10; Ephesians 4:11-32; Hebrews 1:1-14.

Prayer

Lord, while you never change, you nonetheless manifest your presence for us in many callings and revelations. Give us eyes to see your truth so that we do not fall into sin or vice, but always pursue the path you have lit ahead of us in our pursuit of you, your will, and your holy virtue. Amen.

DAY 170

Not all of us can pray as incessantly as a monk or nun. Such is not everyone's vocation. Nonetheless, what St. Catherine tells us today is of great value, lest even our time in prayer becomes an occasion for the Devil to tempt us, making even our prayers a burden. We have all experienced times when, tired of what seems to be prayer without progress or clear answers from God, we begin exchanging our time set aside for prayer for other tasks. We tell ourselves we will get back to it later—but then forget about it and complete the day without any prayer at all. The key, as St. Catherine describes, is to persevere and pray regardless of what we might have on our agenda, or how tired we might be, or how burdensome prayer might be.

Meditations from St. Catherine

"WHEN the soul has passed through the doctrine of Christ crucified, with true love of virtue and hatred of vice, and has arrived at the house of self-knowledge and entered therein, she remains, with her door barred, in watching and constant prayer, separated entirely from the consolations of the world. Why does she thus shut herself in? She does so from fear, knowing her own imperfections, and also from the desire, which she has, of arriving at pure and generous love. And because she sees and knows well that in no other way can she arrive thereat, she waits, with a lively faith for My arrival, through increase of grace in her. How is a lively faith to be recognized? By perseverance in virtue, and by the fact that the soul never turns back for anything, whatever it be, nor rises from holy prayer, for any reason except (note well) for obedience or charity's sake. For no other reason ought she to leave off prayer, for, during the time ordained for prayer, the

Devil is wont to arrive in the soul, causing much more conflict and trouble than when the soul is not occupied in prayer. This he does in order that holy prayer may become tedious to the soul, tempting her often with these words: 'This prayer avails you nothing, for you need attend to nothing except your vocal prayers.' He acts thus in order that, becoming wearied and confused in mind, she may abandon the exercise of prayer, which is a weapon with which the soul can defend herself from every adversary, if grasped with the hand of love, by the arm of free choice in the light of the Holy Faith."

A Treatise of Prayer

Additional Biblical Reflections: Jeremiah 33:3; John 15:7; Romans 8:26.

Prayer

Lord, the Devil once came upon you to tempt you during your forty days of prayer in the wilderness. So, too, does he tempt us during our time of prayer, to dissuade us from this holy task. Sustain us with a spirit of perseverance so that we will not be deceived or abandon our prayers but might, in such times, pray more fervently than before, knowing that you are the one who defeats the great tempter on our behalf. In Jesus's name. Amen.

DAY 171

O nce again, in today's meditation, St. Catherine, in the form of a vision granted by the Lord, tells us not to remain content with vocal prayer—since many pray with mere words without love—but not to abandon vocal prayer either. By these methods, we are told, we can advance in degrees. A single conversation might not spark intimacy between a man and a woman, but such conversations plant the seeds of love that could, if properly nurtured, sprout in a beautiful blossom of love and intimacy. So, too, in our prayers with God, the words of prayer alone are not so important as the relationship that is nourished as we persist in vocal prayer, and our affections and heart are gradually taken hold of by His presence in holy conversation.

Meditations from St. Catherine

But do not think that the soul receives such ardor and nourishment from prayer, if she pray only vocally, as do many souls whose prayers are rather words than love. Such as these give heed to nothing except to completing Psalms and saying many paternosters. And when they have once completed their appointed tale, they do not appear to think of anything further, but seem to place devout attention and love in merely vocal recitation, which the soul is not required to do, for, in doing only this, she bears but little fruit, which pleases Me but little. But if you ask Me, whether the soul should abandon vocal prayer, since it does not seem to all that they are called to mental prayer, I should reply 'No.' The soul should advance by degrees, and I know well that, just as the soul is at first imperfect and afterwards perfect, so also is it with her prayer. She should nevertheless continue in vocal prayer, while she is yet imperfect, so as not to fall into idleness. But she should not say her vocal prayers without joining them to mental prayer, that is to say, that while she is reciting, she should endeavor to elevate her mind in My love, with the consideration of her own defects and of the Blood of My only-begotten Son, wherein she finds the breadth of My charity and the remission of her sins. And this she should do, so that self-knowledge and the consideration of her own defects should make her recognize My goodness in herself and continue her exercises with true humility. I do not wish defects to be considered in particular, but in general, so that the mind may not be contaminated by the remembrance of particular and hideous sins. But, as I said, I do not wish the soul to consider her sins, either in general or in particular, without also remembering the Blood and the broadness of My mercy, for fear that otherwise she should be brought to confusion. And together with confusion would come the Devil, who has caused it, under color of contrition and displeasure of sin, and so she would arrive at eternal damnation, not only on account of her confusion, but also through the despair which would come to her, because she did not seize the arm of My mercy. This is one of the subtle devices with which the Devil deludes My servants, and, in order to escape from his deceit, and to be pleasing to Me, you must enlarge your hearts and affections in My boundless mercy, with true humility.

A Treatise of Prayer

Additional Biblical Reflections: Jeremiah 29:12; Matthew 6:5-8; Luke 11:9; Colossians 4:2.

Prayer

Lord, let us neither be content with praying in words alone nor let us grow weary of such prayers that we imagine they are fruitless. For you have commanded us to pray not to please you by obedience alone, but that through our obedience to prayer, bathe us in your love. Amen.

DAY 172

In today's meditation, St. Catherine, again in a rapturous vision, describes the conversion of St. Paul—undoubtedly the most remarkable and one of the most dramatic conversions in the Bible—from God's perspective. We hear how it was Christ crucified alone who affected such a radical change in the former Pharisee. In Christ crucified, St. Paul saw the image of dying as self-perfect contrition—and there also he found the strength to take up His cross and endure pains for the sake of the very Lord whom he had persecuted before. There is no instrument more effective in converting the godless to the godly than the truth of Christ crucified—for the radical change from death to life can affect each of us, no matter how far into mortal sin we have fallen, and restore us in His image.

Meditations from St. Catherine

"Paul, then, had seen and tasted this good, when I drew him up into the third heaven, that is into the height of the Trinity, where he tasted and knew My Truth, receiving fully the Holy Spirit, and learning the doctrine of My Truth, the Word Incarnate. The soul of Paul was clothed, through feeling and union, in Me, Eternal Father, like the blessed ones in Eternal Life, except that his soul was not separated from his body, except through this feeling and union. But it being pleasing to My Goodness to make of him a vessel of election in the abyss of Me, Eternal Trinity, I dispossessed him of Myself, because on Me can no pain fall, and I wished him to suffer for My name; therefore I placed before him, as an object for the eyes of his intellect, Christ crucified, clothing him with the garment of His doctrine, binding and fettering him with the clemency of the Holy Spirit and inflaming him

with the fire of charity. He became a vessel, disposed and reformed by My Goodness, and, on being struck, made no resistance, but said: 'My Lord, what do You wish me to do? Show me that which it is Your pleasure for me to do, and I will do it.' Which I answered when I placed before him Christ crucified, clothing him with the doctrine of My charity. I illuminated him perfectly with the light of true contrition, by which he extirpated his defects, and founded him in My charity."

A Treatise of Prayer

Additional Biblical Reflections: Acts 9:1-19; 1 Corinthians 1:23-24; Galatians 1:11-24.

Prayer

Lord, you once turned a persecutor into an apostle to the nations. Let us ever be mindful of Christ crucified so that you will turn us from our wayward path and various forms of disobedience and restore us to be used as the instruments of your will. Amen.

DAY 173

In today's meditation, St. Catherine describes a mature posture of faith. This posture sees a brother or sister who excels in holiness, and, in doing so—rather than despising them for exceeding one's piety—one develops a "holy envy," which emulates the other, finding their pious brother or sister inspiring, and thus not begrudging them not at all. When one who is mature in the faith sees one of a lesser estate—someone poor or lacking in holiness—they do not imagine themselves greater than the other but rather does as our Lord does and embraces the poor, dining with them in a holy fellowship. We see here a pattern whereby the Lord uses us to help one another excel in holiness. Casting aside all pretenses of pride, jealousy, or status, we embrace one another and are thankful for what the Lord has ordained in each of our present estates in His desire to bring us all, together, toward Him in greater holiness and obedience.

Meditations from St. Catherine

"The obedient man wishes to be the first to enter choir and the last to leave it, and when he sees a brother more obedient than himself he regards him in his eagerness with a holy envy, stealing from him the virtue in which he excels, not wishing, however, that his brother should have less thereof, for if he wished this he would be separated from brotherly love. The obedient man does not leave the refectory, but visits it continually and delights at being at table with the poor. And as a sign that he delights therein, and so as to have no reason to remain without, he has abandoned his temporal substance, observing so perfectly the vow of poverty that he blames himself for considering even the necessities of his body. His cell is full of the odor of

poverty, and not of clothes; he has no fear that thieves will come to rob him, or that rust or moths will corrupt his garments; and if anything is given to him, he does not think of laying it by for his own use, but freely shares it with his brethren, not thinking of the morrow, but rather depriving himself today of what he needs, thinking only of the kingdom of heaven and how he may best observe true obedience."

Treatise of Obedience

Additional Biblical Reflections: John 8:39; Hebrews 13:7; 2 Thessalonians 3:7-9

Prayer

Lord, let us not consider ourselves greater or lesser than our fellows but, rather, help us to see them as a gift from you—either that we might emulate our brothers and sisters in their greater obedience or cherish our impoverished believers and embrace them in the opportunity to demonstrate your charity. We pray that through all these things, your body will be built up in love and in the image of Christ crucified, rather than perplexed by human pride and jealousy. In Jesus's name. Amen.

DAY 174

Today, St. Catherine ponders the proper attitude we must have when receiving the Eucharist or Holy Communion. By it, we are led to contemplate the mystery of our Lord's holy incarnation and, alongside it, brought to holy contemplation on our need for the Sacrament through meditation on our sins and faults—the very sins Christ atones for through His holy sacrifice.

Meditations from St. Catherine

We have seen that we must seek the kingdom of Heaven prudently: now I answer you about the attitude we should hold toward the Holy Communion, and how it befits us to take it. We should not use a foolish humility, as do secular men of the world. I say, it befits us to receive that sweet Sacrament, because it is the food of souls without which we cannot live in grace. Therefore no bond is so great that it cannot and must not be broken, that we may come to this sweet Sacrament. A man must do on his part as much as he can, and that is enough. How ought we to receive it? With the light of most holy faith, and with the mouth of holy desire. In the light of faith you shall contemplate all God and all Man in that Host. Then the impulse that follows the intellectual perception, receives with tender love and holy meditation on its sins and faults, whence it arrives at contrition, and considers the generosity of the immeasurable love of God, who in so great love has given Himself for our food. Because one does not seem to have that perfect contrition and disposition which he himself would wish, he must not therefore turn away; for goodwill alone is sufficient, and the disposition which on his part exists.

To Messer Ristoro
Canigiani

Additional Biblical Reflections: Mark 14:22-25; John 6:51; 1 Corinthians 10:16-17.

Prayer

Lord, you have given us the blessed Sacrament of your body and blood so that we might truly feast on you, for you are the nourishment of both body and soul, and through our encounter with your presence, we might be more aware of our need of you and your desire for us. Grant us a holy desire for your Sacrament so that we might be nourished in the faith unto life everlasting. In Jesus's name. Amen.

DAY 175

It is a wondrous thing of our faith that the youngest child can take hold of it, and aged theologians still contemplate its truths. Today, St. Catherine reminds us that knowledge is the foundation of it all—the goodness and love of God, the law of God, which reveals our sin, and an awareness of our wretchedness. With this knowledge at the forefront of our minds, we know all we need to take hold of Christ and advance our knowledge of the faith.

Meditations from St. Catherine

What do we need to know? The great goodness of God, and His unspeakable love toward us; the perverse law which always fights against the Spirit, and our own wretchedness. In this knowledge the soul begins to render His due to God; that is, glory and praise to His Name, loving Him above everything, and the neighbour as one's self, with eager desire for virtue; and the soul bestows hate and displeasure on itself, hating in itself vice, and its own sensuousness, which is the cause of every vice. The soul wins all virtue and grace in the knowledge of itself, abiding therein with light, as was said. Where shall the soul find the wealth of contrition for its sins, and the abundance of God's mercy? In this House of Self- Knowledge.

*To Messer Ristoro
Canigiani*

Additional Biblical Reflections: Exodus 20:1-26; Romans 7:1-25; 1 John 2:1-29.

Prayer

Lord, you have given us your law not that your demands might burn us but that we might become more aware of our need for you and your mercies. Grant us sufficient knowledge so that we might seek you more and grow in more knowledge of you and, even more, in greater obedience to your perfect will. Amen.

DAY 176

The Lord is no miser. Everything we have in this world and everything He has promised us in the world to come is given us by His gracious heart. Today, St. Catherine reminds us that all His gifts come from His character. She exhorts us to ask the Lord and not withhold our requests because out of His great love, He desires to bless we who seek Him aright with abundance.

Meditations from St. Catherine

You know that God is supremely good, and loved us before we were: and is Eternal Wisdom, and His Power in virtue is immeasurable: so for this reason we are sure that He has power, knowledge, and will to give us what we need. Well we see, in proof, that He gives us more than we know how to ask, and that which was not asked by us. Did we ever ask Him that He should create us reasonable creatures, in His own image and likeness, rather than brute beasts? No. Or that He should create us by Grace by the Blood of the Word, His only-begotten Son, or that He should give us Himself for food, perfect God and perfect Man, flesh and blood, body and soul, united to Deity? Beyond these most high gifts, which are so great, and show such fire of love toward us, that there is no heart so hard that its hardness and coldness would not melt by considering them at all: infinite are the gifts and graces which we receive from Him without asking. Then, since He gives so much without our asking— how much the more will He fulfil our desires when we shall desire a just thing of Him? Nay, who makes us desire and ask it? Only He. Then, if He makes us ask it, it is a sign that He means to fulfil it, and give us what we seek.

To Messer Ristoro
Canigiani

Additional Biblical Reflections: Jeremiah 1:5; Matthew 7:71-11; James 4:3.

Prayer

Lord, you exhibited your abundant generosity from before the time we were made, even when you were determined to speak and thereby created the world and all creatures. Let us learn to ask you for whatever we need in confidence, knowing that you will grant us what we seek whenever we ask in accordance with your will. In Jesus's name. Amen.

DAY 177

Christianity has known many movements focused on charismatic gifts rooted more in feelings than in true effect. In other words, many have mistaken God's genuine presence and gifts for feelings that may or may not be indicative of God's affirmative response to our petitions. Today, St. Catherine reminds us that God sometimes withholds feelings from those who would make more of the feelings than the gift. However, at the same time, He grants deep feelings to others who might require such confirmations of His presence. As always, it is God's intimate knowledge of our hearts that determines, in wisdom, how He chooses to bestow feelings or withhold them.

Meditations from St. Catherine

Sometimes He will do us the grace by giving it to us in effect though not in feeling. He uses this means with foresight, because He knows that if a man felt himself to possess it, either he would slacken the pull of desire, or would fall into presumption; therefore He withdraws the feeling, but not the grace. There are others who both receive and feel, according as it pleases the sweet goodness of our Physician to give to us sick folk; and He gives to everyone in the way that our sickness needs. You see, then, that in any case the yearning of the creature, with which it asks of God, is always fulfilled. Now we see what we ought to seek, and how prudently.

To Messer Ristoro
Canigiani

Additional Biblical Reflections: Jeremiah 17:9; Proverbs 28:26; 1 Corinthians 14:33.

Prayer

Lord, when we ponder your gifts aright, many of us cannot help but be moved with gratitude. Still, it is not the feelings that are the gift; the gift itself is good regardless of our feelings. Grant that we might cherish your gifts, and when such feelings come, let them not become idols unto themselves but an overflow of gratitude for your generosity. Amen.

DAY 178

Today, St. Catherine reminds us how self-love can lead us astray in various ways. Accordingly, she bids us consider the example of Jesus, who was moved not by His love of His glory but rather set His glory aside out of love for us.

Meditations from St. Catherine

So you see, dearest brothers and lords, that self-love ruins the city of the soul, and ruins and overturns the cities of earth. I will that you know that nothing has so divided the world into every kind of people as self-love, from which injustice is forever born. Apparently, dearest brothers, you have a desire to increase and preserve the welfare of your city; and this desire moved you to write to me, poor wretch that I am, full of faults. I heard and saw that letter with tender love, and with wish to satisfy your desires, and to exert me, with what grace God shall give me, to offer you and your city before God with continual prayer. If you shall be just men, and carry on your government as I said above, not in passion nor for self-love or your private good, but for the universal good founded on the Rock Christ sweet Jesus, and if you do all your works in His fear, then by means of prayer you shall preserve the state, the peace and unity of your city. Therefore I beg you by the love of Christ crucified— for there is no other way— that since you have the help of the prayers of the servants of God, you should not fail on your side in what is needful. For did you fail you might to be sure be helped a little by the prayers, but not so much that it would not soon come to nothing; because you ought to help, on your part, to bear this weight.

To the Anziani and
Consuls and Gonfalonieri
of Blogna

Additional Biblical Reflections: 2 Chronicles 7:14; Mark 10:45; Philippians 2:5-11.

Prayer

Lord, your word has revealed that pride cometh before the fall. Spare us from self-love and let us learn, instead, from the example of you, who in humility came to us even as a child in a manger, ate with sinners, and died alongside criminals. Grant that we might follow your path of humility so that all we do and say reflects your righteous path glorified before the world. Amen.

DAY 179

Today, St. Catherine reminds us that the Sacrament itself leaves, even after the accidents of bread and wine are consumed, an indelible grace that sustains us in the world. Knowing that we are creatures with five senses, the Lord chooses to engage our human senses through the sacraments so that His graces would not be mere ideas but tangible, tasted on the tongue, and thereby confirmed by His promise.

Meditations from St. Catherine

"See, dearest daughter, in what an excellent state is the soul who receives, as she should, this Bread of Life, this Food of the Angels. By receiving this Sacrament she dwells in Me and I in her, as the fish in the sea, and the sea in the fish -- thus do I dwell in the soul, and the soul in Me -- the Sea Pacific. In that soul grace dwells, for, since she has received this Bread of Life in a state of grace, My grace remains in her, after the accidents of bread have been consumed. I leave you the imprint of grace, as does a seal, which, when lifted from the hot wax upon which it has been impressed, leaves behind its imprint, so the virtue of this Sacrament remains in the soul, that is to say, the heat of My Divine charity, and the clemency of the Holy Spirit. There also remains to you the wisdom of My only-begotten Son, by which the eye of your intellect has been illuminated to see and to know the doctrine of My Truth, and, together with this wisdom, you participate in My strength and power, which strengthen the soul against her sensual self-love, against the Devil, and against the world. You see then that the imprint remains, when the seal has been taken away, that is, when the material accidents of the bread, having been consumed, this True Sun has returned to Its Center,

not that it was ever really separated from It, but constantly united to Me. The Abyss of My loving desire for your salvation has given you, through My dispensation and Divine Providence, coming to the help of your needs, the sweet Truth as Food in this life, where you are pilgrims and travelers, so that you may have refreshment, and not forget the benefit of the Blood. See then how straitly you are constrained and obliged to render Me love, because I love you so much, and, being the Supreme and Eternal Goodness, deserve your love."

A Treatise of Prayer

Additional Biblical Reflections: Exodus 12:21-18; Matthew 4:4; 1 John 1:1-10.

Prayer

Lord, you have given us true signs of your grace so that we might take hold of you in our earthly estate and thereby ascend to you in the heavens through faith and obedience. Grant that we might avail ourselves of all your gifts and lack none of them, so we can endure in an abundance of grace throughout our lives. Amen.

DAY 180

In today's meditation, St. Catherine reminds us not to judge our fellows. We live in a world where, with little understanding, many are ready and eager to pronounce judgments on others. However, this is a grave error, one that presumes we are equal to God just as the serpent first tempted Adam and Eve that they, too, might know good and evil and play the role of judge. Instead, St. Catherine tells us that we should rest in God's grace and mercy and recognize that God wishes to bestow the same on those whom we would judge. In the end, His justice will prevail—but we are not the executors of His justice; we are the recipients of His mercy and grace.

Meditations from St. Catherine

From living faith one will derive a will in accord with that of God, and will quench in heart and mind the human instinct of judging. The will of God alone shall judge, which seeks and wills naught but our sanctification. In this wise one is not shocked at his neighbour and does not criticize him. Nor does he pass judgment on a man who talks against him: he condemns himself alone, seeing that it is the will of God which permits such men to vex him for his good. Ah, how blessed is the soul which clothes itself in a judgment so gentle! He does not condemn the servants of this world who do him injury; nor does he condemn the servants of God, wishing to drive them in his own way, as many presumptuous, proud men do, who under cloak of the honour of God and the salvation of souls, are shocked by the servants of God, and assume a critical attitude under cover of this cloak, saying: "Such words do not please me." And so a man becomes disturbed in himself, and also makes others disturbed with his tongue, claiming that he speaks through the force of love— and so he thinks he does. But if he will open his eyes, he will find the serpent of presumption under a false aspect, which plays the judge, judging in its own fashion, and not according to the mysteries and the holy and diverse ways in which God works with His creatures. Let human pride be ashamed, and consent to see that in the House of the Eternal Father are many mansions. Let it not seek to impose a rule upon the Holy Spirit: for He is the Rule itself, Giver of the Rule: nor let it measure Him who cannot be measured. The true servant of God, arrayed in His highest eternal will, will not do thus; nay, he will hold in reverence the ways and deeds and habits of God's servants, since he judges them fixed not by man, but by God. For, just because things are not pleasing to us and do not go according to our habits, we ought to be predisposed to believe that they are pleasing to God. We ought not to judge anything at all, nor can we, except what is manifest and open sin. And even this the soul enamoured of God and lost to itself does not assume to judge, except in displeasure for the sin and wrong done to God; and with great compassion for the soul of him who sins, eagerly willing to give itself to any torture for the salvation of that soul.

*To Sano Di Maco
and all her Other Sons in
Siena*

Additional Biblical Reflections: Matthew 7:1-5; Romans 14:1-23; 1 Corinthians 4:1-5.

Prayer

Lord, let us not again commit the original sin that we would see ourselves become like God by judging others. Instead, let us only do what you command: To love one another while reserving judgment to you. For you know the hearts of all people, and we see only the outward works of one's hands. Grant us humble hearts, Lord, that recognize if we were subject to the judgments of men, we, too, would be condemned. Rather, let us rest in your mercy, who judges rightly and redeems abundantly. In Jesus's name. Amen.

www.ingramcontent.com/pod-product-compliance
Lightning Source LLC
Chambersburg PA
CBHW070942100426
42737CB00011BA/1340